# LEADERSHIP JUNKIE

# LEADERSHIP JUNKIE

*Fables and Parables from
One Who Just Can't Quit*

## DENNIS HUNSINGER

DONNYBROOK PRESS • LANGLEY, WASHINGTON

Published by
Donnybrook Press
Langley, Washington

Leadership Junkie: Fables and Parables from One Who Just Can't Quit

Internet addresses in this book are offered as a resource. They are not intended
in any way to be or imply an endorsement by the author, nor does the author
vouch for the content of these sites for the life of this book.

Disclaimer: Although this book contains references to U.S. military services,
the thoughts, opinions, anecdotes, and lessons contained in this book belong
exclusively to the author. There is no official endorsement of this book or the
material within by any element of the Department of Defense, the U.S. Air
Force, or any of the military units he was assigned to during his career. The use
of the terms Air Force or Department of Defense, FEMA, or Department of
Homeland Security are simple references and in no way are intended to imply
official sanctioning by those Departments. This book contains no classified
information, and no references are made that would endanger military personnel or operations.

ISBN: 978-0-578-46453-4

Book design: Gray Dog Press, Spokane, Washington

Printed in the United States of America

# Dedication

Why am I writing this book? I'm writing it for my kids, my grandkids, my great grandkids, and for all of the future generations of my family that I'll never meet; it's to them that I dedicate this book. I want them to know who I am, what I did, and more importantly, what I think about life and leadership. I'm writing it because it's a hard, tough world out there and there are things they need to know. If they glean anything from this book, I hope that it's not so much how to act as a leader; but, more importantly, how to be a better person. My hope is that just one of them will pick this up someday and read it; and then perhaps years after that, he or she will reflect back on at least some of the leadership lessons and say "you know what…the old man was right!"

The things that I take most seriously, that are the most important to me, are my integrity and sense of honor; as every leader should. After that, it comes down to taking care of my family, my friends, and those loyalists who worked for me that shared the same values. In that respect, I feel a sense of uncommon fellowship. I've learned many lessons through the school of hard knocks, but I've also been blessed with a great support system, and a wonderful life and career.

# Contents

# Introduction

*Then I heard the voice of the Lord, saying, "Whom shall I send,
and who will go for Us?" Then I said, "Here am I. Send me!"*
—Isaiah 6:8

Hello. My name is Dennis, and I am an addict.

Yup, I'm addicted…can't stop. I've been at it for more than 40 years and I've got to have more. You see…I'm a leadership junkie. I look for opportunities to lead. Give me more! I'm the guy that jumps up and down and yells "put me in coach!" Why? Like an athlete that wants to be the guy that takes the last shot in the championship game, I want to be THAT guy. I crave being in charge and having responsibility; the more, the better. I want to be handed the reins of command when the pressures and stakes are the highest. I love serving my country, and I enjoy making an impact, whether it's on a company or directly on someone's life. If there's anything I enjoy more than turning an organization into a winner, it's developing leaders. I don't know if I'll ever be able to stop; so maybe there's a leadership anonymous group out there for me. I definitely need help…I just <u>can't let go</u>.

Why should I let it go? As I sit here writing this, I'm thinking about all the years that have gone by. I've gained all this knowledge, all this experience, and all this leadership savvy (or at least so says me). Now, conventional thinking (and culture) tells me it's time to retire? Seriously? I'm a marketable commodity, aren't I? Think about that a moment! As I move into my senior years, it's like I've fallen into the spam file of life! And now it's just time to go home? With well over 40 years in government, I'm at the top of my senior leadership game, and there's no one in the office more experienced than me. Oh sure, there are plenty that are smarter. In fact, I've said many times that I don't claim to be a particularly smart guy…just well educated. With age also comes experience, and that experience is easily transformed into wisdom. So, a combination of a good education, a lot of experience, and common sense in applying both, has given me the wisdom that many junior leaders lack. Oh yeah; they think they have wisdom. Many junior leaders also think that because they can manage their lives through a smartphone "App" they are, therefore, tech savvy and leadership just boils down to some algorithm or mathematical equation they can fit into a computer model and it'll spit out the right answer every time. I remind them time and again that leadership isn't so simple…it's not so much a matter of the head as it's a matter of the heart. More often than not, you have to <u>feel</u> your way through problems, and frequently through some very tough, if not hurtful lessons. That's where experience and wisdom serve senior leadership best.

So, what's leadership? There are many who have tried to define this very elusive concept. How does it differ from the principles of management? I would start the discussion by describing what it's not, rather than what it is. I don't believe it's found in Total Quality Management or Management by Objectives, or other management "crutches." These are nothing more than aides to help the unimaginative manager try to put structure to his or her organization. A true leader needs little of this. In short, the principles of management are taught in an academic environment; the hard lessons of leadership are learned in the classroom of life. Simply put, leaders inspire; they provide vision and strategy and for the most part stay out of the weeds. Managers, however, just keep employees moving in (hopefully) the right direction; they manage processes and usually implement someone else's vision and strategy.

How do I spot a good leader? I want intrinsic qualities such as charisma; however, I don't believe leadership is an inherited trait. Nor is it necessarily a learned skill. It comes down to basic human decency…practice of the "Golden Rule." It's treating people fairly, honorably; but with standards, discipline, and most importantly consistency in applying both. People will follow you if they can believe in you; they'll believe in you if they can trust you; they'll trust you if you are honest with them. The concept of honesty also includes the setting of standards and the enforcing of discipline; and doing it fairly and equitably while, again, treating everyone with dignity and respect. You have to be a person "of your word." That means you are consistent, fair and predictable. They know what they're getting each and every time.

In most cases, no matter how good or seasoned a leader you are, you won't be blindly followed like sheep over a cliff. You have to give people a reason to follow you beyond their assessment of you as a good leader. They need to be able to see what <u>their stake in the outcome is</u>. If you're going to succeed as a leader, you have to first be successful in translating to them this single concept – just why is this important to me? More on this later.

Beyond what I've already shared with you, if you are looking to get right to "the one thing", then skip to Chapter 7 where I talk about what I believe to be the sacred trust of leadership. If you stick with me over the next several chapters, I'll do my best to guide you through some of the perils of leadership, the life-lessons I've learned, and perhaps a few other issues for you to ponder. I'm not the expert, but I've been around the block once or twice and now have a story or two to share; and that's what makes this book different from many others on leadership. It's not written by some professor who spent his or her entire adult life in a classroom studying and writing on the subject. My life has been an on-going leadership laboratory.

So yes, what you are about to read is certainly autobiographical. Some of it glorious; some of it deeply personal, if not painful. Most of the lessons I've learned revolve around many of my personal experiences. They're the things I write about because they're the things I know and experienced; the military and federal government, and the highs and lows. I believe they're relevant, and I hold them reverently; as much so as my colleagues in business would hold theirs.

I hope you enjoy the journey. This won't be nearly as exciting as when I lived it.

r

# 1

# Milk and Cookies

## *(Or, Are You Tough Enough for the Job?)*

*"The cowards never started…and the weak died along the trail"*
—Kit Carson

### *The Faint of Heart*

Of all the speeches I've ever heard, there are only a few that truly inspire me. One that I've come back to time and again – one that resonated with me during my military career, as it did throughout my professional life – is Douglas MacArthur's farewell speech to the 1962 graduating class at West Point. MacArthur's "Duty, Honor, Country" speech is one that almost every senior military officer has heard at some point, and usually as they've transitioned through one of the War Colleges. It is, in fact, one that I keep handy and listen to from time to time as a reminder of certain guiding principles that keep me grounded, and perhaps bring me back to some reality of purpose. It doesn't matter whether you're from a military background or not, the principles of staying focused and true to your purpose are translatable to any business. It's a reminder of your success; why you've made it as far as you have!

As MacArthur built his presentation around "those three hallowed words" of duty, honor, country, he reminded military officers what their primary (if not sole) objective was and is – to fight and win our nation's wars. Everything else is "corollary", secondary, subordinate, if not unimportant, next to that primary mission. The American public expects it; they demand it. For us to fail means the country will not survive. He argued that military officers must let others dwell on the issues of the day; politics, science, the economy, international relations, and other things that "divide men's minds." There is but one single purpose for the military officer; to answer the call in protecting our nation and winning its wars. It's

1

a life-altering commitment, and an awesome responsibility. Failure is not an option.[1]

I've told several people that when I retired from a nearly 30-year career with the Air Force, I was struck immediately by a void in my life that I didn't think was possible to fill. Where would I find a job — a calling — that was as rewarding or fulfilling, or as honorable and noble as defending one's nation? I couldn't imagine anything, anywhere that would give me that single-scope of purpose that MacArthur describes of the American soldier. Nor did I believe I would ever find an Agency or mission that would test my mettle as a leader, or stretch me intellectually, if not physically and emotionally, in a way that I had previously experienced. But it wasn't long before I found that sense of fulfillment with the Federal Emergency Management Agency (FEMA). While the military places its emphasis on external threats to our nation, FEMA's primary focus is an inward one; one that is directed at natural and man-made hazards. Yet, the concept of absolute service within the two disciplines remains the same. Moreover, the parallels between what MacArthur describes as the awesome responsibility of soldiers to stay resolute in their single purpose, and the similar public expectations of FEMA and its employees, are more than striking. Like the military, FEMA's employees know and accept the fact that more is expected of them.

FEMA is an Agency like no other in government. In "peacetime" they plan and prepare, they offer guidance and assistance, and they administer a variety of grant programs. But in times of catastrophic disaster, <u>FEMA is the final line of defense between order and chaos</u>. Yes, and let there be no doubt, they are responders. They may not be first responders; but they are, nevertheless, responders. Their job is to be there to answer the call. The American public expects it; they demand it. For them to fail means the nation fails. In many cases, there are others that respond ahead of FEMA; local and state emergency management officials are charged with certain responsibilities in protecting their citizens. But FEMA is the last line. We saw it during and after Hurricane Katrina and we've seen it since. We will see it again. The public expects their Federal government to be there for them. It transcends political parties and Administration changes. It is the Agency's primary focus. Anything short is failure, and that is unacceptable.

---

1 Duty, Honor, Country Address at West Point" by General Douglas MacArthur (1962) is in the public domain. Taken from Department of Defense Pamphlet GEN-1A, US Government Printing Office, 1964.

Theirs is an awesome responsibility as well; a commitment; a calling; and it's not for the faint of heart.

So, who is this "faint of heart"? In 1975, as a young security police Lieutenant, I faced probably the toughest period of my entire Air Force career. I was stationed at McChord Air Force Base near Tacoma, Washington and was assigned to a squadron of about 350 people. I was placed in charge of a security police flight of about 60 troops[2] and worked rotating swing and midnight shifts. We were charged with base law enforcement as well as security of our aircraft, the flight line, and a small nuclear weapons depot we had at the time. It was a staggering responsibility, given the number of armed posts and patrols on duty during an average shift as well as both the nuclear and conventional missions at the time.

It was a <u>horrible</u> time in our nation's history (at least from my perspective). We were a very permissive (if not promiscuous) society.[3] Everything from fashion to music revolved around a culture that gave tacit approval (or at least turned a blind eye) to a very prevalent drug culture. Drugs were everywhere. We had just pulled out of Viet Nam, and were rapidly closing the rest of our operations throughout Southeast Asia. I had troops rotating back to the US monthly from Thailand and the Philippines as we continued to draw down from the war. And for the large part, many of these were troops that had picked up horrendous habits from their assignments overseas. For many their hair was outside of compliance standards for the Air Forces; their uniforms were sloppy; their military bearing lacking; and, I place blame for all of this on their leadership. No one seemed to be enforcing the rules overseas.

It was sometime in the fall of 1976 that the Air Force Office of Special Investigations "broke the case." The case? In one night more than 100 security policemen from McChord AFB were relieved of duty for using drugs (mostly marijuana). And of the more than 100, almost a third, came from my security flight. These were the guys guarding our most sensitive assets in the weapons storage area. As the investigation unfolded, it was learned that some of our noncommissioned officers were passing marijuana in the box lunches as they went from post to post during the shift. I remember

---

2 I use the term "troops" throughout this book. Granted, it's a military term. But I use it synonymously (interchangeably) and affectionately with "employee" throughout.
3 Most would probably say things haven't changed since, or have even gotten worse. Perhaps so, but the 60s and 70s were the break-out period, where culture (to include morals and values) took a sharp turn from the more conservative decades preceding. Sex, drugs, and rock and roll, baby!

reading one report about how the Lieutenant (me) attempted to make a check of one of the tower posts. As he attempted to climb the ladder, other security guards talked him out of it, saying the tower had just been freshly painted and they wanted to keep as many people out of there as possible for the next few hours. What was really happening was that several of the guards were in the tower smoking marijuana. I fell for it.

I don't know how I survived that investigation, or that assignment. In one instance, we failed an Operational Readiness Inspection, and for an entire month the Vice Wing Commander attended shift changes to conduct dress and appearance inspections. I accept my share of the blame in our performance at the time. However, I was a young and inexperienced officer who was given tremendous responsibility with little or no mentorship. The squadron was a mess, and the senior leadership above me was failing to fulfill their duties frequently. For a young officer like me, just beginning his career, it was humiliating.

I learned a lot during my stay at McChord…mostly about trust, or that is, the lack of it. My NCOs failed me. Before the investigation, I had great respect and admiration for them; I trusted them to carry out their responsibilities honorably. They didn't do that; instead, they violated my trust and, in the process, let me and the organization down. I also, up to that point, had placed great trust and confidence in my senior leadership; that they wouldn't let a young and inexperienced officer fail. But they did; they failed to provide me that necessary training and supervision for me to be successful in that situation[4]. In terms of hard lessons, this definitely was one. As a result, I learned that I shouldn't take things for granted; that I shouldn't to be so naïve; that I should follow-up on people; and, that I shouldn't so blindly trust those around me (a sad realization, but it's true). Consequently, I advise young leaders today they shouldn't necessarily develop a skeptical or even cynical outlook as a leader, but they most definitely want to be aware of the situation around them and with their antenna up at all times.

So again, who is this "faint of heart?" It's not me! I had an opportunity to cross-train into another career field, but didn't. I did think about it.

---

4  It was sometime after this incident, and not necessarily because of it, the Air Force changed its training program for new officers coming into the career field.  In 1975, the Air Force placed a sudden, renewed emphasis on how we would perform our nuclear security mission. Consequently, they flooded the career field with newly commissioned lieutenants (me being one) in order to have an officer on duty at all times at every nuclear base. There was little formal training offered; most of us just went to work.

It was about that time that my father died and I was struggling with the decision of whether or not I should get out or stay in. I had applied to be an Island County Sheriff's Deputy. I ended up 8th on a very long list of candidates vying for three jobs. I assumed that my chances for being hired were very slim when, about a month later, they suddenly called and offered me the job (apparently others had declined or had fallen off the list and they worked their way down to me). I thought about it, but decided to stay. Why? Because I had managed to survive the hard lessons of bad leadership, a failing squadron, and a toxic environment. Moreover, I had an opportunity to move deeper into the Air Force; take another assignment and prove to any doubters, and to myself, that I was a much better officer than the reputation we all had from those days at McChord. To this day, professionally, it was the best decision I ever made. Despite all that I had gone through in the early years, I was not a quitter and was not faint of heart. No, I decided to stick with my career field, not have milk and cookies with someone else, and have never regretted that decision.

## *Milk and Cookies*

I owe the concept of "milk and cookies" to a crusty old Command Sergeant Major (CSM) by the name of Washington. When I went to Army jump school at Fort Benning, GA, every night after a long day of training we would march back to the barracks in formation. As the formation came back to the training area, the drill sergeant would give the command to halt, and then he gave the command for left-face. There on the steps of the barracks was CSM Washington, standing with a bag of Oreo cookies and a jug of milk. At that point, every night, he would ask if there was anyone in the formation that wanted out. "It's a tough course" he'd say. He'd go on (the same speech every night)…"I know it's hard. But don't be embarrassed. Just come into my office, have some milk and cookies, and I'll find you a flight home tonight." Amazingly, every night, one or two guys took him up on it. Still, to this day, I won't eat cookies and drink milk together.

I've used the term "milk and cookies" for many years when describing someone or something (either an agency or even an entire avocation) that I didn't think measured up to my (admittedly arbitrary) standard. Rightly or wrongly, it is the lens by which I view people and things. I've taken plenty of criticism for apparently disparaging others by its use. I've never intended to offend anyone. Nor am I'm an elitist. I've never claimed to be. But I did survive CSM Washington's course, which does put me ahead of many others.

As a society, we spend far too much time trying to avoid offending everyone and not enough time preparing our young for the harsh, cruel realities of life. The one certainty in life is that it's a dog-eat-dog world out there. The problem is we're no longer stressing competitiveness. We teach our young to be open-minded, accepting of everyone, and tolerant. All of that is good...to an extent. But the world is full of bullies; domestically and internationally. China and Russia are bullies. If we don't go back to emphasizing (instilling) competitiveness in the development of our young, the future leadership gene pool will shrink. Yet, there will always be parents (and other leadership) that coach and mentor competitive skills within that shrinking minority; and future leadership will emerge from that very small group.

Late in my Air Force career, I commanded a security police squadron at Fairchild AFB near Spokane, Washington. One day I had a young lieutenant come into my office, literally crying that the senior non-commissioned officers didn't respect her and the junior airmen made fun of her.

Let me stop right here and address something. I've told this story a couple of times and have been accused of being almost misogynistic (or at least insensitive) because I refer to her as "her" and that she cried, which she did. I don't know how else to tell it. The fact is she was a she, and she did come in crying. Those are the facts. I've seen men cry as well and, in fact, I've made a couple of them cry (not proud of that but that's a fact too). The point is, it surprised and disappointed me. I thought this officer was stronger. The larger point or lesson to this story is that it's a nasty, brutal, unforgiving world out there and you need to be tough enough to succeed in it...or, you can be a shrinking violet and just go hide under a rock. Or, take the safe path your whole life and never make a bold move. So there it is. Think of me what you will. Now on to the story.[5]

My first thought was (and I told her) that if she cried in front of them, they certainly wouldn't respect her, and probably would make fun of her. Nevertheless, she felt that our career field was too hard and she wanted out.

5 I've worked with, and for, some pretty outstanding women leaders in my Air Force and civil service career. As with them or anyone else I've ever been associated with, I judge, in part, by their ability to perform; whether in a leadership or technician role, show me what you can do! I'll judge you by that, as well as by the quality of your character. Race, gender, age, religion, and sexual orientation are irrelevant.

She had, in fact, found a job that she wanted to cross-train into – the Social Actions career field. Social Actions is the Equal Employment Opportunity (EEO) branch of the Air Force. It is a sub-discipline of the Personnel business; a pure staff-function, which she saw as an opportunity to get into guidance and counseling work. I saw it as a wimp's way out and told her so. I was extremely disappointed with the direction this officer was heading. I had previously seen her as strong, motivated and someone with a very bright future in our business; however, she wanted the soft life of a Social Actions Officer. So I gave it my best shot to dissuade her. I told her that ours was the toughest job in the Air Force. The hours were long and the conditions were harsh. The leadership challenges were arduous. The troops get bored on post and it takes a special person to motivate them daily to rise to their potential. It was a job with high demands and equally high risks. Yet, at the end of the day, at the end of a 20-30-year career, you may or may not get promoted to Colonel, but you will definitely feel fulfilled. You will have eventually met and fulfilled that awesome responsibility of "command", and you will walk away knowing that you took the best and worst the Air Force had to offer – you will have faced their most difficult leadership challenges and excelled. Or...you can go have milk and cookies with one of those other career fields.[6]

I told this young lieutenant that on the balance of 20-30 years, she would probably do as well in her promotion opportunities with Social Actions, but would never realize the exhilaration of "command", nor would she ever face the test of her mettle as a leader. Unfortunately, she chose milk and cookies with Social Actions. In my opinion, she was faint of heart.

The milk and cookies parallel is something I found striking within FEMA. While I was there, we had a few that had left the Agency for a variety of reasons; and some of them left for the milk and cookies provided by some other career choice. Over time, I had more than one employee come into my office and tell me that they'd had it, it was too hard, it was a thankless job, the working conditions were poor, and they just couldn't

---

6 To add stress to an already stressful situation for her, we had recently experienced what became known at Fairchild as "Hell Week." On June 20, 1994, a recently discharged psychiatric patient returned to the base hospital and killed his two doctors. He then proceeded on a shooting rampage throughout the hospital ultimately killing 5 and wounding 22 before he was killed by a responding patrol. Later that week, on June 24, 1996, a B-52 crashed on base killing all four crew members. Ours was a very demanding and stressful job at that time, securing a crime scene and a crash scene, and she was (understandably) having a difficult time with it all.

take it – and on several occasions I was disappointed that I couldn't convince them to stay. I had, on one occasion, an employee tell me he was leaving for a job with the Social Security Administration that paid the same but was far less stressful. Of course, I tried to appeal to a sense of calling; would Social Security give him a feeling of self-fulfillment at the end of a meaningful career? Instead, did he really want to have milk and cookies with the very comfortable, safe and secure environment the Social Security Administration was offering him? He chose milk and cookies. He was… faint of heart.

Now, some will criticize me for this too. "Of course, he'd leave for the same pay and less stress. Anybody would, wouldn't you?" No! I wouldn't; and that's the point of this whole book.

Notwithstanding, I was more than pleased by the quality of many of the people that had joined and remained with the Agency before and after Hurricane Katrina. They seemed to understand the gravity of our charge, the complexity of our business, and the demands that would be placed upon them. I'm grateful that it left me with a core of dedicated professionals who, on balance, placed responsibility and commitment above all else.

In the context of what MacArthur described as the nation's demand for focus of its military officers, and a similar challenge that I believe continues to face FEMA, they are clearly not a milk and cookies Agency. For them, the bar has been set very high – higher than for any other Agency. Their hours are long and the conditions harsh. And while there are Federal agencies that plan business trips in and around some of the garden spots of this country, when FEMA takes a business trip to somewhere like Florida it's usually because a hurricane has come through and decimated the local economy. There are few hotels open, the power is out, there's no potable water or available food, and who has time to lay on the beach anyway?! They work twelve or more hours a day. They miss ball games, birthdays, and graduations. They are frequently a media target (whether it's one ice truck too many or one ice bag too few). Their summers are spent preparing for hurricanes, and their winters are spent dealing with floods and ice storms. In the meantime, they deal with wild-land fires, and standby for the inevitable earthquake. All of this while many (not all) of their sister agencies work a 40-hour week, enjoy a stable life-style, and do it for the same pay. FEMA, on the other hand, just seems to shake it off; with most of their employees continuing to come back, both for the challenge, and for the altruistic sense of purpose it brings. In many respects, they have taken the best and worst that FEMA has to offer – they <u>have</u> faced the Agency's most difficult leadership challenges and many have excelled. They are not the faint of heart.

## *The Warrior Ethos*

Willie Nelson sings that his heroes have always been cowboys. Well, my heroes have always been soldiers, sailors, airmen, and marines.

When I was a young kid, my heroes were men in uniform. I idolized the Mercury, Gemini, and Apollo astronauts. I was in complete awe of the men fighting and sacrificing during the Vietnam conflict. For much of it, I was too young to understand its complexities; and for all of it, the men that I admired were distant figures that I didn't even know. But years later, that all changed when I began to show up at duty locations where many of them were serving. I've been fortunate, and honored to have served with, or worked for, some of this nation's true heroes. For a short time from 1992-1993 I worked for Barney Barnum, a retired Marine Colonel and Medal of Honor recipient when we were both working drug control policy issues in the Office of the Secretary of Defense. Over the years I worked for Special Forces Colonel Craig Chamberlain, a Distinguished Service Cross recipient; SEAL Admirals Irish Flynn and George Worthington and Captains Lou Boink and Rick Woolard, all legends within the SEAL community; and with countless others during my years in special operations that were all multiple combat medal recipients. Many of these gentlemen were involved in sensitive operations that ranged from the Son Tay raid in Vietnam, to Desert One in Iran to Operation Just Cause in Panama. I relieved Lt Col Garth Wright (one of only two security police Air Force Cross recipients) when he left command at Peterson Air Force Base in 1981.

Three additional heroes of mine are my Dad, my father-in-law, and my step-Dad. Don Hunsinger, Fred Frei, and Nick Hebert were three of "The Greatest Generation." Dad and Fred were both B-17 crewmembers during World War II. Nick was aboard the battleship USS Indiana. All of these great men were my heroes, and all of them possessed a warrior ethos that not only defined them in their craft, but also as the men they were in general; men of honor and conviction. But these great Americans were also men of a generation and, consequently, an ethos, if not a toughness that I believe are beginning to fade.[7]

My Dad and his crew in 1945. Donald Vernon Hunsinger is the skinny kid
on the left. His pilot, J.B. Giles (kneeling, center) told me years later that
he was the youngest and smallest so they "elected" him as the ball turret
gunner. Dad wasn't too happy about that.

I'm worried, and I feel compelled to comment on what seems to be a
troubling trend in our society. As I guess I've already suggested, in leadership, one has to wonder if we're toughening-up our young people that will
eventually inherit the most senior positions. Are they tough enough to take
the really tough jobs? Lord knows…we've become a society where everyone
has to have a trophy; where we now insist on the passage of hate crime laws
for bullying. To be clear, hate crimes are wrong. Discrimination in all of
its forms is wrong. Sexual abuse, and abuse of any kind toward women is
wrong. It's also wrong that I have to say all of that here because, if I didn't,
I'd be criticized for being too insensitive; which leads me back to the question…are we preparing our kids to be competitive world leaders, or for
mediocrity as colossal underachievers (wimps!)?

---

7 To be sure, there are some heroic young men and women coming out of the conflicts
in Afghanistan and Iraq that might be our last best hope for this nation.

My father-in-law, Fred Frei. Fred flew 44 missions over Europe (including two on D-Day). After 25 he came home. While home, his airplane was shot down and much of the crew didn't survived. Nevertheless, Fred volunteered to go back for another 19 missions.

Image 3.jpg Caption:
My step-Dad, Nick Hebert, aboard the USS Indiana (row 3, 6th from the right). He said they sat off Iwo Jima for 9 days, shelling the island, trying to soften the beaches before the landings. Often under frequent Kamikaze attack throughout the war, he spent 13 months aboard ship, at one point, without touching land. How's that for an afloat tour, Navy guys?

I want our public service sectors (police, fire, emergency medical, emergency management, and others) to be tough, competitive, to some extent aggressive; but also compassionate, given the nature of their public service role. And I certainly don't want them (metaphorically) eating cookies and drinking milk in the fire house.

As for our Armed Forces…I want my military to be mean and lean. NEVER faint of heart. I want them to be highly competitive in their daily culture, and almost ruthless in the prosecution of our nation's wars when no one else is available or willing to do it. In short, I want them to maintain a warrior's ethos and spirit.

Not long ago the Department of Defense reversed its policy on gays in the military. I've never taken an anti-gay stance, nor am I now. Sure, I'm pretty conservative on most things. Personally, when I was on active duty I didn't care if someone serving next to me was gay or not. Someone taking a shower or sleeping next to me was of little concern as well. We're all adults. We know the rules and can (or should) follow them. We can and will respect each other, and each other's privacy.

Lt Col Garth Wright at our change of command in 1981.

What concerns me, though, is that this action is just one more in a long line of steps that continue to slide us down a slippery slope toward something <u>different</u>. What I'm really concerned about is a fundamental change in our military culture, which could be dangerous if not fatal to our nation. Years ago, drill instructors were ordered to stop physical touching in basic training and boot camp. No longer could they push, or shove, or physically touch trainees; but you could still yell at them. These changes were probably necessary following a number of ugly incidents where a few troops were injured. Nevertheless, even with these changes our front-line combat skills retained a certain traditional warrior ethos. Will they continue to?

With a number of actions involving social policy in the military, to include a growing number of women and trans-genders engaging in combat, will all that change? Will we move down a path that continues to "soften" what has always been a highly competitive, almost ruthless, combatant culture? Will we evolve into a kinder and gentler military because we're now concerned about some troop who tells his Drill Instructor that "yellow makes me sad"? I hope none of this is true. I hope, institutionally, we never dilute our training regimens to appease the politically correct. Or worse yet, we never see the day a platoon sergeant takes a tactical course of action under fire that endangers the whole platoon, not because he thinks it's the correct decision, but because he is concerned about someone in his charge that wasn't there before – like his girlfriend (or perhaps, boyfriend as the case may be).

Is the unintended consequence of all this that we'll start grooming military leaders that are no longer type A personalities; no longer red meat-eating cannibals that will devour each other and their young at the first sign of weakness? I hope not, but I fear we're already down that path. I'm one who firmly believes that if you can't keep up, or cut it, regardless of gender, you SHOULD be weeded out. For THAT is the competitive culture presently found within all of our combat specialties. For at least the moment, they are not part of the milk and cookies crowd, and we need to keep it that way.

As Douglas MacArthur suggested, our military exists to fight and win our nation's wars; nothing more, nothing less. This is not a social experiment. Our military shouldn't (but it does) exist to provide jobs to the disadvantaged, or temporary careers to college graduates seeking a way to pay off their student loans[8]. Perhaps as a consequence of the all-volunteer

---

8 Many are affluent kids who are coming in for the wrong reasons. "I need to pay off

force, we have lowered our standards (and our expectations) in order to meet enlistment quotas, and we are letting far too many that are faint of heart into our military; and it is poisoning the rest. Yet equally disturbing is that without a draft our military is unfairly over-represented by the poor, disadvantaged, minorities, and people of color; and I guarantee you…far, far superior numbers of these folks are NOT faint of heart, with many having been thrust into a career decision with none of the alternatives other, more privileged, kids have. As the "advanced" nation we are, when are we going to stop using primarily underprivileged kids to do the nation's dirty work? I know these are strong, contentious statements, but that's my opinion. It's time for a draft again.

Some will argue that most of our major allies have begun the transition, successfully, of recruiting a more socially diverse population, with service already alongside of us in places like Iraq and Afghanistan. But really? Are we really comparing apples to apples? Most of our allies were largely in support roles and were not in Iraq and Afghanistan in any great numbers. The US carried a disproportionate share of the combat load in both countries. In fact, none of our allies that have reversed their similar policies have ever been tested under conditions that really matter; conditions where intense, consistent combat is the norm; or worse yet, conditions where their national security, their very existence, is on the line.

I'm seeing a basic lack of leadership accountability at the highest levels when these trends are allowed to happen. Senior officers appear to be more concerned with holding on to their "stars" than protecting their heritage (or perhaps more importantly, their country). They have taken their eye off the ball, and that I find disturbing.

But there's more. I was struck several years ago by a story where the commanding officer of the USS Enterprise was relieved of his command for inappropriate behavior that had occurred years earlier.[9] Seriously? We

---

my student loan", or "I need job experience", and "holy crap! I didn't know I could get killed!" Few of us enter the military for the right reasons; perhaps Pat Tillman, who gave up his lucrative career as an NFL star, and then later his life, when he joined because he felt a sense of patriotism, altruism, and duty. The rest of us were either drafted or joined for opportunities that weren't otherwise available. Truth be told, I decided in the fall of 1972 to join the Air Force because my wife was pregnant with our first child. I was in a low skilled, minimum wage, no benefits job with little future. I was not born into an affluent family, nor did I marry into one. I saw the Air Force as a means to an end; pay for the birth of our son and finish my education. While many of us don't enter the Service for reasons of duty and patriotism, most of us stay for exactly that.

9  According to en.wikipedia.org/wiki/Owen Honors, on 3 January 2011, Captain

are casting aside a proven warrior because he offended someone's sensitivities? I certainly don't condone his actions, it was clearly poor judgment at the time, and I'm disappointed in him for that action (read the footnote for more). But neither do I condemn it now, several years later. What I am disappointed with is the apparent lack of leadership at every level above him. Perhaps there's more to the story that we'll never know. But by appearances, they seemed to have caved on the issue. In the Captain's case, the events occurred years before. Many in senior leadership later knew of it when it happened, and said nothing until the media made it a headline story. And when something like this breaks as a news story, the immediate response is that someone needs to be fired. For decades the liberal media has been quick to label military culture as war-mongering, when I don't know of any culture more blood-thirsty than theirs (except maybe Congress).

Just what is our expectation of our senior military leadership – any senior leadership for that matter? In the case of the military, we strive to recruit aggressive, hard charging, type A personalities, and then spend millions of dollars and the next 25 years trying to instill a warrior spirit and culture. On the one hand, we hope he (or now she) becomes the trained killer we need to defend us in, again, those times our national security is in peril and no one is available or capable to do it. On the other hand, we expect him or her to be kinder-gentler in today's "multicultural" military. Moreover, we've come to expect they'll act more like corporate executives than the hardened killers we need them to be. My point, and hope, is that people need to wake up and realize that our military should be of one culture...the warrior culture. Would/did Eisenhower dump Patton for slapping a soldier (or for a variety of reasons he could have)? No. He realized Patton was his best field commander; the warrior he needed at the time, and that far surpassed the need for political correctness.

We need to decide what role our military plays in our larger society.

---

Owen Honors was under investigation for videos he produced, one set entitled "XO Movie Night", filmed on the USS *Enterprise*, and aired via closed circuit television on select Saturday evenings, while he was Executive Officer of the *Enterprise*.[7] Three complete videos, produced for distribution over the ship's closed circuit video system, have been released by *The Virginian-Pilot*.[8][9][10] One video shows two male Navy sailors standing in a shower stall pretending to wash each other, and two female sailors pretending to shower together to conserve water; sailors parading in drag; homophobic slurs; and there are scenes of simulated masturbation and a simulated rectal exam.[11] The videos were shown on board in 2006 and 2007.

Where it intersects, and when it clashes, we need to figure out how we deal with that. Unfortunately, we have non-military cultures (the media and political leaders in particular; many of whom have never served) applying standards of conduct that might just be irrelevant. Our military culture has always been one where we feed on the weakness in each other. It's competitive, almost brutal; and only the strongest survive. Are they tough enough for the job? Some would argue that we've made them too tough. I don't think so (if anything, not tough enough) and I don't want to lose that culture because we're worried about hurting someone's feelings.[10]

So what about our senior leadership in the civilian sector of government? During the Eisenhower Administration the "plum book" was developed. This is a list of all the senior positions within the federal government to which the President could make political appointments. Some require Senate confirmation, some do not. But all positions within the plum book serve at the pleasure of the incumbent Administration. The rest of the Executive Branch of government consists of career civil servants, many of whom are career senior executives. The system was designed to ensure there was a cadre of career employees, at every level, that remained unfettered and unaffected by the whims of political will. These leaders would give advice and make the tough call without concern for their standing, or threat of losing their job. Unfortunately, under two Administrations where I served as a career civil service employee (one of each political party), I saw a number of career senior executives marginalized for standing up for their principles. Consequently, I've seen other senior officials bend with whatever direction the political wind may be blowing in hopes of keeping their job (or landing a better one). It's partly for this reason that I left government. Sadly, many (to include many in FEMA and the larger Department of Homeland Security) have been bullied into submission, and have abandoned their culture and ethos.

I think the phenomenon that I found most troubling was a tendency for the Administration in power at any given time to see its career civil service (particularly career senior leaders) as "holdovers" from the previous Administration. Yet, to external customers, past relationships and loyalties were flipped like a light switch. For instance, years ago I took a business trip to Alaska shortly after we had transitioned from the Bush Administration

---

10 Someone once asked me, in the course of a conversation about jobs and the economy, if I considered myself to be "middle-class." I thought about it for a moment and responded "no, I consider myself to be part of the warrior-class."

to the Obama Administration. As I customarily did from time to time, I scheduled an office call with Congressman Don Young's chief of staff. I had always had a very amicable relationship with all of the congressional delegations. But when I walked into his office this time, the mood was different. It was tense and edgy. When I walked out later, it occurred to me (hit me like a ton of bricks) that I was now seen by them as "the enemy." I was now an Obama-man; and on some level, I guess they were right. But the hardest part to accept, which became more and more clear as the months went by, was that the Obama Administration (and particularly my senior FEMA appointed leadership) saw me as a Bush holdover. I was somewhere in the middle; trying to appease everyone, but not appeasing anyone. The consequence to these perceptions is that our career civil service becomes much maligned by the media and others as mindless bureaucrats that are just coasting to a fat-cat government pension.

Shishmaref, AK in 2008 with Senators Ted Stevens and Mary Landrieu, to survey coastal erosion issues.

I don't have a clear answer to fixing the opinions about our career civil service. A lot has to do with politics and how election banter is spun by sleazy politicians, and a dishonest media that promotes ratings by fanning the flames of dissent.[11] It's disgusting to see those that lean on catchy

---

11 To be clear, the media is not a public service. They will hide behind the first amendment when they feel threatened. But they are a business; they are in it to make money

phrases like "drain the swamp." Drain the swamp of what? What if someone campaigned on an initiative to drain Wall Street of everyone with a financial or economics background or who's been there for more than a few years? Let's just devoid the world's largest financial sector of anyone that has any background on keeping the thing running. Sound ridiculous? Well, it is; and it's equally ridiculous to suggest we should dump everyone in Washington that has spent their life acquiring education, honing skills, and developing personal and business contacts that keep the nation's political and administrative systems running. We need a professional career civil service that is (largely) unfettered and unaffected by politics. Probably a noble, but unattainable goal.

Nevertheless, my caution to all, whether it's military leadership, other sectors of public service, or even private business...don't abandon your culture, your principles, your ethos (who you are) for political expediency. Your employees can sense it and that's probably the fastest way to lose them.

## *Your Sense of Honor*

*"Life every man holds dear; but the dear man holds honor far more precious dear than life."*
—William Shakespeare

There are countless times in my professional career (both military and civil service) where I crossed paths with senior leaders that were successful at balancing both their ethos[12] and their compassion for their subordinates, with their sense of honor. But there have been only a few that I've found to be truly inspirational at it.

Years ago, I worked for a man that, regardless of the differences in

---

pure and simple. If you think otherwise, you are either naïve or stupid. Good news is bad news, bad news is good news. It's all about ratings, and slamming government employees is an easy score.

12  As I speak here of "ethos" I'm speaking in far more general terms than just the military and a warrior ethos (although that too is included). In a more general sense I'm speaking of one's commitment to the mission, and as that relates to the culture of one's agency. Some of us are warriors, while some of us provide a service to our customers. Whatever the case, we should all embrace our organizational ethos.

our political philosophies, I'll admire for the rest of my life. In the twelve months that I worked for Mort Halperin, I learned more about honor than the entire balance of my 42 combined years in government. I am, by nature, a fairly conservative fellow. So, I was a little alarmed when I heard that the Clinton Administration had picked a guy to be an Assistant Secretary of Defense that had just recently run the Washington DC office of the ACLU, and was (reportedly) wearing a pony tail.

My boss at the time, the Assistant Secretary of Defense (ASD) for Special Operations/Low Intensity Conflict had been detailed to be the Acting Undersecretary for Policy in the final days of the George H.W. Bush Administration, and was responsible for overseeing a smooth transition of many of the Office of the Secretary of Defense (OSD) offices to the Clinton Administration. He called me in one day to tell me that Mort had been designated to be the new ASD for Democracy and Peacekeeping, and asked if I would consent to a detail to assist Mort in establishing his office. I agreed and within a couple of days we were in business. The detail was supposed to last for a few weeks, until Mort could hire more permanent Military Assistants, and then I would return to my job in Drug Enforcement Policy and Support.

My first encounter with Mort was almost surreal. As I walked into his office for the first time, General Ron Fogleman (Commander of the Air Mobility Command, and later Chief of Staff of the Air Force) was walking out. We introduced ourselves to each other, shook hands, and then he moved on to his next appointment. I guess the point to that part of the story is that little did I realize it would be a common occurrence for the next year to have someone like General Fogleman in the office, or be with Mort as he visited someone else's office, or to be escorting people throughout the building that would then, or later, be major players on the world stage.[13]

Mort entered the office in February of 1993 as a Presidential nominee.

---

13  At the time, Kofi Annan was the Deputy Secretary General of the United Nations for Humanitarian Affairs. Of course, later he became Secretary General. He was a frequent visitor to Mort, and I would sign him in at the River entrance to the Pentagon and escort him throughout the building. Over the course of the year, Mort was active in the formulation of the "Don't Ask, Don't Tell" policy. We had frequent visits by representatives of the gay and lesbian communities, and I would sign them in and escort them throughout the building. It was not uncommon to answer the phone and have Sandy Berger, George Stephanopoulos, Daniel Ellsberg, and others on the line. It was an interesting year to be sure.

That meant that he needed Senate confirmation before he could officially assume his duties. But from day one, we proceeded along two concurrent paths. One, that he needed to prepare himself for the long and ultimately painful confirmation process; and two, that the President's business needed to get done so, confirmed or not, Mort needed to quickly (but respectful of the Senate's role) get to work on issues.

Mort Halperin and me in his office in 1993

Mort left the Pentagon in February 1994, having lost his confirmation battle. It was a grueling year for all of us. In the meantime, we built a 96-person office that developed major US Government policy for DOD's role in both humanitarian and peacekeeping affairs. But the confirmation process itself was nothing short of disgusting; it was brutal, vicious, completely partisan, and dishonest. It was my first real exposure to partisan politics at a senior level, up close and personal.

Mort, at the time, had written about 14 books and countless papers and articles on subjects ranging from the US role in humanitarian relief to arms control and nuclear proliferation. The entire year was a coordinated and deliberate attempt to discredit, if not slander, Mort by distorting many of the things he had written. I saw occasions where editorial writers took passages from one page in a Halperin book, and then piecing that together with another passage from a different page of the book, and then representing that as a direct quote. Chief among the critics was an editorial writer for the Washington Times by the name of Frank Gaffney…a man that I have little if any respect for to this day.

The partisanship was uglier than anything I'd seen before or since. One has to remember that Mort was considered by some to be probably the most liberal person to come into the Pentagon, perhaps ever (even though he had previously worked there). Equally important, was Mort's history with conservatives. He was alleged to have been the person that helped Daniel Ellsberg steal the Pentagon Papers in the late 1960s; his house had been bugged on the orders of Henry Kissinger in the early 1970s and Mort, in fact, sued Kissinger for illegal wire-tapping and won; he was listed as number 8 on Richard Nixon's infamous "enemies list." So it was no surprise that the entire confirmation process (controlled by Republicans) was neither honest nor honorable. But that's politics.

The most salient point to this story is that, while others weren't, Mort was a gentleman, and one of the most honorable men I've ever known. He conducted himself accordingly until the bitter end of that confirmation process. He remained composed and dignified throughout, even in the presence of his most vicious critics. I knew there were times when it was wearing him down, but he rarely let that show. Mort was not faint of heart, nor did he choose to have milk and cookies elsewhere; he stuck it out. Through and through, he was one of the toughest guys I've ever known. What I learned from this great man were the virtues of honor, grace, control, dignity, and a commitment to your principles in all that you do[14]. Mort was probably the smartest person I've ever been around. While he had little patience for people that couldn't intellectually keep up (still not sure why he kept me), he also had a sense of charm that I saw him use as he dealt with everyone. I've tried hard over the years to instill those qualities in my personal leadership style.

In another instance, during the summer of 1996, and following the devastating bombing of Khobar Towers in Saudi Arabia, I was plucked from Fairchild AFB and given 10 days to report to the Commander of Joint Task Force-Southwest Asia for a one-year tour to rebuild security

---

14 I also learned that in the world of political appointees, what motivates them is rarely any of the qualities that I'm trying to highlight throughout this book. Many aren't motivated by their honor or integrity, but more often than not, by their political loyalties and the Administration's agenda (whether liberal or conservative). I've alluded to this somewhat already and more of this to be discussed later; but while hoping not to sound too cynical, I have found there is a sense of honor, if not chivalry, that is needed in senior leadership but is lacking in many political leaders today.

within the region. As it was told to me, General Fogleman (Air Force Chief of Staff) and General Benny Peay (US Army and Commander of CENTCOM) had argued over who to send. General Peay wanted an Army Infantry officer, while General Fogleman argued that the majority of assets within the region were Air Force assets, requiring an Air Force security police officer for the job. I was told that several records of SP officers that were already pinned-on Colonels or were Colonel-selectees (as in my case) were presented to him for selection. Because of my previous years in the Pentagon, writing DOD policy on combatting terrorism[15], he picked my records out of the pile and said "This guy!" So, in August of 1996, with little notice, the Air Force "frocked" me to Colonel (a rare event in the Air Force) and off I went.

I stopped at the Pentagon on the way over to meet General Wayne Downing, whose commission had just left the region and was in the process of writing a rather scathing report on the state of security at US installations. He gave me, not a draft of the report but, essentially a list of things that he thought needed to be done.

I then went through CENTCOM Headquarters at MacDill Air Force Base in Florida, where I met with the CENTCOM Director of Operations, Maj Gen Joe Hurd. General Hurd's instructions were slightly different. He asked me to do an assessment of Air Force security in the region as fast as I could, and report to him my recommendation on whether the air base defense mission should be taken from the Air Force and given to the Army. There was no mistake…he was asking me to make a recommendation that could ultimately strip the security police career field of its primary core mission; a mission that had been central to its heritage since before Vietnam. What General Hurd told me, very candidly, was that many people (non-Air Force and even some Air Force), in expressing disappointment with Khobar, placed some of the blame on the Security Police inability to adequately conduct their Air Base Ground Defense mission; that we were neither organized, trained, equipped, nor qualified to perform a mission that was (in their view) more appropriately for the Army.[16]

When I finally got to Riyadh, Saudi Arabia and checked in with my

15 I wrote the DOD Directive on combatting terrorism. It was the defining document on DOD policy and how we would protect troops, families, and conduct force protection operations around the world. It introduced the Threat Condition (THREATCON) system.
16 This sentiment was also expressed to me in a separate meeting with BGen Fields, USMC, who was the CENTCOM Inspector General.

immediate boss, Maj Gen Kurt Andersen, he reiterated what General Hurd had asked. By this time, both Generals had told me that there was pressure to bring the Army in. Although the Downing Report had never openly criticized Security Police, there was nevertheless an effort afoot to put an Army infantry battalion in at Dhahran to protect Khobar (post bombing) and then Prince Sultan Air Base, where all U.S. and allied forces would eventually move. Surprisingly, both Hurd and Andersen were Air Force general officers, yet they seemed to be driving me toward a recommendation that would be counter-productive to the Air Force. What I learned was that career survival instincts are a very powerful and compelling force. Following the bombing, commanders in the field were paranoid as hell. They kept diaries of every action they took and did almost everything they could to divest themselves of responsibility. It was shameful. While on the one hand, legitimate questions were being asked about the Air Force's training and capability to do the mission, on the other hand, I saw it as a deliberate attempt to get out of the mission if at all possible. For some senior Air Force leaders, it was to pass it off to the Army. For me, any notion to do that was sacrilegious. Nevertheless, I worked hard to give an honest and fair assessment of who should be doing air base defense, despite the heavy-handedness.

Members of the team in front of Khobar Towers in the Fall of 1996. I'm second from the left.

Adding to that pressure, within a month or so on the job, I met Lt Gen Carl Franklin, 9th Air Force commander, who was stationed in South

Carolina but came to the desert frequently. General Franklin would repeatedly press me for an opinion on security (as I was the "expert") and then would ridicule me for my position. In this respect it was a frustrating and pressure-packed year for sure.[17]

I don't mean to drag this story out. But I ultimately did my assessment, and reported back to all that in my opinion the Air Force security police were trained, equipped, and had adequate leadership to successfully perform the air base defense mission. The problems leading up to the Khobar Towers bombing were not those of a poor security force. The issues involved poor intelligence sharing (mostly from the CIA[18]) and a lack of cooperation among the interagency community that created a perfect storm for Osama Bin Laden and Al Quida to carry out their mission. For the nine months I was there, I travelled from site to site with my team of professionals rebuilding the security posture. We re-strung concertina wire and re-stacked sand bag fighting positions; reviewed and validated security plans; and generally presided over an enhancement of force protection within the region.

The view of Khobar Towers on page 23 (with me and the team) is the one most Americans saw at the time. It's what the press showed in their reporting of potential incompetence; implying that it was one high rise building, why couldn't the US commander secure that building? This view is what Khobar Towers (plural) truly was. It was a huge international mission at the time, with US, British, French, and other forces occupying most of these buildings. This is the challenge, and awesome responsibility, the US commander had. (The destroyed building is front left)

---

17 There was an onslaught of oversight and criticism throughout the year I was there; several outside assessments (Marine Corps Red Team, GAO, Joint Staff, and others).
18 Retired CIA Director John Brennan was the Station Chief in Riyadh at the time, and responsible. As Forrest Gump would say…that's all I have to say about that.

As for my Three Amigos (the three Air Force Generals); Hurd and Andersen generally accepted my recommendations and left me alone. Franklin, on the other hand, continued to refute our findings, without founded facts. Based on the timing of his visits, some speculated that he was definitely focused on taking advantage of the tax free status of being in that area of operations (AOR), versus the problem.

The points to this story are both of honor and responsibility, which I'll cover in more detail next. It's important to note, however, that I was placed in a position where I could have easily compromised my values of honor and integrity, and consequently could have shirked my responsibility. I didn't. I guess I hope there are some that will agree that I was tough enough for the job. The pressures at the time were tremendous, and I ultimately survived it. It goes to show that it's not always easy to do the right thing.

## *Your Sense of Responsibility*

I have found over my many years in leadership positions that, of the most unflattering words that you can either speak or hear, "it's not my fault" are just about at the top of the list. That small, concise statement tells me volumes. I used to teach my own children that their action (or inaction), no matter how small, could have affected an outcome. "Dad, it's not my fault. The alarm didn't go off." Yes, but who is supposed to set the alarm? "Yeah, but the clock was defective." Yes, but shouldn't you have checked that out before going to bed?

This conversation could go on forever (and frequently did). I think my kids ultimately realized that there is always some action we could've taken to affect the outcome. Unfortunately, I think a growing number of people from younger generations have learned the art of scapegoating, or responsibility-dodging. I don't know, but I suspect that it goes back to our failure to instill that competitive culture in our kids that I discussed earlier. But I think there is a larger problem. As parents, we've done (in some cases, not all) a horrible job of instilling basic responsibility in our kids. We let them make excuses, or worse yet, we make excuses for them. It is far easier to divest yourself from responsibility and to divert it to someone else.

It was sometime around 1984, I was sitting at my desk when my secretary walked in and said there was a Mr. Jones (I've changed the name here) on the phone for me; that he wanted to discuss his son. I knew immediately who it was and why he was calling. As I answered the phone, Mr. Jones began a tense but cordial conversation. He was upset that I was in the process of discharging his son for illegal drug use. He wanted to know the facts of the case, and while I was under no obligation to even speak with him about his adult son, I did. I gave him as much information as I could legally do, and I tried desperately to reason with him as he grew angrier with the situation and my apparent intransigence on dropping the charges. Suddenly in the conversation he began chastising me for my failures as a commander. It was suddenly all my fault that his son had strayed, and that he was disappointed in me for not turning his son into a responsible man; after all, that's why he encouraged him to enlist. As you can imagine, the conversation deteriorated rapidly.

Again, in many instances parents aren't exercising the responsibility they should. So why should they expect their son or daughter will have learned some basic concepts of honor, integrity, loyalty, and yes responsibility, in the first place? Mr. Jones just didn't get it!

While I was on active duty, we (at least most of the organizations I was associated with) had countless successes. Nevertheless, there were also times when I had to stand up and accept responsibility for some pretty dumb things that we did. Here are some of my more stellar examples:

While at Peterson Air Force Base my K-9 trainers lost a heroin training aid for 24 hours. While one may not understand the significance of that, it is a very serious event, and was a monumental blunder. Drug training aids are tightly controlled by the DEA. The aid is weighed and accounted for every shift, and stored inside a locked safe within the armory. One afternoon, the team was doing drug dog training and left one of their aids (about 2 ounces of pure heroin) in a hangar on base. Apparently, the dog never found it, and the team just forgot it. It was all very innocent, but when that happens the aid has to be sent back to the DEA to be tested to ensure that no one cut or diluted it (after all, it was out of our control for about 24 hours); and in doing so it destroys the aid. It all came out well, but I was in serious trouble for a few days. I could have easily blamed it on the team, but I took full responsibility for the incident because it happened under my command.

In a similar incident at Fairchild Air Force Base in 1995, we lost a prisoner out of our jail. He just walked out! As it turned out, he spent several days watching guard procedures, as well as their habits. When one of the guards left the jail, the prisoner slipped a piece of paper into the locking mechanism just before it automatically closed. When no one was looking he walked away. That too, was a serious security breach that got plenty of attention from our headquarters. Again, as the commander I immediately stepped up and accepted full responsibility.

One of my favorite quotes came from legendary coach Bear Bryant, who said "If anything goes bad, I did it. If anything goes semi-good, then we did it. If anything goes real good, then you did it." Now, there is a man that took responsibility. But what's also revealing about that quote is that he gave responsibility, and the credit, as well.

I've been so lucky over the years to work for leaders that gave me room to grow and, therefore, a lot of responsibility. I have what seems like countless stories to tell, but one of my favorites involves the night we invaded Panama under Operation Just Cause. I was working the night shift in the Defense Secretary's Crisis Coordination Center. Throughout the night as events unfolded, my partner and I would coordinate with the Joint Staff for updates and would keep the Secretary (and others) informed. As morning approached and the air drops were now complete, it appeared that all was going to plan, but no one could find Manuel Noriega. He, to this point, had escaped capture. At about 6 AM, the Assistant Secretary of Defense (ASD) for Special Operations and Low Intensity Conflict came in and gathered the team. He wanted recommendations on what we (the US Government) should be doing next. He said that he needed to see Secretary Cheney within the next hour and he would be looking for ideas to present to the President. Now, I was the junior guy in the room and was just a little intimidated by the experience. Also, my immediate boss was there and we hadn't had a chance to discuss any of this, and I didn't have a chance to give him some thoughts. So, when the question was asked, and there was a long pause in the room, I spoke up. I suggested that we offer a reward for Noriega's capture. The ASD said "brilliant!" and wrote it down quickly. He then asked how much we should offer. Again, silence. So, I said "how about a million dollars?" He said "brilliant!" and wrote that down quickly. Then he asked the room if there was anything else. Again, silence. So I said "let's offer a reward for each rifle or handgun that the public turns in; that would get weapons off the streets." Once again, "brilliant!" and he wrote it down. He asked "how much should we give them?" by this time everyone was just looking at me so I said "how about $150 for each weapon? He wrote that down quickly and was off to see the Secretary.

I signed off my shift and went home to get some sleep before needing to be back again that night. When I got home, I was more than amused by the whole event, and told my wife Jeanne the whole story; and then went to bed. When I got up at about 5 PM and came down stairs for dinner, Jeanne was watching CNN. She simply said "I think you might want to watch this." When the headline came up at the top of the hour the lead story was "The President has authorized a one-million-dollar reward for the capture of Manuel Noriega and $150 for every weapon that Panamanian citizens turn in." Needless to say, I was floored. As it turned out the ASD submitted my suggestions to Secretary Cheney, and he took them directly to the President. Of course, none of that would have happened if I hadn't had leadership that gave me responsibility and encouraged me to be bold confident, and innovative.

On another occasion, while assigned to USCINCPAC (US Commander-in-Chief of the Pacific) headquarters at Camp Smith, Hawaii in 1987, I was tasked to be the lead on what became the largest national counterterrorism exercise in our history (certainly up to that point). I was a young Major in the Special Operations Division, entrusted with an awesome responsibility.

We'd been approached by the Joint Special Operations Command (JSOC) from Ft. Bragg to set up a complicated dual scenario that would involve a cruise ship assault and recapture by SEAL Team 6 and a hijacked airline rescue by Delta, all simultaneously. The scenarios were linked where intel from one would drive events in the other. The ship scenario[19] would take place in Hawaiian waters and the aircraft scenario would occur in Thailand. As lead exercise planner, my job was to build the scenario, put together that master events list, and then act as a controller during the exercise.

This was an event that consumed my time for about 8 months, beginning with a preliminary exercise where SEAL Team 6 was to conduct a practice assault and recapture of the cruise ship about 4 months before the full-scale exercise. In the early fall of 1986, I flew to Virginia and then, by C-5 transport, to California with SEAL Team 6. The day after arriving at Moffett Field in California, I boarded the cruise ship in San Francisco and sailed through the Golden Gate as the ship was on its way to Hawaii after being refurbished during their off-season.

19 The ship was a Hawaiian-based luxury cruise ship that we rented for a week at a cost of $850,000 in 1987. We called the 25th Infantry Division at Schofield Barracks and asked if we could "borrow" about 200 soldiers to play the role of hostages. We told their command they should only tell their troops to pack beach wear for a week. Boy, were they happy and surprised when they saw what they were getting into.

One of the many papers from across the nation the morning after the Panama invasion in December 1989. (Photo by permission of *The Arizona Daily Star*)

The plan was for SEAL Team 6 to "assault" the ship off the coast of Monterey as it was sailing to Hawaii. As luck would have it, we ran into weather just after leaving San Francisco, and the exercise was cancelled. Suddenly I found myself on a cruise ship on its way to Hawaii. I was supposed to be extracted by SEAL Team 6 after the assault, but with weather conditions (mostly heavy fog) they could no longer fly. I called my boss via the satellite radio I was carrying to tell him I'd see him in five days when the ship arrived in Honolulu. Not surprisingly, his reply was "not so fast."

I got a radio call back about an hour later and was told a Coast Guard cutter would pick me up about 20 miles off the coast of Monterey. I have to tell you that transferring ships in the middle of the ocean is not something I want to do again. I almost lost all my communications gear (and nearly my life) trying to get into a small zodiac with swells that were approaching ten feet.

When I got back to Hawaii, and it was time for the major exercise to take place, my boss asked me which one of the simultaneous take downs did I want to cover. I told him I'd already done the cruise ship (thank you very much), so I'd go to Thailand and cover Delta's operation.

About three or four days before the exercise was to start. I headed off to Thailand. Since we hadn't fully negotiated everything on the Thai side, I took an Army Major with me who was also a contracting officer. He served as the exercise's contracting officer, while I was the dispersing officer (DOD required two people for those roles). When I left Hawaii, I was handed $25,000 in travelers checks and a cashier's check for $300,000. We had tentatively worked a deal with Thai International Airways to rent two of their A300 Airbuses for four days (one to be used as the hijacked aircraft and the other for Delta to practice their operations plan on).

To our surprise, when we got to Bangkok, the embassy warned us that Thai International Airways wanted an emergency meeting to discuss details. The embassy's prediction was the price had suddenly gone up. The problem I had was, we had negotiated for $300,000 for both airplanes, and that's exactly the amount of the cashier's check I was carrying. When we got to the meeting it was me, my Army major, and an embassy contracting officer on one side of the table, and the President of Thai International Airways and the Chief of Staff of the Royal Thai Army on the other side. No question, it was a power play on their part. Of course, as expected, they wanted more money. Now, I'm not sure if they saw a couple of young Majors they could steam-roll, or if they suddenly decided the United States had deep pockets and they could squeeze just a little bit more.

As negotiations commenced, I had no choice but to learn fast how to play hard ball with the big boys. I had no other money with me and failing to close the deal for these airplanes would result in catastrophic failure; we had major forces moving already and this was to be the largest counterterrorism exercise our country had ever attempted; not to mention the most complicated as well.

We argued back and forth for a while, and had taken a couple of breaks. It seemed like we were getting nowhere when I decided enough was enough and I needed a "hail Mary." I walked back into the conference room, sat down and looked that Thai four star right in the eye and said "General, we negotiated $300,000 in good faith. I'm getting up from this table right now and calling Admiral Hays to tell him you've backed out of your agreement. He will call you, you'll have to face him on this issue, we will ultimately have to cancel this exercise, it will be a stain on US-Thai relations, and it will embarrass your country."[20] At that point, I started to get up and he said "wait, we need another break."

With Major General Anujit (on the right), Thai National Security Council, conducting final negotiations and planning for a major bilateral counterterrorism exercise in 1987.

So, to be clear, I've never even met Admiral Hays and there was no way I was going to call him to admit defeat. I'm not even sure I could have gotten through. The fact is, I was bluffing and wasn't sure what my next move would have been. We came back together after about 10 minutes and the President of Thai international Airways (the guy that had been holding the line on money) suddenly announced that $300,000 would work just fine. I signed over the check, we all shook hands, and off we went. It was clear to me I'd hit a nerve with the General and he, in turn, had words with the

---

20  Admiral Ronald Hays was the US Navy four star in charge of the US Pacific Command; about five levels above me.

airline. The next day, the Thai army gave me a helicopter and crew to fly up to Korat Air Base to ensure that critical equipment was moving from there to U-Tapao Air Base in southern Thailand.[21]

I met the Delta operators at U-Tapao for the major exercise a couple of days later, setup and paid for all the food and other incidentals. And, when it was all over, flew home...exhausted.

The point to this story is to highlight the tremendous responsibility my bosses placed on me (a young officer) with monumental (international!) consequences at stake. I delivered and they weren't disappointed. It was a lesson I learned about giving responsibility to people you recognize that can handle it, trusting them, and then holding them accountable.

The point I hope you're getting from all this is that responsibility, when given, is yours. Accept it. But an important point, as well, is that if you ever find yourself in a leadership position, it's NOT necessary for you to lead from the front every time. Sometimes it's equally important, if not more, for you to lead from behind and push your people up front. Allow them to (make them) take responsibility. I was a guy that was lucky enough to have leadership throughout my career that followed this basic principle. And I know there are many that have worked for me throughout the years that have wondered why, at times, they found themselves suddenly in the spotlight when they least expected it. It's because I've long embraced the concept of delegated responsibility as the best way of nurturing future leadership. Have I been burned by it? Sure. But in the vast majority of cases pushing younger/junior people up front, and providing them both experience and exposure, helped me develop a quality leader that was ready for the tough jobs later in life. And again, in the vast majority of those cases, they didn't disappoint me.

## Final Thoughts

By now you probably feel you've gotten a healthy dose of military and federal civilian culture. I'm sorry about that, but again, it's what my experiences are based on. I don't mean to suggest that only these cultures are the truly tough ones. Instead it's to drive the point that it's a cruel, harsh world out there. It's extremely competitive, and if you're not ready for it you probably won't survive; much less succeed.

---

21 The story about having to drag my aircrew out of a local bar to make the return flight is a wild one...for another time.

I heard someone once say, what's not important in life is the job resume you build, but the character resume. What do you want as your legacy, and how do you want people (your great, great grandkids, for instance) to remember you? Above all, strive to treat people fairly, equally, with dignity and respect. Not that I would suggest that you make life unnecessarily harsh for yourself, just don't always look for the easy way out; especially at the expense of your sense of honor or your sense of responsibility. Be bold and brave always. Reach for responsibility. If you're lucky enough to work for a boss that relinquishes it, seize the opportunity. If not, then look for opportunities; but don't shy away from either responsibility or an opportunity to excel at the toughest someone has to offer. I guarantee rewards will follow.

I told my young nephew, Nathan, who was about to be commissioned as an officer in the United States Army, that he needed to be in excellent physical shape for the basic infantry course, and for jump school, and especially for Ranger school. But beyond physical strength, success in all of these courses was more about strength of character; a strength that almost wills your success; that you refuse to fail. I believe this principle applies almost universally.

And then there's my older brother, who once told me that at least in the business world "sometimes success comes from knowing when to raise your hand in time to say 'me too.'" I think that often applies universally as well.

*"If not you, then who? If not now, when?"*
—Hillel the Elder

# 2

# Loyalty

## *(Or How to Fake it)*

*"The only people I owe my loyalty to are those
who never made me question theirs."*
—Anonymous

My son once said to me when he was dating a young lady that was beginning to question his level of commitment…"Dad, the key to any relationship is sincerity; you have to learn how to fake sincerity."

As funny (or as sad to some) as the statement above sounds, it's often true. The problem I've encountered throughout my career is that too many leaders (and far too many followers) are faking sincerity in their organizational relationships. They aren't serious about their loyalty to senior leadership, the organization, or even their subordinates. Too many are in it (the job, that is) for one reason only; a narcissistic self-promotion. Everything seems to revolve around them. Some are more open than others about it, and they're not shy about admitting their motivation to get to the next level of promotion. Others are just trying to politically survive, and consequently, most of their decisions have that underlying element to them. Regardless of which type, they would all throw you and me under the bus if there was any threat to their political standing. The worst of the bunch (and there are many that do) are those that fain loyalty to their boss, and then run him or her down to the troops. In my view, they're the most despicable of leaders.

This idea of self-promotion is something I was warned of early in my career. I was told that it doesn't reflect well on your character; and, no matter how well you think you might be hiding your true intentions, everyone else sees it. More on this in a later chapter.

## *Never Step in Front of Your Boss Unless it's to Take a Bullet*

In the early 1980s I was the Chief of Security Police at Peterson Air Force Base in Colorado Springs. I was a young Captain at the time. Peterson was, and is, the home of NORAD and the Space Command (it is also NORTHCOM today). The four-star commander at the time was General James V. Hartinger[22]. Now, I didn't work directly for General Hartinger; but I did interact with him on some level a couple of times a week. I was either speaking with him about the alarm system at his house or we would see each other at the base passenger terminal where we were often providing security for distinguished visitors coming through. On one of those occasions General Hartinger seemed to be in an exceptionally good mood and decided he would spend a little time mentoring me[23]. He told me several things; that the most meaningful promotion he ever had was when he made Sergeant in the Army, because sergeants were supervisors and that was important to him; that the second most meaningful promotion was when he made Colonel, because as a colonel he would be eligible to become a wing commander (and besides colonels put their rank on their mail box when they retired; I don't); and, despite those two meaningful promotions, he said…"but there's nothing like being a four-star."

In the course of the conversation he gave me what he considered to be the Hartinger secret formula for success…absolute loyalty to whomever you work for, and do everything you can to make your boss look good. General Hartinger then told me the story about the time he was the Director of Plans at Headquarters NORAD in the early 1970s and took a trip throughout the Pacific with the four-star commander at the time. He said it was amazing to see how many senior officers would trip over themselves to look good in front of the boss. They would sit in a number of briefings throughout the trip asking questions or offering facts that were clearly intended to make themselves the most knowledgeable in the eyes of

---

22 Senior officers were as frightened of this guy as I've ever seen. He certainly had the power to crush careers on a whim. Whether he did or not are only matters of speculation, if not legend. He did have quite the ego, however. He wore two different name patches on his flight suit. One had his wings and "Jim Hartinger, World's Greatest Fighter Pilot". The other had his wings and "Grrrrrrr" (His nickname was the Grrr).

23 It's not uncommon for most senior officers to take a junior officer aside and pass along some of their stories and lessons learned. I had the good fortune to be on the receiving end of that from Gen Hartinger a few times.

the boss. Hartinger said he took a different approach; he would find interesting facts about the location or organization they were visiting, and then whisper suggested questions the boss could ask during the briefing. All the while Hartinger would remain silent. He'd suggest "Hey boss, why don't you ask them about that green latrine they built last month" (an example he actually used). As he told me this story, he said he used that tactic frequently and "guess who got promoted?"

General James Hartinger "The Grrr"
(Air Force file photo)

From that day forward I learned the lesson that you should never step in front of your boss unless it's to take that courageously noble action of self-sacrifice; in other words, to take a bullet. Your job is to make your boss look good, and to give him or her (as well as your subordinates) all of the credit. I also learned that you don't ever have to think <u>like</u> your boss, but you do have to think about the things your boss thinks about. Do everything you can to stay one step ahead of the boss by anticipating what he or she will react to next. Your focus needs to be on the boss's agenda… not yours!

## Who's Sitting Next to the Boss?

I'll never forget the time, while at Peterson Air Force Base in the early 1980s, I was down at base operations waiting for a distinguished visitor (DV) aircraft to come in; and this was no <u>routine</u> DV aircraft. At that time (and they may still do so), the Air Force had a program where they would send a KC-135 tanker around the country to pick up retired four stars and bring them to the Pentagon for a series of briefings. They did this quarterly (as I recall), and it was a program where retired senior officers could both stay current on issues and impart sage advice on things they may have encountered throughout their careers.

This particular aircraft was coming from somewhere in California and had retired General Curtis LeMay on board. Waiting in the DV lounge were four retired four stars that would board the aircraft when it landed. I had the great fortune to be a fly on the wall and overhear their conversation as the aircraft was on final to Peterson. After all the years, there was still a great sense of respect and admiration, if not a sense of reverence, for this iconic man. Yes, loyalty, still. A couple of these guys had worked for General LeMay when they were junior officers. Their loyalty for him never wavered or waned. It was almost cute, if not a little surreal, to hear them discuss who would get to sit next to the old man on the airplane.

I had the honor of shaking General LeMay's hand when he stepped off the airplane. An honor I hold dear today, given the historical importance of the role he played in WW II and the early development of the Air Force.

## Is it Really Loyalty You're Seeing, or is it All a Fake?

OK, maybe I shouldn't be that cynical about it, but I know that some really do fake it. I recently had a relatively young GS-15 working for me whose concept of loyalty extended to his GS-13 wife and their two kids, and that's it! As hard as I tried over the years to mentor and teach this young man as much as I could about the concept, I failed. <u>I consider this to be the biggest failure of my professional career</u>, and one that will haunt me for the rest of my life. Despite my efforts, he never got it. He never understood the value (to his integrity, if not his self-respect) to take care of those around him, up and down the chain, sometimes at his own expense. For him, it was all about him. But because of that, and all of my failed attempts to influence him, I came to realize that some people reach adulthood, and ultimately leadership positions, without having the basic concept of loyalty ingrained as a building block of childhood development. I mentioned this as a function of parental responsibility in Chapter 1. This man apparently never got that from his parents, and that's both sad and dangerous at the point where he was in his career. In his case, he has learned to fake loyalty whenever it suited his purpose. On at least two occasions (once with another agency and once with me) he had sued his employer when a personnel decision made by management didn't favor his personal situation.

When you ascend the leadership ladder, at some point (the clear bright line is usually when you begin supervising people) you have to "flip the switch" and become a member of the management team. It doesn't matter what type of organization it is. Whether it's military, civil service, or the corporate world, the principle remains the same. You are no longer one of the troops! That doesn't mean you don't care, or that you don't work to take care of their interests. Your job is exactly that; to supervise, manage and nurture your employees…to lead! But you can no longer hang around the water cooler and commiserate. You can't stand on the back loading dock twice a day and smoke a cigarette with the troops, all while bashing senior leadership (I actually had a senior leader I worked for doing that…to himself and his organization!…"Yeah, we all suck!"). But the young GS-15 I'm referring to did that and more. He would fain loyalty to senior leadership and the organization, and then undermine it when it suited his needs. Like my son joked, this guy had learned how to fake sincerity; across the board, to his troops and to his bosses.

But maybe it's more than just loyalty. Maybe it's more of a sense of honor this guy (and many others) lacks. It's my firm belief, that loyalty and honor are in fact personal values that are ingrained in you early in life; they are part of your morality system. You either have them or you don't. They're not something that can be instilled later. They are personality traits…by-products of upbringing. There are many influences on a child in their early developmental years; to include this sense of honor and chivalry. Yes, loyalty was developed along with everything else then, or it was not and will never be developed later. Those that I have encountered throughout my life that lack the ability to be loyal, have an almost sinister aura about them. You can spot them a mile off. Call me a cynic if you like, but I truly believe this.

I believe, and have always believed, that my professional value system is driven by an ingrained sense of loyalty to whomever I'm working for. And regardless of my personal or political beliefs, I've been able to keep them in check and conduct business professionally. To do anything less would be an affront to my personal code of honor. But despite all that, what follows is one of the most frustrating chapters of my life as it relates to the issue of loyalty.

During my last two years with FEMA, while I was the Acting Regional Administrator for an extended period (the first year and a half of the Obama Administration), I worked as hard as I could to convince the Administration that I wanted to be part of the team. I travelled to Headquarters and visited with the incoming FEMA Administrator. I worked the incoming political appointees very hard to sway their opinion of me and the region. But as time went on in the early months, I became increasingly aware that I was seen as a "Bush holdover" (something I also talked about in Chapter 1). Now, granted, I was hired during the Bush years and I am a retired Air Force Colonel, so one could probably correctly assume that I'm a rather conservative guy. Nevertheless, I was a career civil servant; and one that took his charge to serve every presidency to the best of his abilities. Notwithstanding, I was, and remained to the end, an outsider.[24]

At one particular meeting where the FEMA Administrator had all of his Regional Administrators around a table, we were discussing his new reorganization plans. I raised my hand and asked a simple question; "Have you ever considered…?[25] He became somewhat red faced, and visibly upset that I would ask such a question, and cut me off by saying he didn't think the law would allow what I was asking, but he would check. Very soon after, the meeting ended. The next morning his Director of Operations started the meeting off by saying he had just come from the Administrator's

---

24 This was exceptionally disappointing for me. For all my time at FEMA, I received nothing but superior ratings and, at this point, there was no reason for me to believe that I wasn't anything but the next Regional Administrator. I believe to this day that their leadership (or lack of) failed me; they were disingenuous with me. Ironically, I encountered a lack of leadership at the beginning of my career, and then again at the end of my career. I'm not as naïve as I once was. Nevertheless, still disappointed.

25 The content of the question dealt with a classified component and is really irrelevant to this discussion; but it was what I thought at the time to be a very innocuous question.

office and a meeting where they discussed our meeting from the day before. At the previous day's meeting, someone had asked a question that basically challenged the entire foundation of the FEMA reorganization and their (the political leadership's) capability to make sound decisions. He went on to say that if there was anyone in the room that thought they could do better, or more directly, if such acts of disloyalty continued with people questioning the direction the Administrator was taking the Agency, then those people needed to resign, retire or move on immediately. I was mortified! Clearly, he was talking about me.

FEMA Director Craig Fugate and me in 2010.

At the break I pulled the Director of Operations aside and quickly confirmed that I was the subject of the discussion. He said there was a perception that I, and my entire regional staff, seemed to question every decision that was coming out of Headquarters; and that was unacceptable during this time of transition, rapid growth and change. We needed to "get on board!" He told me that this Administrator "has a very close circle of advisors and was not seeking input from others."[26] I responded by saying two things: First, OK, good to know, thank you; now that I know that

---

26 So here's a classic example of myopic thinking; but, then, I guess that too is certainly one leadership style. A sign of good leadership is to recognize that often (very often) better ideas come from people in the trenches that have been thinking about this stuff for years. Don't ignore or dismiss them out of hand; which was clearly happening in this instance.

he doesn't want my input I'll keep my mouth shut and my region in line. Second, and for the record, just because we ask a question or offer an input, that should <u>never</u> be seen as a sign of disloyalty. Good Lord! There seemed to be a certain level of paranoia that I'd never seen before. I told him we are, in fact, committed to serving the President, this Administrator, and the Administration as vigorously and professionally as we would any other.[27]

I spent the next year and a half trying to rebuild my Headquarters relationships. The incident above was something I don't think I ever recovered from with those in the Obama Administration.

My role as the Acting Regional Administrator for FEMA Region 10 was to chair the Regional Advisory Council. I'm here with civic leaders from throughout the four-state region.

The point to all this? No matter how hard you try, no matter how well–intentioned you are, sometimes, the deck is just stacked against you. Regardless, don't ever waver on your values. I value loyalty extremely high. I proceeded with the next year and a half trying at every opportunity to

---

27 It was this single meeting that drove the climate of future weekly Regional Administrator's video teleconferences with the FEMA Administrator. He would sit on that VTC, frustrated at times, that no Regional Administrator had anything to say. He often remarked, and on at least one occasion chastised them, that he didn't understand why he even had the regions on if they weren't going to contribute. He just never got it (or he was oblivious to what had gone on).

demonstrate my loyalty to the organization. Why...because it was important to me to preserve my professional integrity and my personal sense of honor. If at any time you feel you can't support the boss you work for, or you feel that your effectiveness has been diluted by some notion that you're disloyal, then perhaps it's time to move on. Ultimately, I failed in my attempts to become a "member of the team", and after months of their continued marginalization of my role as a Deputy Regional Administrator (a lack of support from the political leadership on a variety of issues), I left in the summer of 2011 for a promotion as Regional Director for another agency within DHS. As disappointing as that was to leave FEMA, it was the right thing to do at the time.

## *Loyalty Up and Down the Chain*

During the early 1980s I was assigned to Headquarters Strategic Air Command in Omaha, Nebraska (the two coldest winters of my life, by the way). My job was to be the Executive Officer to SAC's Chief of Security Police. As a young Captain, I ran all things "administrative" for the boss, but also for his staff of about 40 people. Some staff elements at SAC Headquarters would often use an officer from the administrative career field for this function, but our philosophy was that we needed a career security police officer who could understand paperwork as it flowed through the office for its subject matter, and then decide who should work it and what priority it should carry. This practice worked extremely well, and I was enough of a generalist in our career field to have a pretty good grasp on what was and was not a hot issue to work.

My (our) boss was a crusty old Colonel that was short on both personality and patience. He was a Colonel, operating in a world of Generals, and often reminded me that he was a General Officer equivalent and wanted to be treated accordingly[28]. I remember on one occasion his air travel got mucked up; I can't remember what went wrong, but he was left standing at the passenger terminal for about an hour one day before I realized it and finally got a car to pick him up. He came in the next morning, walked straight past my desk into his office, looked at me, pointed, and said "that's one!" Believe me; I never let him get to two. All in all, he was a decent guy;

---

28 Egos are a funny thing; but someone once told me that "if you have the word equivalent next to your title...it means you ain't."

and I'm sure he had everyone's interest in mind. It's just that he had a difficult time showing it, and an even more difficult time relating to his troops.

His two Division Directors were a different story, however; two Lieutenant Colonels, and both full of personality. Lt Col Lars Vedvick and Lt Col Steve Heppell were extremely gifted and talented leaders. They were career cops, where the boss was not.[29] I attribute their leadership style and their troop-savvy ability to relate to those around them, and working for them, to their backgrounds as cops. They came up through the trenches of the security police career field. They knew the struggles and challenges of leading men (and later women) in what was one of the most boring jobs on earth; standing a post for eight hours in a 40-degree drizzle with a poncho, getting one or two latrine breaks and 15-20 minutes to eat your lunch. In an era before alarms and sensors, troops had to stand their post regardless of the weather conditions.[30] Consequently, and perhaps due to the rigors of our line of work, they developed a very intense sense of loyalty to those loyal to them; especially to those with the same commitment to making life easier for troops on post.

I suppose my time with Steve Heppell and Lars Vedvick did as much to shape my view of loyalty than anything else before or since. They also taught me very valuable lessons on how to lead from below. In short, they taught me how to lead up and down the chain, and how to have multiple loyalties (how to split, but not compromise, my loyalties to each of them and the boss).

As the Executive Officer to the Chief of Security Police, my job was really to serve him; or at least from his perspective that was my duty, and for the most part that was true. He needed a junior officer that could get things done; someone who would track "suspenses" (or tasks) and keep the staff moving. He also relied on me to be his eyes and ears, a spy of sorts, on all things involving the staff from operational planning to morale. I would keep him posted on what issues were being worked, what issue may walk through his door, and to the extent that I could I would give him all the

---

29  The Colonel was a career pilot who had been given the job as SAC Chief of Security Police in a time during our history when cops were deemed incapable of leading themselves. It took a pilot to be a true leader in our Air Force (sarcasm). Consequently, there was a glass ceiling for most security police officers that wasn't broken (with a few exceptions) for another 10 years.

30  There is a long-standing story about how Air Force regulations required K-9 handlers to kennel their dogs when the outside temperature reached a certain point below freezing. The handler would then go back to his post by himself.

background information available to prepare him for the issue before it got to him. In most cases I would offer him a question or two that he might ask as the staff briefed him on a specific topic. As his "gatekeeper" I spent a great deal of my time at my desk just outside his office, but I also spent a great deal of time throughout the building interacting with the staff on action after action.

As I became more comfortable with my job as an Executive Officer an odd, if not funny, relationship began to develop (that I later realized was the mark of a truly successful, if not good, Exec). While the boss saw me as his eyes and ears for all things involving the staff, the staff saw me as their eyes and ears for all things involving the boss. I began to realize that I was spying for both sides. Holy cow! In no time, I had become a double agent.

As I had done with the boss, if I felt an issue was brewing that would catch the staff by surprise, I quickly took it to one of the Division Directors (Vedvick and Heppell) to give them a heads up. As I mentioned earlier, the boss was a gruff old Colonel that on occasion would shoot first and then ask questions. If I sensed that he was upset about something, or even if we had an issue coming down the chain of command, I took it as fast as I could to the appropriate staff element. On countless occasions I walked into one of their offices and said "he's coming down the hall right behind me, here's the issue, here's what I know about it, and here's what I recommend you say or do for now." I never once revealed information given to me in confidence, nor did I ever conspire behind my boss's back. But I did everything I could to keep order and harmony within the staff. I felt that if the boss could get the results he was looking for, and his subordinates could look good in the process, it was a win-win for everyone. You can only imagine how appreciative my two Division Directors were. I never sought glory or recognition for anything; but they knew that I knew that I had saved their butts more than once. When I left the staff, Lt Col Steve Heppell, who worked most of the staff's follow-on assignments, had me placed as a Squadron Commander at Peterson AFB in Colorado Springs; an extremely rare opportunity for a Captain within the Strategic Air Command at the time.

This story about my time as an Executive Officer at SAC Headquarters carries an important lesson about loyalty; loyalty up and down the chain and to the organization as a whole. But I've also seen the antithesis. I've seen Exec Officers on power trips; they "wear their boss's rank." I've seen Exec Officers who are disloyal to the boss and who are not discrete with information that was to be held in confidence. I've seen Exec Officers who will purposely torpedo other staff officers just to make themselves look good. I've seen a number of examples of Exec Officers who were patently disloyal. My advice to any of you that ever gets an opportunity to fill such a role to embrace it for the chance to learn from seasoned veterans; embrace it for an opportunity to have an impact organizationally where other junior people don't; but embrace it with a pure heart and mind – be loyal up and down the chain because when you aren't, others notice.

There were a couple of times in my career that I encountered a person or two that were blatantly disloyal, but nothing like I faced in my final role with the Federal Civil Service. To be clear, I hold most of the people I worked with in extremely high regard. But, nevertheless, there were those above me and below me who failed to embrace the concept of loyalty. It was unlike anything I ever faced in the military, where the loyalty to each other has been proven in study after study as the key reason why soldiers fight (they fight for each other, not for their country). In Federal Civil Service that commonality of purpose doesn't exist. They aren't facing "harm's way" and, consequently, don't need their buddy's loyalty in order to survive (in the literal sense). Accordingly, for some, the loyalty they get and give is nothing more than a commodity they will spend as they need. They have no compunction about using people if it somehow propels them to the top. They will use their friends, abuse their subordinates, and climb over their boss if it suits their needs. Again, this is not to characterize all civil servants; the vast majority are outstanding patriots. But those few to several that do exist only serve their own interests and poison the cohesive climate of an organization. They are the bad apples that can spoil the barrel.

When I left the military and entered the "other" government work-force, I was very naïve to believe the old adage that "loyalty begets loyalty." Not true. It doesn't matter that you give it completely or unconditionally. You're nuts if you think that devotion to an employee, a colleague, or a supervisor will be returned, in kind, every time; in fact, some will fake it. I learned this the hard way – from below and above…at the same time in one instance! More on this later too.

I have given you my opinion on what loyalty is or is not; by now you can guess that loyalty is at or near the top of essential qualities for any leader, and certainly a member of my team, to have. Your integrity and your sense of honor are also paramount. But if you are an honorable person with great integrity, _and_ you are loyal, then little else matters to me. I'm pretty forgiving when it comes to mistakes. In relative terms, it matters little to me how talented you are, how brilliant you are, how hard you work, or what a great guy you appear to be. If you cheat or steal, I may not be able to help you; but if you are loyal, I will do all I can for you within the limits of my honor and integrity. Unfortunately, I have done this from time to time to a fault; I've even been loyal to those that haven't been.

And never forget this bit of advice… When you do leave the organization, move on! Don't expect old "loyalties" to continue on; if they do, great. But in many cases what you thought was a loyal relationship was merely an association of mutual convenience. Now that you have nothing to mutually offer, your loyalty might not matter at all to them, and their loyalties do often shift (and do so swiftly). When you walk out the door, some will forget who you are ten minutes later.

There is one more thought on loyalty that has to be conveyed here and now. During the first year of his Presidency, the media and the left (which are often the same) have been apoplectic over Donald Trump's demand for loyalty from key members of his staff. He is said to have demanded it from his former FBI Director and his Attorney General, as well as many other members of his Administration. Folks, I am here to tell you something you should already know…that is his right! And to be absolutely clear, it is everyone's responsibility as a member of the Executive Branch to be loyal to the President of the United States of America. As long as he is taking action that is legal, ethical, and moral, he has the right and duty to take the action he sees fit (and be very careful of interpreting on your own what is legal, ethical, and moral). Whether it's Donald Trump or Barack Obama, the duly elected President ran his campaign on a specific platform that got him elected. He has the right and obligation to voters to implement that platform. And you, as a civil servant, have the obligation and responsibility to support the President's agenda. If at any time you don't believe you can do that…then get the hell out! You, as a private American citizen (meaning, not in your official capacity), have a right to question, criticize, or even disparage the President and his Administration…that is what truly makes us Americans. But you cannot, must not, obstruct!

As simple as this concept should be, there are plenty in congress, the media, civil service, and even ordinary citizens that just don't get it.

# 3

# If They Don't Have Stake in the Outcome, You're in Trouble

*A genuine leader is not a searcher of consensus but a molder of consensus.*
—Martin Luther King, Jr

### *There Once Was A Guy Named Brad*

As I've already mentioned, many years ago I was the commander of the security police squadron at Fairchild Air Force Base, in Spokane. I had a very large squadron of about 440 people that was responsible for law enforcement on base, as well as security of our most sensitive assets (to include our flight line and aircraft, and a nuclear weapons storage site). In the fall of 1994 we received word that we'd undergo an inspection – a Nuclear Surety Inspection (NSI) – that would occur in the spring of 1995. So that you understand clearly, this is a big deal in the Air Force, or anywhere else within the Department of Defense. Careers, over the years, have been made and broken over how well you did or did not do during one of these inspections (and rightly so, given its nature). In fact, in recent years there have been a number of prominent national news articles about Air Force commanders either cheating on or failing some of these inspections; with severe consequences for doing so.

This inspection, however, was coming at the worst possible time. As footnoted earlier, during the previous summer we had experienced what became known at Fairchild as "Hell Week." On June 20, 1994, a recently discharged psychiatric patient returned to the base hospital and killed his two doctors. He then proceeded on a shooting rampage throughout the hospital ultimately killing 5 and wounding 22 before he was killed by a responding bicycle patrolman; and later that week, on June 24, 1994, a B-52 crashed on base killing all four crew members. So, it was a tough time for the whole base, and particularly for our squadron, who had to manage a complex crime scene, a large crash site, and endured months of follow-on investigations into both incidents. For me personally, it was the roughest time in my life. Less than three weeks after the B-52 crash my oldest son Don was killed in a horrific accident. I was crushed personally. Honestly, many of the events late that summer and throughout the fall were a blur. If it hadn't been for the quality of the staff surrounding me, I'd have never made it through. Two of my officers, Benny Martin and Ted Shelton, and my Chief, Joe Markin, propped me up and kept me pointed in the right direction. There is no other way to put it. Their loyalty to me personally, and to the success of the unit, professionally, ensured the success of everyone over those next few months and beyond. I'll never be able to thank them enough, or many of the other officers and NCOs that rallied to my side at the time. But the remarkable thing is, as they came together for that common purpose, they also jelled as a team. More about that...

Part of one of the best teams I've ever been associated with. Ken Staley, Ted Shelton, me, Benny Martin, Scott Kolar. Wish the rest of them were in this picture (Joe Markin, Scott Dearduff, Jay Colt, Gary Rhome, and many others).

What I can't tell you is how it all began. As we were moving in the direction of preparing for this major inspection, things just seemed to come together. I had taken over the unit about eight or nine months previously and realized that while we were adequate, we just weren't hitting on all cylinders. We were a collection of sub-units (individual shifts, known as Flights), but there really wasn't a "team" concept. In the fall of 1994, headquarters sent us an assistance team to look at procedures and documentation to help get us ready for this major inspection. What they found validated my assessments that while we were "OK", there were a number of things that needed to be addressed both procedurally and administratively that would bite us if they weren't fixed now. I went one step further…I shook up the entire leadership team.

What I realized then, and have never been afraid to do elsewhere in my career, is make the necessary changes (without regard to hurting someone's feelings) whenever and wherever it was necessary to do so. One of my leadership strengths is the ability to recognize strengths and weaknesses of those surrounding me[31], and therefore the ability to capitalize on their best attributes while minimizing others. You see, I don't believe in casting off someone just because he might be difficult to work with; he might also be a brilliant technician. Although, as I've alluded to previously, it has bit me on one or two occasions. Generally, though, you just need to find the right spot for that person to flourish. So, we made changes in our leadership team. I had two guys in my unit that just happened to be good at everything they did, but in this instance had a particular gift for both attention to detail and the ability to communicate it to <u>anyone</u>. Captain Ted Shelton and Master Sergeant Scott Dearduff were the guys I put in charge of getting us ready; and oh, how they did!

I can't describe to you the months of preparation that went into that inspection. But Shelton and Dearduff led the effort to re-write post orders, cleanup documentation, and establish new standards of conduct and performance. But they weren't the only heroes in this effort. It was contagious. It started small. The training section (Rudy Luna), Stan/Eval section (Jay Colt), and others, all stepped up their efforts as well. Before long, all the Flights[32] were in a friendly competition to see who could out-do who in everything from dress and appearance to response procedures. That is…all flights but one.

Brad was a Master Sergeant in charge of D Flight. Reports were coming back to me that D Flight just wasn't holding up their end. Their daily

---

31 There are countless times in my career where I moved employees around based on their most redeeming quality. People, in general, come to the organization with a variety of skillsets (and flaws). But everyone has something to offer. Some are great briefers; others are frightened at the thought of standing in front of a crowd, but might be great writers; and so on.

32 We operated on a four Flight system with a dayshift and rotating swing, mid and break shifts.

inspections didn't measure up, their paperwork was sloppy, and their response drills lacked the effort and enthusiasm seen elsewhere in the unit. You see, Brad was a 20+ year NCO that had announced his retirement, and he had a pending job interview with the Spokane County Sheriff's Office. Although the inspection we were facing would occur in just about two months (April of 1995), Brad's retirement date was in about three months. Frankly, he didn't care; his focus, interests and attention were elsewhere now, and his Flight's performance reflected his attitude. Brad no longer had a stake in the outcome of what the rest of the unit was facing. He no longer had anything to gain or lose.

My team came to me with the problem and recommended that I remove Brad immediately from his Flight and replace him with another NCO. I thought about it for a while and then had them bring Brad in to see me. In about five minutes with Brad, and in front of witnesses (dangerous, but I really wanted the story to circulate), I told Brad that he had two choices. First, he could get on board with his colleagues; for the next two months put his heart and soul into this single inspection goal and, do everything in his power to bring his Flight's standards (morale, appearance, performance) up to those of the other Flights. If he did that, I promised him that he could use my name as a reference anywhere, and that I would be happy to call anyone (to include my friends at the Sheriff's office) to help him with his job search. Or…second, he could continue down the path of complacency and mediocracy that he seems to have chosen. In which case, I promised him that I'd see to it that he <u>never</u> worked law enforcement in the Spokane County area…ever. I said like the guy on the old Men's Wearhouse commercial, "I guarantee it."

Suddenly, Brad had stake in the outcome; skin in the game. He didn't think about it for long. Within days his flight began to turn a corner. They were completely on board, and now in full-fledge competition with the other flights. As it turned out, they were some of the stars of the inspection. In the spring of 1995 the Air Force sent their Nuclear Surety Team to Fairchild. What they found was a security police squadron like (I believe) no one had ever seen before or since. Every single troop on post, every troop encountered throughout the four-day inspection turned in a phenomenal performance. If you've ever visited a security troop on post, they will often ask (rather obligatorily) if you'd like to receive a post briefing. Within our career field, it's a matter of culture. This is what we do. It's the only career field in the Air Force that starts its day with a formal open-ranks inspection, and then requires it posts to report to senior leadership as they approach. It is found nowhere else in the Air Force. When a senior leader approaches and receives a guard's post brief, there is rarely any standardization to it; and often, you never truly know what you're going to get. But in this week, for this inspection at least, it was a sight to behold. Not just standardization, but an aggressiveness by the troops that none of us had ever seen. They hunted down the inspectors and demanded they hear their post brief! One inspector came to me during the inspection and said he literally had tears in his eyes when several troops recited the Rifleman's creed[33]… before going directly into a capabilities brief on the M-16 rifle…before going into their post brief! In all his years (and mine) he had never seen anything like it. In another instance, an M-60 machine gun crew on day shift was demonstrating to inspectors how fast they could disassemble and reassemble their weapon via stopwatch. When one of the night shifts heard this, they began demonstrating to the inspectors how fast they could do it in the dark! And it just got better and better as the week went on. Bottom line? Certainly, the best inspection results any of us had ever been associated with; and by all accounts, the best ever seen…period. In the course of an inspection like that, usually about 3-5 "Outstanding Performers" are named. In this case, the inspection team named every member of the unit (all 400+) as "Outstanding Performers."

In terms of management and leadership style, this was classic me. But it's also a leadership style that was influenced by both years of trial and error, as well as countless courses and readings on the subject.

Douglas McGregor, a scholar from MIT's Sloan School of Management

---

33 The USMC Rifleman's Creed (public domain):
"This is my rifle. There are many like it, but this one is mine.

My rifle is my best friend. It is my life. I must master it as I must master my life.

My rifle, without me, is useless. Without my rifle, I am useless. I must fire my rifle true. I must shoot straighter than my enemy who is trying to kill me. I must shoot him before he shoots me. I will…

My rifle and I know that what counts in war is not the rounds we fire, the noise of our burst, nor the smoke we make. We know that it is the hits that count. We will hit…

My rifle is human, even as I, because it is my life. Thus, I will learn it as a brother. I will learn its weaknesses, its strength, its parts, its accessories, its sights and its barrel. I will keep my rifle clean and ready, even as I am clean and ready. We will become part of each other. We will…

Before God, I swear this creed. My rifle and I are the defenders of my country. We are the masters of our enemy. We are the saviors of my life.

So be it, until victory is America's and there is no enemy, but peace!"

from the 1950s to 1960s, for one, postulated Theory X and Theory Y approaches to management.[34] McGregor suggested that Theory X managers believe employees are inherently lazy, they dislike work, they need to be forced to work, they require constant supervision with significant controls, and they must be threatened with discipline in order to be effective. Theory Y managers, however, operate under the assumption that employees like to work, they will motivate themselves, they will take the initiative if given the opportunity, and they will commit themselves if they can see the self-benefit (their stake in the outcome).

The truth is, neither approach, in its absolute form, will work. I've always believed in a major Y and minor X hybrid approach to leadership. I just choose to believe, and I think it's been proven to me more often than not over my career, that people are inherently good and industrious if you give them the chance. But McGregor's writings, and others like him, had a significant influence on how I developed as a leader.

Why did we do so well at Fairchild? Because I let them be themselves and encouraged camaraderie, teamwork, competition, and innovation. I instilled a pride in them they didn't have. That doesn't mean there wasn't discipline; we were, after all, a military unit. But after setting ground rules, to include bright lines that should never be crossed, the rest of your energy as a leader should be to encourage critical thinking and innovative ideas.[35] People are generally creative by nature (the theory Y in me). So beyond showing them why it's important to them, what they have to gain or lose, you have to provide an environment (culture) that allows them to flourish.

In the end, it's hard to say for sure how the whole thing with Brad and his flight happened, or when it really even started; but again, I have a pretty good sense it was during one important conversation. Stake in the outcome, or skin in the game? Sure, by that point. The point to this story is that you have to have it or find a way to instill it in your team. But to

---

34 *The Human Side of Enterprise*, Douglas McGregor, 1960, McGraw-Hill, New York
35 It doesn't matter what environment or type of organization. The leader, on day one, has to stand before his or her people and tell them in no uncertain terms what is and is not acceptable behavior; and then should do that repeatedly over the course of time. This doesn't have to be a threat or be done in a threatening tone. But the facts are, if you break the law, there is nothing I can do for you. There are other pass/fail items depending on the organization. As government employees (a specific issue while at FEMA) I had to remind them to leave their personal politics on the bumper of their car…it was not to come into the building in any form.

also be clear, the level of "stake" required is relative. For some (Brad for instance; or even me) it had huge career implications. For others, as the weeks went on, it was a pride (if not peer) issue…no one wanted to let their buddies down. I think most of those folks are proud still today. I certainly am.

## There once was a Guy Named Bud

As we'd been recovering from the devastation of the hospital shooting earlier in the week, the Wing Commander decided we would continue with an already-planned open house and air show. His thought (and most thought a good one at the time) was to get everyone's attention focused away from the shooting and back to something positive, if not fun.

So to back up for a moment…on about Wednesday of the previous week (before Hell week) I was sitting through a briefing to the Wing Commander on air show operations. My part of the meeting was to discuss base security, and probably more specifically, how and where we'd park cars for all the visitors on base during the coming weekend. What I witnessed was an amazing thing. While I sat along the side of the room (tiered seats, and I was actually sitting in the second row), Lt Col Bud Holland was sitting at the foot of the conference table with his back to the Wing Commander, very casually, if not flippantly, briefing the boss on his portion of the air show. There were only just a handful of people in the room at the time, and Bud's piece was actually the center of the briefing. As he continued to brief (with big sweeping arm movements and his back to the boss), what struck me most was his arrogance and the fact that everyone (including the boss) let him get away with it.

I come from a completely different community and culture; something far more formal than what I've seen over the years from the flying community. As I mentioned, within security police/security forces, we began every duty day with a formal guardmount…an open-ranks inspection of the troops. When a senior supervisor would visit a troop on post, that troop would come to attention, render a hand salute, and "report" his or her post (a short recitation of post duties, post limits, and that his or her post was secure). For me to witness this outright display of insubordination was both disgusting to me and embarrassing. I had one of my NCOs with me, and I was almost humiliated to see a fellow senior officer acting this way. Nevertheless, I kept my composure (and my mouth shut) and just watched in amazement as the conversation unfolded…something like this…[36]

Bud: So, I plan to make a pass over the airfield and then execute a 360 around the tower at a 60-degree bank.

Wing Commander: No…you will only execute a 40-degree bank.

Bud: 60, 40, whatever.

The rest is now a sad part of history. As I sat along that wall listening to all this with my NCO, I leaned over and whispered "this guy's gonna get somebody killed." As I also found out later, even the Wing Commander didn't have the authority to approve a 40-degree bank.

About ten days later, on June 24, 1994, while practicing for the air show to be held the following day, Bud Holland augured his B-52 into the ground while executing a 360 around the tower at a bank greater than 60 degrees. His airplane became almost vertical and he lost all lift. The saddest part of the story is that he took three others (all friends) with him. Col Bob Wolff was the retiring Vice wing Commander. He was sitting in the jump seat and this was to be the final flight of his career; his family and the fire department were waiting at base ops to hose him down after the flight was over. Lt Col Ken Huston was the navigator.

Lt Col Mark McGeehan was the co-pilot. Mark and Bud were NOT friends. Mark was a professional in the truest sense of the word and had expressed his displeasure with Bud and his distrust of him. As reports go, Mark would not allow any of his squadron crew members to fly with Bud…so Mark agreed to do it himself that day. I can only imagine Mark trying to wrestle the controls away from Bud in those final seconds.[37]

---

36 To the best of my recollection, this is what I testified to at the Accident Investigation Board.

37 In one of the great ironies of my life, Mark had called me earlier that morning. He was Chair of a base committee that oversaw the care and maintenance of Warrior Park (a park on base that had several static airplane displays). Mark wanted to propose renaming Warrior Park to Andy Brown Warrior Park, in honor of our troop that had responded to the base hospital shooting earlier in the week. I told Mark that I didn't think it was a good idea, since most naming conventions were done in honor of posthumous candidates. We both agreed to table the discussion for some time in the following week. Today, the park is still Warrior Park. But Mark's name is on the B-52 static display there.

Call sign Czar 52 in its final seconds. The speck to the right is a blown
hatch as the result of Mark McGeehan trying to eject.
(Aircraft accident investigation photo)

Not much to say about this.
(Aircraft accident investigation photo)

Lt Col Mark McGeehan. The embodiment of leadership. He flew so that
his troops wouldn't have to. I won't provide a photo of Holland.
(Official U.S. Air Force photo)

To be clear…Bud Holland had NO STAKE IN THE OUTCOME; nothing to gain or lose in the success or failures of the Wing's performance. You see, the air show was to be Bud's final flight as well. He was retiring. No one, up and down the chain of command (except Mark, and perhaps only Mark) realized what a liability, if not a danger, Bud was to himself and those around him. He had a long-standing record and pattern of similar behavior, had been passed from supervisor to supervisor, with no one taking action. His behavior went unchecked for years, and in the final years became even more brazen and dangerous. He was retiring as a Lt Col no matter what. He didn't care what others thought, and certainly didn't live in fear of reprimand or demotion. Nobody had the guts to cross him, or the leadership courage to make the right call when it needed to be made. Bud was just coasting along and taking his unit (and leadership) along with him.

## *So How Do You Build Stake in the Outcome?*

*"Outstanding leaders go out of their way to boost the self-esteem of their personnel. If people believe in themselves, it's amazing what they can accomplish."*
—Sam Walton

As illustrated by the two examples in my life (above), you've got to start with people who have a reason to want to do good; people who are in the job because they are driven by the results of their performance. If their performance doesn't matter; if doing marginal nets them the same result as doing well, I believe human nature defaults to the easiest approach. That said, I also believe human nature is such that rarely does anyone come to work in the morning saying "I want to do bad things today." At most, it might be complacency (boredom) arising from an unimaginative job and an uninspired employee; and again, a lack of stake in the outcome.

So, your first challenge is to find out what motivates them; and believe me, everyone has something that motivates them.

Beyond that, you can start by building a sense of inclusion and involvement in, if not policy, at least procedure. Many leaders are reluctant to include the rank and file in matters of policy; believing that to do so undermines their authority to make that final decision to move in a specific direction. Not me. Granted, there's always a danger in asking employees their opinion; doing so then implies (to at least some) that you're now on the hook to accept whatever you get back. It depends on how you approach them. You'd be a fool to say "give me your input and we'll go with what the majority wants." Their input needs to be one of many factors to be considered in making a final decision, and they need to know that up front.

I believe firmly that policy development is similar to the "test-before-training" model[38]. I would encourage every leader going onto a new organization to ask the following questions in his first staff meeting: What do we do well? What are we proud of? What is it we don't do well? What do we do we shouldn't be doing? What do we not do that we should be doing?

You might be surprised at the reaction you get with such questions. In many cases, no one has ever asked them their opinion. Sure, some organizations have a "suggestion box" nailed to the wall. Some unknown person opens it every few months, collects whatever is inside, and nothing is ever revealed (I've seen it many times). But to do it in an open staff meeting takes some level of courage; although it's much easier if the leader is new to the job. Get it out in the open, white board it, and track it. That type of exchange with your employees builds trust and confidence, and yes, begins to establish some level of stake in the outcome of the organization they may not have had.

TV personality/commentator/frequent blogger Mike Rowe gave a video commencement speech to new graduates about following their passion; how that is bad advice. He said you should take your passion with you. He said the people he was most impressed with were those that saw people going one direction and they went somewhere else. He told a story about a guy who owned a septic business; the business wasn't his passion, but he was good at it. And because he <u>had</u> passion, he was highly successful and ended up developing passion about what he was doing. He said the key is to follow the opportunities, not your passion, and success will result. According to Mike, just because you're passionate about something doesn't mean you won't suck at it. Mike's passion was to be an opera singer…he's now a very good blogger, and passionate about it.[39]

---

38  A very successful training model is to establish a base of knowledge first by testing your subject to see where you need to focus your course content. In this reference, one should first seek a baseline of policy issues and perspectives from those who are dealing with it daily.

39  Rowe, Mike, retrieved March 30, 2019, "Mike Rowe on why you shouldn't follow your passion" https://www.wimp.com/mike-rowe-on-why-you-shouldnt-follow-your-passion

I have absolutely no problem with Mike's advice on <u>following the opportunity</u>. I think it's spot on. But to add context to it, Mike is talking to and about younger people; newly minted college graduates. My focus is on newly minted senior leaders, and what they might face walking into a new organization; particularly one that has a history of morale and performance issues. Presumably, employees at such an organization are there because they did follow the opportunity at some point; on some level it's either why they came or why they stayed. But that's not always true either. To some, it may be "just a job" or a paycheck and it will never be anything more. Those are the people I actually pity; to come to work every day and punch a clock without ever realizing some grander purpose, to me, is sad and pathetic. But it happens, and it requires a great deal of work on the part of leadership. The others may have followed that opportunity because they had passion about it early on and that passion has grown, or they acquired their passion later (as in the case of the septic guy). Or, they had passion at one point and lost it; discouraged and hopeless as the result of poor leadership. All of these cases present unique leadership challenges in themselves.

So, for you as a new leader, what it basically comes down to are two types of employees: those with passion, who need to be channeled; and, those without passion, who need to be inspired. Sounds easy, right? It's not.

Despite my love for FEMA, I found many of them to be the most cynical people I've ever met in my life. And not to be too critical of the organization, while I did find it to be one of the most over-worked agencies in federal government, I found FEMA to be populated at the mid to senior leadership level with an over-representation of unskilled and under-educated employees that worked their way up in a system that rewarded tenure and cronyism. Many got their first job in FEMA, at a very low entry level (usually because they accepted frequent disaster duty) and because they knew someone (or worse yet, had a relative that pulled them in). The culture throughout the Agency (not just my region) was one where an employee could navigate the career ladder with an expectation that "I've been here the longest, I've paid my dues, and I'm next in line for that job opening." It was an agency culture that displayed resentment, if not outright hostility, to a senior leader being hired from the outside.

In my first staff meeting at FEMA (as a Division Director) I had one employee ask "So, Dennis, just how in the hell did you get this job?" My response? "Well, Andy, I guess they just saw something in me that they didn't see in you." I recognized early that while my military career prepared me for a lot of things, it was a hindrance and it inhibited the free flow of conversation between certain employees and me. Some seemed to be genuinely afraid of me. I swear, I think many of them thought I'd come in at 5AM, have them fall into a formation, and then conduct a forced march for 10 miles with full ruck. They were certain that FEMA had just hired a dictator to oversee them. I actually spent years trying to overcome that image of the military officer. Don't forget (at least for the Air Force), with the elimination of the draft and the advent of the all-volunteer force, we now have to work hard to recruit and then retain service members. We found a long time ago that the key to that process was recruiting and retaining the spouse. Consequently, senior leadership in the Air Force is more of a corporate leadership style; with a greater emphasis on family quality of life. But to be clear, there is still a military rank, order, and discipline structure within the Air Force.

So just how does a senior leader channel or inspire passion? Creating stake in the outcome for employees is often directly linked to tapping into their passion. I believe it's human nature to become passionate about something when either you can figure out, or someone can articulate why it's important to the organization and what's in it for you. What's in it for them is probably the key. It's an art form; your ability to translate organizational goals and objectives into something that is meaningful and relevant to the employee.

In August of 2008 I had taken over FEMA Region 10 (all things FEMA for Alaska, Idaho, Oregon, and Washington) as the Acting Regional Administrator (RA). This was a position I eventually held for two years. But up to that point, I had been the Deputy RA since 2005 (the senior career employee in the region, reporting to the Presidentially-appointed RA). I was (but wasn't) in charge. I was the right hand of the boss; I had an entire regional staff of career employees working for me; I provided expertise, guidance, counsel, and leadership to the boss; but I was not in charge and wasn't responsible for establishing goals and objectives to implement the President's priorities. As I look back on that, in every sense of what I described, I failed my regional staff. Here's what I mean:

Sometime shortly after taking over, we had an off-site regional leaders meeting. The Division Directors within the region asked for it as an opportunity to get our collective act together pending what we thought would be a new Regional Administrator announcement very soon. Our goal was to build transition briefings and other materials that would bring the new leader on board as efficiently as possible.

It was sometime during that first morning of that two-day meeting that one of my Division Directors, Pat Massey, approached me. He recognized that everyone seemed to be struggling with how to explain the relevant fit of their division within the context of the Region's overall goals and objectives. Why? Because we didn't' have any! I had never pressed it with the previous Presidentially-appointed RAs. They had come into what I always assumed was a well operating and efficient regional office. The fact was, we weren't that efficient. No one (least of all me) had stood before the regional employees and given them regional goals and objectives. The reason for that is because FEMA hadn't published an agency-wide strategic plan in years.[40] Without regional goals and objectives, there was no way to really articulate to employees how they fit in the overall mission scheme and why that was important to them. We had not created buy-in for them. Sure, we'd been marginally successful as an agency up to then; and most of that success was on the backs of tribalism. The response people did their thing, the recovery people did what they always do, and so on. It was actually their passion for the work that had propped us up all those years. Many FEMA employees are "disaster junkies." They love the adrenalin rush of deployments and field conditions; they get great satisfaction out of helping people (and rightfully so).

Even after Pat approached me I hesitated (only for a few minutes). Pat is a former military officer and was familiar with military planning. He suggested I give them my "commander's intent" as done in military planning.[41] So why did I hesitate? Because I had worked so hard for years to devoid my leadership style of any association with the military; especially military jargon. But it had to be done if we were to move forward.

40  There were a lot of organizational issues with FEMA. Before and after Hurricane Katrina, the Agency was criticized for the way it hired people and spent money, among many things. There was no budget process, literally! FEMA managed a budget line called the Disaster Relief Fund, which, Congress kept filled with up to $3B on any given day; and it's even more than that now. If FEMA needed new computers, they would order them and charge it to a current disaster. That's how they funded themselves for years. The Post-Katrina Emergency Management Reform Act of 2006 changed all that.

41  The commander's intent succinctly describes what constitutes success for the operation. It includes the operation's purpose and the conditions that define the end state. It links the mission, concept of operations, and tasks to subordinate units. (US Army Field Manual)

I moved quickly to the front of the room, grabbed a big Sharpie pen and stepped to the easel. I wrote down four RA priorities. And then I began to explain the relevance of each.

- Response
- Program Delivery
- Outreach
- Employee Development

We had failed miserably at our response mission during Hurricane Katrina. At the time of this meeting, that event was only three years in our past. While some then and now will argue whether or not FEMA employees are first responders (or responders at all), the fact is, the American people believed we were. FEMA had always argued that they weren't responders, and that American citizens needed to be able to support themselves for three days (make a plan, build a kit, rehearse with your family, and so on). But that's not reality. The American people expect more out of their federal government, and in particular, FEMA. I told the staff that, at least in Region 10, every employee is a responder first. Everything else is secondary. I told them that if we failed in our response mission again, we would never get to number 2 on my list of priorities. They would never get to implement all the various programs FEMA administers because congress would take them away from us. FEMA would be disbanded, and those of us that survived would be transferred to other agencies along with the programs. I told them the American Congress and public would demand it. And I believed it; and in turn, I think it fueled their passion once again.[42]

I had suddenly articulated a stake in the outcome that no one had ever given them. We moved forward quickly from that point, developing a region strategic plan, as well as metrics to track the monthly progress of our goals and objectives. It was clearly rough at the start, but we were light years ahead of the other regions. I found a sympathetic ear in the Deputy FEMA Administrator at the time, who wanted to implement a form of monthly metric tracking for the Agency. Both he and I recognized from our military background how important strategic planning was at every

42  Program delivery meant administering everything from disaster relief monies, to flood insurance, to Homeland Security grants. Outreach related to our continuing effort to reach deep into our state and local jurisdictions for planning and preparedness. Employee development involved the recruitment, hiring, training, and continual development of top flight talent for the region.

level to building that stake in the outcome. Strategic planning is hugely important in the way our government works. How do you justify anything you've asked for in your budget if you can't articulate to the President, and ultimately Congress, what <u>their</u> stake in the outcome is and what the consequences are if they don't support you? And you have to begin that process by selling it to your employees first.

## The Potential Danger from Not Having a Stake

February of 1986 was one of the most interesting, if not surreal, months of my entire life. I was assigned to the Combatting Terrorism Group (CTG) of Headquarters USCINCPAC at Camp Smith, Hawaii[43]. I'd been there for several months when an opportunity suddenly arose for me to travel to the Philippines. I was assigned to the CTG as a counterterrorism officer; and as a security policeman, a sure anomaly that I can't and won't get into here. My boss had me attached to a team that would be going to the Philippines on the 20th of February for a series of security surveys at Naval Air Base Cubi Point, Subic Bay Naval Base, and Clark Air Base.

To be sure, this was a troubling time in the Philippines. President Ferdinand Marcos had undergone a number of high profile scandals, with serious allegations about corruption within his government and by him personally.[44] It was becoming clearer by the day that his time in power was becoming more and more tenuous. The only real questions were how much longer, and will it be a peaceful transition?

At this point it's important to give a little of the back-story about why I was there. Without question, I was a security (antiterrorism) expert, and was becoming more and more comfortable in my role as a counterterrorism officer. But I had also spent three months during the previous winter attending the FBI National Academy in Quantico, Virginia. The FBINA is considered by many (nationally and internationally) as the premier senior executive law enforcement school in the world. In fact, the FBI brings in a

---

43  We were a combined unit of J-36 Special Operations Division and SOCPAC (Special Operations Command of the Pacific).

44  There had been an election on February 7th. Corazon Aquino was the opposition candidate. Marcos was declared the winner by the official elections commission, while another election observer, the National Movement for Free Elections, had Aquino winning. While there were reports of widespread cheating on both sides, the declared results fueled what became known as the People Power Revolution beginning on Feb 22.

relatively large number of international students for each three-month session. One of my classmates, Al, was a police Lieutenant Colonel who was in charge of investigations and intelligence for the Manila Police Department. Al and I had become fast friends while at the academy. He was without a car and I had driven to Virginia from my base in Illinois. Several of us had formed a small group early on and I chauffeured them around the greater DC area for the three months we were there; to the Smithsonian, dinner, Pentagon tour, and various other places. This trip to the Philippines presented itself as the perfect opportunity for me to visit Al!

We arrived at Cubi Point on February 20th and immediately went to work on our assigned mission. I think it was sometime the next day that I reached Al; I told him I was in country and would love to see him. He was ecstatic! I told him that I'd be spending a couple of days at Cubi Point/ Subic Bay and then would be moving over to Clark AB near Angeles City on the morning of the 25th. He said that was perfect; it was only about a 90-minute drive from Manila, and he would come out and pick me up.

Graduating class (140th session) of the FBI National Academy in 1985.
I'm third row, third from the right. Aladdin (Al) Dimagmaliw is front row,
fourth from the left.

On the afternoon of February 25, 1986, I checked out with my boss one more time before departing for Manila. Al was right on time and we jumped into his car and headed out. To be clear, at this point, I already knew what was going on. There had been a series of disturbing, if not dangerous, events throughout the week. There had been an attempted coup on Marcos, and Defense Minister Juan Enrile and Armed Forces Vice Chief of Staff Fidel Ramos[45] had been implicated and, by this time, barricaded themselves inside of Camp Crame in downtown Manila. The People Power Revolution was in full swing, with massive demonstrations in Manila demanding Marcos resign and the military mobilizing for an apparent fight…and me heading right into the middle of it.

Al Dimagmaliw and me in his office at the Manila Police Department on the evening of February 25, 1986.

On the way downtown I asked Al where we were going and what his plan was. He kept telling me not to worry about anything, he had a big surprise in store. I said that was great, but was there any chance we could swing by the police department and he could show me his operation? He responded, saying that was exactly where we were headed. When we got there, the place was abuzz with activity as you might imagine. To my surprise, Al walked me straight into the Chief's office and introduced me to the Chief of Police. Now I was ecstatic because I had never expected access like this! And then this is when it all got bizarre…

The FBI National Academy is a big deal in the Philippines (it is in the US as well, but Philippine law enforcement reveres it as a tremendous

---

45   Ramos was also dual-hatted as head of the Philippine National Police.

professional accomplishment). The Chief, a graduate himself, told me "well, as you can see, we have this little problem going on right now. And, at any other time it might consume all of our time and energy. But the way I see it, it's really an Army and federal government problem, not ours. I'm planning to send some patrols in the vicinity of Camp Crame for crowd and traffic control…but that's it. We've planned a party in your honor tonight. Several FBINA graduates from our National Bureau of Investigations are planning to attend. So we're all going to a local restaurant for a party."

Folks, I ain't making this up. This dude had convinced himself that he had no stake in the outcome. The Chief was, in fact, a Marcos man. Some would argue that it's likely he decided on the better part of valor; knowing the Philippine Army was changing sides quickly and they outgunned him, he elected not to engage. Instead, he turned his back and let the scenario play out. If that's the case, perhaps his stake was more than I give him credit.[46] Nevertheless, his entire country was about to collapse, and we spent the next 4-5 hours at a local restaurant eating and drinking and listening to the revolution on a police radio! It was certainly not how I had planned to spend the evening. But certainly interesting, surreal, and insightful. I was the only US military officer in downtown Manila that night. As far as I know, the embassy had sheltered all of their people in place, anticipating that things would get ugly. Fortunately, it didn't.

We (the US Air Force) extracted Marcos and his entourage from the palace via helicopter that night at about 9pm. They were taken to Clark AB and billeted in the bachelor officers quarters overnight, and then transported to Hawaii via C-130 the next evening. After the party, I was deposited into the Hilton Hotel as the guest of the Manila Police Department (not sure who, if anyone, ever paid for that). When Al took me back to Clark the next day, I found that all of my personal effects had been packed up and moved to another room. Someone from the Marcos delegation was now occupying mine.

So, that's the story. I once sat through an entire revolution (and partied all night). But what's really the lesson here? Again, I observed a senior leader that believed he had no stake in the outcome. Notwithstanding the fact that he had patrols in the vicinity, and that he was monitoring events, what if it had gone bad? How do you explain, in an after-action review, the

46 Perhaps his "Blood-stake"? During WWII everyone had a stake in the outcome. It was a blood-stake where everything was on the line. The ultimate buy-in. You see this in combat. If so, my personal opinion is that he cowered; easy for me to say, but my stake was my personal safety that night.

optics of hosting a party (for an American!) while your country is burning? I do know this. Just a few months after the change in government, the Chief lost his job to General Alfredo Lim (a no nonsense, hard liner) who, in my observations, took a much more hands-on approach to leadership.[47]

This next story is equally disturbing (at least to me). In the spring of 2009 Washington State experienced a rain event that resulted in unprecedented flooding throughout the western part of the state. Several rivers had reached or exceeded flood stage, particularly along the Cowlitz and Toutle rivers in southwest Washington. As the Acting FEMA Regional Administrator, I oversaw the response and recovery efforts for that Presidential declaration; and by all accounts, things were moving along well toward full recovery. But sometime a couple of months after the rain event, a couple of members of the staff walked into my office and told me they had just returned from a meeting with the US Army Corps of Engineers District office in downtown Seattle. What they proceeded to tell me was nothing short of shocking. The Corps had briefed them that the spring rain event had also severely damaged the Howard Hanson dam several miles upstream from the cities of Kent and Auburn, Washington, along the Green River. In fact, the damage was so severe that there was a legitimate threat of dam failure. If the dam failed, it could catastrophically flood the entire Green River Valley (the cities of Auburn and Kent and the second largest warehousing district on the west coast).[48] Yet, more shocking to me was what the Corps team told my employees after the meeting. "We have to keep this a secret; we can't tell <u>anyone</u>."

Now, I once had a boss that told me "you never want to be the senior guy holding a secret." So, I immediately called the Corps District Commander…and sure enough…he detailed the gravity of the situation, and then explained that I needn't worry about the dam failing because he guaranteed that it wouldn't fail. He said that for the next major rain event, he was planning to begin releasing water well before levels reached

---

47 General Lim later became the Mayor of Manila and a Senator. About a year after the revolution, the government was still in tremendous turmoil with massive demonstrations still in the streets. I was in downtown Manila for one of largest of them. Gen Lim took me to lunch afterward. As we sat there, he said "you know Dennis, it seems like every time you come to town, something happens." I never went back to the Philippines again ☺

48 In briefing headquarters, and the severity of the issue, I tried to relate the impact on some of the nation's critical infrastructure. When I told them the Starbucks Roasting Plant was in the flood plain, they finally sat up and listened.

the damaged section of the dam; but not to worry, the dam is safe. So I asked him what the impacts would be to people downstream of an early release. He said "oh, for sure, everyone is getting wet. Our models show up to 3-7 feet of water throughout the valley floor. But don't' tell anyone!" I thought about it for a moment and then quietly said "Oh no, I'm not telling anyone. Because you're going to tell everyone. We're going to make appointments with the Governor and her staff, as well as the congressional delegations and the mayors of the cities involved. You're going to brief them on every excruciating detail about the damage, and I'm going to brief on what we need to do to prepare the community. Then, we're going to hold a series of town hall meetings to get those communities ready."

I was incredulous at what I was hearing. I was working here with a senior officer who was trying to avoid the angst of having to go public, and deal with the public, on such a potentially catastrophic situation. His response to me was that he had a Supreme Court decision that indemnified the Corps against any liability if he made the decision to release water and save the dam, as though it was some larger nobler service to the community. I said "Dude, do not use that line when you're talking to the Governor or the media; just my recommendation." He just didn't care. But I, on the other hand, had a moral obligation and that was my stake in the outcome!

Ultimately, we worked through the issues. The State and local jurisdictions were outstanding; both in their understanding of the issues and their responsiveness in seeking solutions. The congressional delegation worked the funding aspects, and a year later, the Army Corps looked like heroes with a $44M project to fix the dam.

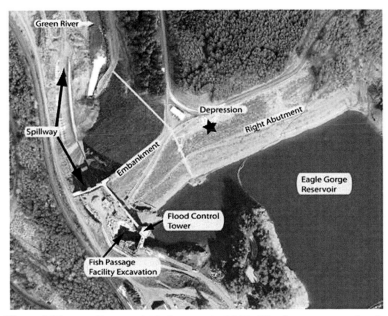

Howard Hanson Dam and it's damage in 2009. The fear was over the depression (star); it could catastrophically fail the right abutment causing the Green River (top of photo) to flood. (US Army Corps of Engineers photo)

Howard Hanson Dam and its impacts from a catastrophic flood (Shaded area). The Kent-Auburn area is the second largest warehousing district on the west coast (Long Beach, CA). And the, of course, the potential impacts on Seattle.

# 4

# Leading the Ineffective Leader

*"The art of leadership is saying no, not saying yes. It is very easy to say yes."*
~ Tony Blair

## *Leading Up*

Earlier I mentioned that a leadership skill of mine is to be able to recognize strengths and weaknesses of those surrounding me, and therefore the ability to capitalize on their best attributes while minimizing others. The context to that statement was as it relates to employees I supervised. Now, it's time to explore the same concept as it relates to those that supervised me.

I've known countless people who are flawed in some way or another; me included. None of us are perfect. We all have strengths and weaknesses. That includes the most respected and revered leader you've ever worked for. If they were <u>that</u> perfect, we'd be worshiping them every Sunday morning, not just admiring them Monday through Friday.

There are two concepts that need to be briefly addressed right from the start; followership and the ability to recognize your leader's strengths and weaknesses.

## *Followership*

You can't be a good leader unless you've first learned how to be a good follower. If you spent the majority of your junior years bitching about the organization and every leadership decision flowing downhill, or worse yet, an inordinate amount of time trying to circumvent and undermine your leadership, you're not likely to make a successful leader later in life. By this time, you've gained too many bad habits, and your head and heart are probably in the wrong place to begin with. Like some of the examples I gave before, you've failed to acquire (or someone failed to instill) basic concepts of integrity, honor, and loyalty. Probably just as important as those qualities, is the development of your work ethic. How well do you take direction, and how well do you apply yourself after you've received it? This is probably an excellent self-assessment process you should consider as you move into a leadership role for the first time. You might just be surprised at what you learn about yourself. The bottom line? How well a follower follows, is probably just as important as how well a leader leads. The forecast of your leadership success boils down to this: You shouldn't expect any more from your subordinates than you were willing to give earlier yourself.

## *Your Leader's Strengths and Weaknesses*

WARNING! As I discussed in Chapter 2, first and foremost, you have a responsibility to take care of your boss. How you do that; how you build and implement an engagement strategy for highlighting strengths and minimizing the boss's weaknesses can become very tricky, if not dangerous.

Everyone's relationship with their supervisor is different, and personal. Some have an already established friendship, while others walk into a situation that is cold and tense from the start and seems to never improve. You have to assess that environment and be sure that you're on firm ground before you directly engage; that's if direct engagement is your strategy.

I once worked as the Deputy for a senior leader that, while skilled in so many ways, was not the polished public speaker she needed to be for the job she was now in. Early, in our time together, we had attended several conferences where she was giving a keynote address. When standing on stage and giving extemporaneous remarks, she had a propensity for saying "uh" or "um" frequently. I cringed at first, and essentially tried to ignore it. After the third or fourth appearance, and after a senior leader from another agency made a passing remark, I finally acted. I walked into her office the next morning, closed the door, and confronted the issue. I also offered a simple fix (and it was simple). We had a public affairs officer within the organization that she had already built trust with; that person was capable and willing to give her a crash course on the do's and don'ts of public speaking. He coached her for about two weeks before the next scheduled engagement.

In the end, all was well. She turned out to be perfect for the role. Quickly, her speaking skills matched everything else she was presenting on stage (knowledge, experience, credibility, and so on). But in the process of our burgeoning professional and personal relationship, I suffered dearly for it; when I closed that door and revealed to her something that she hadn't seen, but others had. She was at first a little embarrassed by it, and then <u>furious</u> with me. She kicked my ass! She was angry, and rightfully so, that I hadn't come to her after the first speaking engagement. I'm very lucky in that situation. She quickly reminded me of what she expected out of her Deputy. I could have lost her; specifically, her trust in me before we ever got a chance to gel as a team. It was an important lesson I learned and you can bet that I never let something like that happen again.

Notwithstanding the example above, you never know. You never really know how the boss is going to take criticism, or even suggestions, until you go for it. Nevertheless, you have to be in the right position and have the right relationship already established. On sensitive, personal issues like this one, it was likely that anyone else but me approaching her would have been catastrophic…for everyone. Just make sure you know what you're doing.

What if direct engagement is not your strategy? What about the boss you can't approach, or you've tried and have gotten nowhere? There are many situations where you need to, and many in my career where I had to, work around the boss. To be clear, that is <u>not</u> to suggest disloyalty or something even more nefarious.

Sometimes there are just issues and situations where the boss just doesn't need to know. Some of those issues could be those that just don't or shouldn't rise to his or her level of interest yet. Specifically, those issues that still need to be worked, with pros and cons being developed along with courses of action and a recommendation. There are plenty of those instances where you don't want the boss to know all the details until you're ready to take your shot at influencing him; and there's nothing wrong with that. Then there might be times when, for personnel actions or program directives, the boss can't legally be involved because he or she is the next appellate authority in the chain. That happens frequently in government.

There are also those times when you are protecting the boss by providing "plausible deniability." Believe me, I've done that more than once with an edgy situation and an eventual decision where I just made the call and "protected" the boss (I provide an example of that later in this chapter).

Let there be no doubt from me, <u>at no time</u> should your attempt to go around your boss be one with malice in your heart; for whatever reason. I think I've been crystal clear on this issue already, but let me state it here again unequivocally. The boss is the boss. He or she was placed in that position by someone or some responsible entity. As long as their decisions are moral, ethical, and legal, they will and should remain the boss until properly relieved. If you can't support that concept, then get out now! It is never appropriate to undermine the authority of your leadership unless they've done something that is not moral, ethical, and legal. In such cases, there are plenty of legal options to rectify that situation.

Then there are times when you just have to step in to save certain leaders from themselves. In the spring of 2009, Alaska was undergoing one of their worst flood seasons in decades. Along the upper Yukon River, for several hundred miles, an early spring thaw was causing large sheets of ice (some a hundred miles long) to break up and move downstream creating tremendous damage and destruction to several native villages.

While still in the middle of the response phase, I flew from my regional office near Seattle to Anchorage to meet with the state. Governor Palin had asked me to assist with damage assessment teams, as she was getting ready to ask President Obama for a major disaster declaration; and both would need my assessment before one could be granted. As I got there with every intention of fulfilling her request, I found her state emergency management team completely immersed in their response operation. While there was no need for federal help during the response phase, it was none-the-less, a major undertaking for the state of Alaska. Again, the impacted area was several hundred miles long, several hundred miles away, and there were no roads in which to get there (most travel in the interior of Alaska is done either by air or river). I found the state emergency management staff to have almost a target fixation with regards to response, at the expense of everything else. They were just too busy worrying about evacuating people down-river of the impending flood, that they didn't have time to discuss actions necessary for the recovery phase.

As tactfully as I could, I invited the State Emergency Management Director into his office, as well as his Deputy, and closed the door. I commended them both for their aggressive approach throughout the response operation, but told them they needed to get "out of the weeds" and up to a level where they could visualize the long-term picture. My message to them was this; while it's late April, winter in Alaska is just around the corner. The construction season in Alaska, especially in the northern interior, is only about 120 days. By the first of September, the snow begins again, and if we didn't move quickly, a large number of native village residents would be going into winter without a home. The message I gave them was that while response was very important, there were many important issues they needed to be working (such as the recovery mission) simultaneously.

Effects of the 2009 ice breakup and flood along the Yukon River in Eagle, AK. Before and after photos showing the damage, and homes we were able to build within the short four-month construction season.

Once I had their attention, I convinced the state of Alaska to set up a housing task force immediately. They did so with their state housing authority, and several federal and volunteer agencies. I finished the damage assessments, the Governor made her request, and the President granted a federal disaster declaration.

The long and the short of this story is that both response and recovery missions were accomplished, and done so superbly by the state. Within 120 days, we rebuilt about 70 homes in several native villages along the Yukon River. But the real point is…I don't know how long they would have floundered if I hadn't spoken up. I certainly didn't want to see them fail, and ultimately me fail in my federal mission. More important than that, we were losing precious time, and our opportunity to adequately care for disaster survivors. Sometimes you just have to throw yourself into the fray.

Finally, let me just add a word of caution about getting too wrapped up in your endeavor to <u>lead up</u>. Don't let the effort consume you to the point of neglecting your responsibility to lead down as well. It's easy, as a leader, to feel like you need to attend to your boss and his or her constant appetite for everything from information to attention. There is certainly a careful balance to leading in both directions. If the majority or your time is spent licking your boss's boots (or kissing something else), your employees are perceptive enough to sense that…and your effectiveness as a leader will bear the consequences for it. Your primary responsibility as a leader is to be there for the folks under your charge. Don't ever forget that.

## *The #1 Key to Successful Leadership*

*"The most dangerous leader is the one that completely ignores the advice of his staff because he thinks he's the smartest guy in the room."*
—Anonymous

In my view, the number one key to success in leadership is who you surround yourself (and your boss) with. You should surround yourself with people that are both the most talented and intellectually brightest minds you can find. Without doubt, there are leaders that want to be (and some think they are) the smartest guy or gal in the room. If they are, or worse yet, want to be, you're in trouble as an organization. They are definitely idiots for not recognizing that particular character flaw, and the catastrophic consequences it can lead to throughout their decision-making process. But you're also either an idiot, or are culpable in mismanaging your organization if, as a deputy, you allow it to happen. You should make every effort possible to surround your boss and yourself with the best, brightest, most competent (and loyal) people available.

Equally important to talent and intellect, are people who are calm, rational, and collected in the face of crisis; people who are rock-steady and you know you can depend on. I read an article not long ago about Astronaut and teacher Crista McAuliffe, who died tragically in the Challenger shuttle accident of 1986, and the selection process she went through to get accepted to the program. From among 11,000 applicants, she was selected in large part because NASA cited the recommendation of a former teacher, who declared that the she was "tops in emotional stability and seriousness of purpose."[49] That is probably one of the best descriptions I've heard of an essential leadership quality, and spot-on of who you want around you.

---

49  https://www.foxnews.com/opinion/remembering-the-space-shuttle-challenger-a-bold-prayer-in-a-public-school-that-brought-comfort-amidst-the-grief

**The Good**

As a newly assigned Chief Executive, as the leader, you should want to be occasionally led. I've had a couple of opportunities in my career, once as a commander (the leader) and once as a Deputy Regional Administrator (the second in charge), where I enjoyed what I thought was the perfect symbiotic relationship between boss and deputy.

From 1981 to 1984 I was the commander of the 1001st Security Police Squadron at Peterson Air Force Base, in Colorado Springs. Let me say this from the start…throughout my Air Force career I was blessed, in almost every situation I faced, with a highly professional staff that in some cases saved me in spite of myself. I've already mentioned the heroics of my folks at Fairchild AFB during and the weeks and months following Hell Week of 1994; I would never have survived without them. But in terms of a one-on-one relationship, the one I had with my Operations Officer at Peterson was unmatched in my Air Force career. Steve Ross came into the squadron a few months after I arrived. He was prior enlisted, experienced, smart, savvy, polished, and unafraid. He was a year older than me, but almost three years junior to me in rank. We were a couple of young 30-31-year olds, both Captains, had the same leadership philosophy, and even resembled each other in appearance to some extent.[50] It was a match made in heaven!

I won't go too deeply into the relationship I had (still have) with Steve. It was and is a deeply close friendship. But it didn't happen immediately. The first time I met Steve we sat and talked on his front porch for about 30 minutes just to get acquainted. I remember walking away from that wondering how well it would all work out. He was quiet and reserved, and seemed unmoved by any of the "vision" I was sharing with him about where I wanted to take the squadron. I asked him about it years later, and he simply said "I didn't know who the hell you really were, or at that point, what type of trust I could have in you." But it didn't take long. We quickly jelled as a leadership team and had a number of tremendous successes while we were at Peterson.

The point to my story about Steve as my Deputy is that, on many occasions, he was the smarter guy in the room. He was my alter-ego, my voice of reason, the guy I could rely on to whisper in my ear and tell me to stop… take a breath. If not Steve, then one of our outstanding Chiefs at the time (Jess Disnute, Tom Niblett, or Bob Lopez). I'm lucky to have served with a long list of outstanding Chiefs in my career. Those mentioned here, and others like John Conley, Joe Markin, Dan Miller, Jack Riling, and Larry

50  Steve and I served together three more times in our careers.

Cayabyab. I relied on the talent and experience around me, and used them liberally. I never felt that my position was threatened by any of them, and they never felt intimidated by me. I learned a long time ago that you never have to remind anyone that you're the commander (or CEO, or whatever). Everyone around you knows it. You don't have to keep telling them. They have built-in respect for that position. So cast your ego to the side. What you hope to gain is respect for you personally; and that depends on how you carry yourself and how you treat others. If you build trust with them (if you place trust <u>in</u> them), they will in return trust and respect you. The decisions you ultimately arrive at will carry significantly more weight than just because you have the legal authority to do it. Trust me! That type of decision-making process is far more constructive and healthier for an organization.

My buddy Steve and me in 1992.

Steve and I were at lunch with a couple of other officers on base when one asked "how do the two of you get along so well as two Captains in the same organization." Steve simply said "it's easy, Dennis is the commander."

During my time as the Deputy Regional Administrator at FEMA Region 10 I experienced the second time in my career where I enjoyed that perfect symbiotic leadership bond.

Following Hurricane Katrina in the early fall of 2005, I returned from my deployment[51] to find a regional staff that was, well, I'm not sure how else to

---

51  I spent a couple of months first in Fort Worth, Texas, and then in Austin. While in Fort Worth, I helped the Mayor and his staff house and care for nearly 30,000 displaced New Orleans survivors. It was a staggering mission that left even me a little scarred.

but it but…broken. When I left for Fort Worth I was the regional Division Director for preparedness. When I returned, I found the Response and Recovery Division Director had quit, the Deputy Regional Administrator had announced her retirement, the (Presidentially-appointed) Regional Administrator (RA) was disengaged and spending most of his time in his office (there hadn't been a regional staff meeting in weeks), and half of the regional employees were still deployed doing post-hurricane recovery work. For certain, Agency morale was at an all-time low. If the Hurricane hadn't kicked our butts, Congress and the media were certainly finishing the job. In the eyes of the public, FEMA had failed and changes were about to be made.

Within the region I quickly (but informally took charge). I assumed the additional duty as Division Director for Response and Recovery, and also agreed to take charge of several disaster close-out activities as a Federal Coordinating Officer (FCO).[52] I held staff meetings and did as much as I could to bring order and discipline back to the regional office, and to quell the chaos. As for more large scale changes…the Deputy retired in May of 2006 and the Presidentially-appointed Regional Administrator decided (I believe mutually) to move on to another career. I was eventually hired in June of 2006 to be the Deputy, and soon found that I was running the place as the Acting Regional Administrator from that summer into the fall.

In an effort to appease Congress for more "professional" emergency managers in key leadership positions (our previous RA had owned a small coffee company prior to being appointed, and was infamously named in Rolling Stone Magazine as being one of FEMA's leaders with a degree from an unaccredited diploma mill), FEMA decided to convert three of the ten RA positions around the country from presidential appointments to career hires. They did this in Atlanta, Philadelphia and Oakland. They kept the position in Region 10 as a "political appointment."[53] Nevertheless, with two years left in the Bush Administration, and a commitment to Congress and

---

52   An FCO is a presidentially-designated position. The FCO is in charge of the Federal response and recovery for a declared disaster in a given state. The FCO is designated by the President in a letter to the Governor. I was originally hired into FEMA as an FCO in 2002 and served in that role several times during my FEMA career.

53   In a previous chapter I mention the Plum Book going all the way back to the Eisenhower Administration. These are lucrative government "plum" jobs the President (more importantly, the party) can use to, in many cases, reward contributors and supporters. Sorry, it's just the way our system works…for both parties.

the American people to "professionalize" FEMA, the President re-tooled the Agency from the top down with new and experienced leadership.

Me, Susan Reinertson, and Dave Paulison (FEMA Administrator) preparing to launch on a Coast Guard tour of the oil terminal at the Port of Valdez, AK, in 2007.

In late October of 2006, Susan Reinertson arrived as my newly-minted Regional Administrator. Susan was young, but experienced. She was born and raised in North Dakota where she graduated from the University of North Dakota with a bachelor's and a master's degree. She also has a master's degree from the Naval Postgraduate School, in Monterey, California. She had worked her way up within North Dakota's Office of Emergency Management to become the State Director. She was, in fact, as qualified as I had seen anyone coming into the Agency! And, I thought at the time (and still do today) the Agency did it right by taking a State Director from one region and making her an RA in a completely different region (it is otherwise inappropriate, if not a conflict of interest, to appoint a sitting State Director as the RA within the same region). I had heard nothing but praise for her, and was thrilled about the selection.

As in my story with Steve Ross, I won't belabor the work relationship and eventual friendship I had and enjoy still today with Susan. I had worked with several presidential appointees before (from Mort Halperin in the Pentagon to the RA just prior to Susan). But Mort was considerably older and far, far more accomplished than I, and consequently the role I assumed was one with much more deference to his seniority. As for the previous RA, I really hadn't served as his Deputy for more than a couple of weeks before he moved on. But with Susan, I saw opportunity; opportunity for both of us to get what we wanted and needed out of our respective jobs. Don't get me wrong, I paid complete deference to Susan as well, but the dynamic was different. She was clearly the boss, and I made sure everyone in the region understood that despite the fact that I had been in charge for a while. It didn't take long before we were friends and we had built mutual trust. Nevertheless, for her it was clearly a career opportunity of a lifetime, and it was also a troubling time in FEMA. While Susan came with the President's vision for revitalizing the Agency, I think there was a general feeling among new appointees at the time that it was "hope to survive this" for those first several months following Katrina. For me, I was hoping against hope for a partnership. What I got was, well, a partnership.

I told Susan very early on that most of us in the region understood the dynamics of the political environment she faced. The opposition (Governors, Senators, and members of Congress from the opposing party) would continue to berate FEMA in the aftermath of Hurricane Katrina, as would the media. That comes with the territory and we deal with it as we go. But even more frustrating will be the pressure from within her own party (those Governors, Senators, and Congressional members that have close ties to the White House and aren't afraid to use them). My promise to her was that I had a professional career staff behind me that was ready to give her pure, unfettered advice on every issue with a non-partisan recommendation on which path to proceed. I, on the other hand, understood more than most, the pressures on her and would always temper my recommendation with those (political) variables in minds. But I also told her there may be times when she feels a need (despite my recommendation or those of the staff) to do the politically expedient thing on her own. There were very few times when that happened.[54] But my pledge was also as long as it's moral, legal, and ethical, I would support her.

Susan was smart enough to surround herself with people that were as smart as, or smarter than, herself. She was also perceptive enough to recognize who the talent was, who the non-performers were, who she could trust, and who would genuinely take care of her and her best interests. I think she recognized early on that I was someone of my word, and a person that just wanted to do good and honorable things; or at least I hope that's what she saw. At one point I told her that I was the guy that would never be afraid to whisper in her ear to tell her she was about to screw up. There were only a couple of times that I did that. But there were also a couple of times that she did the same to me as well, and I truly appreciated it.

At the end of almost two years, Susan left the Region. As I think about it now, I'm not sure I ever had a more consistently fun stretch of time in my entire career. Without question, I've done some pretty neat things throughout my more than 42 years in government. But in those days, I was more in a survival mode myself. By that point in my life and career I'd seen or done it all. It was fun working for a boss (a business partner) that wanted to enjoy the ride too.

In neither case, did I think Steve was "leading me" as an ineffective leader, nor was I trying to lead Susan for the same reasons. But the ability to "lead up" is truly an art form, and in both cases, Steve and I were trying to influence the decision-making process of our respective bosses. I had "surrounded myself" with the right guy in Steve. I think, I hope, Susan felt the same way.

Steve Jobs, of Apple fame, famously quipped, "It doesn't make sense to hire smart people and tell them what to do; we hire smart people so they can tell us what to do." Yet, isn't that what all good leaders want, or should want? The truly good leader wants a divergence of opinion. Nobody in their right mind wants a room full of yes-men or yes-women. If your

---

54 Of note, for almost a year after Hurricane Katrina, the Seattle Post-Intelligencer was still writing anti-FEMA Katrina-related editorials; about one a month. Susan and I finally agreed, over the objections of HQs, to schedule "coffee" with the PI editorial board. We decided to go to them, put a FEMA name and face to the local Agency office, and to brief them on some of the programs and initiatives we had on-going. It was a huge hit with the media! The editorials stopped immediately. HQs wasn't happy at first but they were in the end.

staff meeting is a session on group think, all you will get generally is one thought, one idea, and probably only one bad solution.

*"War has rules, mud wrestling has rules, but politics has no rules."*
—Ross Perot

## The Bad

I've been blessed with countless situations in my life where I worked for a boss that needed very little "guidance" from me. I know that statement can imply a negative connotation. But still, every boss needs to be led to some extent. In fact, if you're doing your job correctly aren't you always trying to get the boss to see things your way? Think about it. You're asked to put a proposal together with pros and cons and, perhaps, three options with the recommended course of action. Isn't that entire process one where you're trying to drive the discussion, and ultimately the decision, in a direction of your choosing? If not, you're a poor staff officer.

But there are times when you're handed the course of action and expected to backward plan it (or justify it). Those are the tough cases where you have to ask yourself if it's legal, ethical, and moral. If it is, you have to recognize quickly that the boss is the boss; and like the case I made earlier about the President and his right to implement his agenda…the boss is still the boss.

Then, there are those cases on the margin; those that'll require you to muster all of your knowledge, experience, and certainly political skill to find a solution to a sticky (often emotional) problem requiring compromise. What you don't want to do is ever compromise integrity. Remain honest, forthright, and committed to the ideals that you've previously championed with your employees. Don't just cave! But try to find ways at getting to a "yes" answer if it's reasonable to do so. Remember this one piece of advice: Senior leaders rarely accept a "no" answer right from the start; they generally don't want to hear the word no. What they'd rather get from you; what they will respect from you, is an answer along the lines of "boss, we can do that, but here is what that decision will cost you." Going back to what I said previously about influencing your boss with pros, cons, options for consideration, and a recommendation, by doing this you're likely to reach a result that is at least a well-thought decision. It may still not be the decision you had hoped for, but at least the boss will have made a fully-informed decision.

I've certainly had a few situations in my career that were on the edge and that did require me to bring it all together; to include, sometimes, my distaste for the dirty politics of it. What follows is an example:

We, FEMA, had been working for years to revise all flood maps throughout the country, and by 2010 we were well along with the process. To be sure, flood mapping around the country was/is a very contentious, if not emotional, issue. The consequences of new (more accurate) flood maps on communities, businesses, and individual home owners has been enormous. It has driven major economic issues ranging from flood plain development to insurance rates. I can say with earnest, of all the controversial subjects I faced while at FEMA, flood plain management (whether environmental or mapping issues) were the most painful; certainly, the most politically poisonous.

In 2007 there was an major flood event that had impacted several counties in western Washington state; one of those counties most affected by the flood was Lewis County. It had devastated a large number of families, businesses, farms, and it had severely impacted significant critical infrastructure throughout the county to include roads and bridges. The flood was deemed to be a "100-year flood." Now, to the lay person that sounds bad, and it is. This flood and its damages were staggering (to at least Lewis County, and others).[55]

Three years later, in early 2010, when the new flood maps were released, Lewis County was almost apoplectic over their maps; the flood plain had been enlarged significantly from previous maps, and now a much larger number of homes, businesses, and farms were included. FEMA mappers had used the data related to the 2007 flood, as well as data from an earlier 1996 flood event, which the county argued had inappropriately skewed the map results. So they immediately engaged with their congressional delegation in an effort to revise the maps. While we walked all parties through

---

55 What people hear on the nightly news is some guy standing there saying "this was a 100-year flood, but we had another 100-year flood in 1996!" Then the media mocks state, local, and federal agencies for referring to it as a 100-year flood. What the media has done, in fact, is distort what a 100-year flood is (partly because they're too lazy to do research and partly because FEMA hasn't properly clarified the term). 100-year flood means there is a 1 in 100 chance that a flood of this magnitude will occur in any given year (it's a probability statement). If it happens, then next year there will still be a 1 in 100 chance of the same flood happening again. Somewhere along the line the term was shortened (probably by some well-meaning staffer) to "a hundred-year flood." I mean, even the dumbest of dumb in the media can't believe that just because we got a hundred-year flood this year means we won't get one now for a hundred years…can they??

the laborious process of map revision, we insisted early on that science is science and data is data. There is a provision in the law that allows for appeal, but that appeal needs to be based on irrefutable (additional) science provided by the aggrieved party; to date they hadn't or couldn't produce enough to satisfy the mappers.

This issue dragged on and, in September of 2010, Senator Patty Murray's office contacted ours and wished to set up a conference call between the RA and the Senator's staff members in Washington DC. The subject of the call was…Lewis County maps; and they had one proviso for the call…the RA and no one else in the room on our end of the call. Upon hearing this demand, the RA simply said "set it up, let's do it."

It was absolutely clear to me and everyone else involved what was about to happen. Our newly appointed RA (an Obama appointee who had been in the job for three months) was walking into a trap; he was about to experience a very heavy lean from his Party. I was, at first angry, and then disgusted, by this blatant attempt to circumvent the established appeal process. It was an insult to the professional staff, who had made it their priority to be fair and impartial. It was also premature, since we hadn't gone through the full appeal process yet. Moreover, it put my RA in a very compromising situation. For the latter, I informed the RA that if we did this, he wouldn't be taking the call alone. He needed at least me in the room as a witness.[56]

After thinking about it for a while, I called the senior staff involved in the decision into my office to see if there was any way that we could get to "yes" on this issue; was there any flexibility in either the law or the Code of Federal Regulations (CFR) for us to consider their appeal. I made it clear that I just wanted them to look at it one more time and tell me it couldn't be done. Without going into the excruciating nuances of the Stafford Act and the CFR, the long story-short on this was that, yes, there was a way to get to yes. It was, in fact, within FEMA's authority to include additional data if it was determined the data used was in "technical" error. The staff, and the mapping contractor, all agreed to consider the additional data.

Without briefing the boss, or gaining his permission, I seized control of the issue and the decision process. I told our Legislative Affairs Officer to contact Senator Murry's office and tell them that Deputy RA Hunsinger

56 The optics of this power play were indescribable. It didn't take long for word to circulate. Many on the regional staff were aware and the worst situation for the boss would have been to be alone on a call with the Senator's staff, followed by a sudden appeal approval.

had made a decision; FEMA will consider additional data. Even given the fact that we could have let the RA be a hero within his Democratic circles, there was no way he'd recover (with the troops and our other jurisdictional partners) from the impression that he caved to political pressure. I felt that I needed to act, and had found a legal and ethical answer that satisfied almost everyone. In a sense, I stepped in front of my Boss to take a bullet. I mentioned earlier sometimes you have to be courageous enough to whisper in your boss's ear that he or she is about to screw the pooch on this issue; it's called leading up. There are also times when you just have to act; that's called leading the ineffective leader.

On another occasion, and I think it was sometime in the fall of 1994 when I was the Security Police Squadron Commander at Fairchild AFB, I got a call from our operations center[57] to respond to the flight line (aircraft parking area)…there was a security incident underway, and a senior officer was needed to resolve it. I hopped in my truck and went straight to the aircraft parking spot where the incident was occurring. When I got there, I found that my young second lieutenant (Lt) shift supervisor had apprehended one of the flying squadron commanders and his crew because they had inappropriately crossed the red restricted area line. So that there's no misunderstanding, in the Air Force, crossing the red line without proper identification is a big deal; but really, it's not that big a deal.

When I got out of the truck and approached the scene it was clear that tempers had escalated. I looked at the security flight chief, a seasoned, older, non-commissioned officer (NCO); the next subordinate person to the Lt. He just shrugged his shoulders as if to say, "sorry Boss, I had no control over the Lt" or "hey, don't blame me, I'm not in charge." When I got to the Lt he was shaken and started blurting out, chapter and verse, the regulations that he was certain put him in the right on this issue.

What did I do? As pissed off as my fellow squadron commander was, the Lt was right. I had no real choice other than to support him. I took the squadron commander aside and explained to him how his actions put both him and me in an uncomfortable position. Nevertheless, I smoothed it over with him, and then sent everyone on their way…except the flight chief and his Lt.

I first addressed the Lt (privately) and gave him my speech about the differences between being in charge and being in control. As the Lt, he was clearly in charge. He was the accountable and responsible official on duty. It

---

57  In the Air Force it was known at the time as Central Security Control (CSC).

all rests on his shoulders. He should take his charge very seriously, and I told him how impressed I was that he had studied the books and knew the regulations so well. But I reminded him that we have a professional NCO corps that are trained to lead during these situations. It was the NCO's flight line to manage, and that he would have been the better technician to handle that particular situation. I essentially gave him a lesson on stepping back and letting his people do their jobs (and taking care of him in the process).

I then turned my attention (again privately) to the NCO flight chief. I told him that of everything that went on out there, his action (or lack of action) gave me the most disappointment. He was a seasoned veteran who knew the ropes. My expectation of him (and all of the NCOs) was that his job was to take care of his Lt. He was to (discreetly) train and mentor him; he was the first step in molding him into a potential squadron commander. As far as I was concerned, the NCO's actions were the primary cause of a very controllable event getting rapidly out of control.

This was clearly a lesson on leading up, as well as allowing yourself to be led from below. It was also a lesson in the need to surround yourself with the right people (although the Lt had little choice in the matter). Nevertheless, I think both guys got the message. Last I heard the Lt was still on active duty as of this writing as a Security Forces Colonel.[58]

> *"Too Many Kings Can Ruin an Army"*
> —Homer

## The Ugly

So, when is it time to leave an organization? When you've surrounded the leader with quality people, but he won't or can't act, or the actions he takes and the decisions he makes begin to affect your personal reputation, it's probably time to go.

As the FEMA Deputy Regional Administrator, I once worked for a presidentially-appointed RA who I believed was ill-suited for the job. He was slow and indecisive (more on that later). He was also easily politically-influenced; and I understand that in itself, on some level, can be expected from an appointee. But I once heard a sports talk radio host describe an NFL player as the type of guy that seemed more interested in being an "NFL football player" than really playing NFL football. As I sat in the car absorbing that statement, it came to me that it described my current RA exactly.

---

58   The Air Force Security Police became the Air Force Security Forces in 1997.

My guy seemed more interested in being a "Regional Administrator" than actually administering a region.

Let there be no doubt, being the RA can certainly be an ego rush. You are king (or queen) of the regional hill. In your four-state region you represent your Agency, if not the President, in all things FEMA. You are sought after for conference engagements, and when you walk into a room, people know you're there. But all I ever wanted out of the job was to lead, be in charge, do good things; I wanted to be accountable and responsible…and also survive as an apolitical person in a very political world. After all, I'm a leadership junkie! I didn't care about the "position", but I was very passionate about the mission and my employees. I enjoyed running the place, setting the tone and culture, and providing strategic vision. I'd say "but I guess that's just me", but it's not; there are countless other leaders out there (and I've named a few) that are very much like me.

Throughout my tenure with this particular leader[59], his style was very much as I described; he liked being the "RA" but didn't necessarily seem to like doing the "dirty work" of running a region. That, he left for me to do. Before he arrived on scene I had held the job as Acting RA for two years.[60] Let me say right up front that my failure in this scenario was two-fold:

First, I had overlooked (violated) a long held military command principle; you can only have one commander at a time. In military tradition, when a commander succeeds another commander, there is a change of command ceremony, the flag is passed, and the old commander rides off into the sunset never to be seen again. There has to be a clean break so that troops understand exactly where their direction is now coming from. If the old commander were to remain in some other capacity, chaos may/would ensue. Despite the fact that all the troops still worked for me, and I now worked for this additional layer of management, I believe some of them were nevertheless confused.

Second, throughout the two years I was Acting RA, I never appointed one of my Division Directors to rise up and serve as Acting Deputy RA; I continued to hold both positions throughout. Consequently, there was no good cop/bad cop relationship between RA and Deputy RA; I was both![61]

59  Just because you've been handed a Presidential appointment doesn't necessarily make you a good leader, or even a leader.
60  My previous RA had left toward the end of the last Administration and it took the new Administration almost two years to finally fill the job.
61  This relationship was part of the successful chemistry I had with Susan Reinertson. We played those roles well, and interchangeably, as the situation dictated.

The problem with this new RA was that good cop/bad cop doesn't always work, especially if one is a weak, ineffective leader (most especially if the subordinate bad cop is the stronger personality of the two). What I found as we went along was that I was always the bad cop because he wanted to be seen as the good guy at all times. If there was bad news to be delivered, or an unpopular decision to be made, I did it. Again, he liked the role of RA and spent an inordinate amount of time "holding court" and pontificating at staff meetings. He's also the guy that spent time on the back loading-dock smoking and commiserating with employees.

My intent here is not to run the guy down. There were plenty of mistakes I made during that time. It didn't take long for some of the more sinister forces within the organization to figure out how to manipulate that situation; to divide and conquer in a form of "organizational guerilla warfare" (to be covered later). If they didn't like something, they heard from me, they'd go to him and get a reversal. Again, if confronted by an employee at the loading dock, he always wanted to come out looking like the hero; he'd make snap decisions that were unstaffed and uncoordinated. There was nothing illegal about what was going on. However, with regards to ethics and morality? It took me too long to accept I couldn't change that toxic environment and realized it was time to go; I worked for a year under him before moving on.[62]

What should/could I have done differently? For one, I should have pushed more of the negative issues in his direction. I let him, too easily, be the hero in all situations. While you should want to take care of your Boss as best you can, you can't do their job for them. They have to step up and be accountable and responsible as well.

A couple of years before, I had one of the state emergency management directors complain to me that certain members of our staff were making (seemingly) arbitrary decisions that negatively impacted their program implementation. One of my hallmarks has been to stress, as an organizational priority, the need to arrive at "yes" if at all possible when dealing with our customers. After all, our whole reason for existence at FEMA was to be in a support role for state and local jurisdictions; we couldn't very easily do that

---

62  I felt a duty to help him until I thought he was secure enough in the role for me to depart. When he came into the position, FEMA lawyers ruled that it would be a conflict of interest for him to preside over issues dealing with the state where he had been state director. I was directed to continue as Acting RA for that particular state for one year. At about 6 months I started looking for another job, but retired (temporarily) after a year.

if we were always saying no. So, I implemented an internal policy where "you can say yes, but only I can say no."[63] That policy was designed to apply only to FEMA program issues. Unfortunately, over time it became the policy with virtually everything. Consequently, it became known throughout the office that if you wanted a <u>no</u> answer go see Hunsinger, but if you wanted a <u>yes</u> answer go see the RA. It took me far too long to realize how unfair I had made that situation for myself. Lesson learned.

## *The #2 Key to Successful Leadership*

*"I have a prodigious amount of mind;*
*it takes me as much as a week, sometimes, to make it up!"*
—Mark Twain

In my view, the second most important key to success in leadership is to <u>your decision-making capability; your ability to react, and just how you go about doing that</u>. Whether it's a split-second decision or something that you carefully contemplate, or whether it's in your professional life or your personal situations, just how you react to things will determine your success.

I read an article some time ago regarding Charlie Munger, business partner of Warren Buffet and Vice Chair of Berkshire Hathaway.[64] Munger, it seems, practices and advocates for a decision-making process (he calls "inversion") where, instead of thinking about what you need to do to accomplish a goal, think backwards about all the things you <u>don't</u> want to happen. An interesting and admirable concept, but hardly innovative. Isn't that really just backward planning that we've done in the military for decades? Or at <u>least</u> a form of it.

---

63   I wanted to empower our employees to give a positive response to their state counterparts (as long as it was legally supportable); in turn, making them the hero. When it was not legally supportable, I wanted them to brief and convince me that the answer should be no. If it was finally a no answer, I wanted to deliver that message to the states myself so that state directors would know that it was a well-staffed and final decision.
64   https://25iq.com/2015/09/12/a-dozen-things-ive-learned-from-charlie-munger-about-inversion-including-the-importance-of-being-consistently-not-stupid-2/amp/. The one thing I like that he said is that you can't tell people how to be happy (only they can do that), but you sure can give them examples of how to make their life miserable.

Backward planning is an important element of good decision making. What is our objective? Where do we want to be at the end of this journey? After those questions have been answered, it should be a methodical process of stripping away all of avoidable obstacles and pitfalls along the path to success. There are countless names for this process, from decision trees to Occam's Razor[65]. My personal favorite is the use of decision trees; and, of course, I have a short story that led me to that bias.

In the early 1990's, I was a doctoral student at The American University in Washington, DC. I was well into my program before I realized that university requirements for a Doctor of Philosophy included the "mastery of a foreign language." Holy crap! I can barely master the English language, much less a foreign language! I took two years of high school Spanish some 25 years earlier, but I hadn't retained enough to converse with anyone. Frantically, I approached my senior advisor for a course of action who quickly said "no problem." The short conclusion to this story is that he directed me to a local small college that offered undergraduate courses in computer programming language. I took a course in FORTRAN programming, got an A in the course, presented that to AU, and I was good to go! I had demonstrated a mastery of a foreign language. Whew![66]

While taking my class in FORTRAN, I began to realize how much my whole decision-making process, everything I had learned in the military to that point was at least somewhat congruent with the FORTRAN model. The whole basic language was founded on the principle that "if…then." With DO, GO TO, IF and other commands, the input phase of the language was in many ways similar to building a decision tree model. That is certainly an over-simplification, since the language is very complex and is used today for scientific and engineering modeling; complex weather predicting, for instance. But still, it resonated with me.

Decision tree modeling for making a quick and accurate decision, in an environment where zero margin of error is needed, captured my attention during my FEMA years. In 2003, I was attending a plume release exercise at the Hanford Nuclear Plant in Washington state. Under the Radiological Emergency Preparedness (REP) program, FEMA's responsibility is to

---

65  Essentially, the path with the fewest assumptions associated with it is usually the right one.

66  If that's all there is to it, you wonder why they even have the silly requirement. Nevertheless, to be a PhD they assume you are more generally rounded than a Doctor of Business, for instance, who would be more specialized. I don't know…still doesn't make sense to me. Otherwise, it's just another hoop.

prepare the community for a potential radiological incident at the local generating station. We provided tone-alert radios, and prepared and exercised the community for potential sheltering in place, or evacuation. The nuclear industry (Hanford, in this case) has responsibility for preparedness and response on the site itself.

As I sat in their control room watching them go through their emergency shutdown procedures for the reactor, I noticed that their entire decision-making process was (for a lack of a better term) a giant white board on the wall with a pre-drawn decision tree. You see, in the nuclear energy business, there are a finite number of things that can go wrong with the reactor (my recollection is approximately 58, but for illustration the actual number is irrelevant). It was laid out in a manner that, once they started reviewing gauges and data, the Senior Controller could go straight to the board and follow the "if this…then this" path very quickly to his correct Protective Action Decision (PAD). It was simple, effective, efficient, and brilliant!

What I described here is an example of how to reach a quick solution for those types of events where opportunity exists for prior planning and, perhaps, even rehearsal. But there are times when you have to make it up as you go along; those situations that are so dynamic and rapidly evolving that require a leader capable of making (sometimes life safety) decisions without the benefit of a "staffed decision."

In the spring of 1998, I was minding my own business as the Support Group (Base) Commander at Andrews AFB, when my Boss called to tell me I had been ordered to deploy to Thumrait, Oman for what was to become Operation Desert Thunder. Since I had been in the Arabian Desert the entire previous year as Central Command's (CENTCOM) force protection guy, I had been to Oman several times. But I had no idea where the heck Thumrait was, or even why they wanted me there. As I soon learned, the 21st Air Force Commander knew that I had all that force protection experience, and he wanted me to deploy with another Colonel from McGuire AFB, NJ, to be his advisor. My specific mission? To go over with the deployed forces and help with the bed-down process by ensuring that all the force protection measures were properly in place; that operations were safely established. I was promised that I would be there for two weeks…max! That should have been my first warning.[67]

67  I was in command of a Group at Andrews that was responsible for everything on base except the flying operation (from the gates in, to include all facilities, services, and base housing). On top of that, I had a Deputy who was about to rotate out to another assignment. I couldn't afford to be gone for very long!

Upon arrival at Thumrait, and for about two days, everything went fine. I was busy getting tent city built, and making sure security forces were properly positioned and the camp perimeter was well established. Then, the Colonel who had deployed with me from McGuire AFB asked me to step into his makeshift office. He had deployed as the commander of this aerial operation, and now as it turns out, he was on his way back home on the next airplane that came in; he had a family emergency that required his presence. The next morning, we all stood on the tarmac and waved goodbye as he boarded the jet and flew off. Suddenly, I was in command of a U.S. Air Force Tanker Task Force. I had command of five KC-10 tankers and 500 people, as we began to finish establishing the 305th Air Expeditionary Group.

In front of tent city at Thumrait, Oman, in 1998. The senior staff and me. I'm third from the right.

Now, some of my Air Force flying colleagues might disagree, but I can't overstate the historical significance of what I'm about to describe. To the best of my knowledge (and I've spent some time trying to research this), I am the only non-rated officer[68] in Air Force history to have ever

_____

68 Pilots and navigators receive an "aerial rating", the rest of us support slugs are just non-rated. It's clever how they perpetuate the myth; how you can do anything if you wear wings, that "universal leadership badge", on your chest. Sorry for my cynicism.

commanded an aviation unit in a combat theater. After it was all over, there are many that just never wanted to talk about it again.

Frankly, I didn't think it would last for long. I quickly jumped on the phone back to headquarters to find out when my relief would arrive… crickets. I waited a couple of days and then called again. This time the conversation with my headquarters contact went something like this: "Well, it seems this deployment has over taxed us on manpower. There are no tanker commanders available to relieve you. The Boss here has talked to the Joint Task Force (JTF) commander there and they've agreed to leave you in place for the duration." For the duration! What the hell does that mean? I found out later that all agreed that since I was the former force protection guy for the theater, and knew the region well, and since I had a very sharp Lt Colonel with me as my rated operations officer, why not just let Hunsinger do it?

I have to tell you, of all the awesome experiences of my career, this one was at or near the top of the list; I could finally tell pilots what to do!! Seriously though, I was immersed into aspects of Air Force operations that I had only seen from the periphery. I was on the flight line all the time watching the maintenance crews swap out this hydraulic hose or change that tire. I flew several missions with the tanker crews, and learned so many things about their business that I hadn't known. Expect for the fact I was away from my "other" command at a critical time, it was an absolute blast. That is, until I met the U.S. Ambassador to Oman.

Frances D. Cook was a career foreign service officer (FSO). FSOs are diplomats; yet, even though they're career employees of the State Department, they are nevertheless politicians. This FSO had been appointed Ambassador[69], and she was as mean as a junk-yard dog.

Once again, I was minding my own business when I got a call from the embassy; they were sending a representative to Thumrait to meet with me the next day. It seems that someone in the Omani Air Force had seen one my security troops on the perimeter armed with a weapon. My reaction? "Let me get this straight. We are U.S. military personnel, deployed to a country inside a hostile fire zone, building an operation with critical U.S assets, with a legitimate/bona fide assessed threat against us, we're getting ready to go to war, and the Ambassador doesn't want us carrying guns? Do I have that right?" The response from the other end? "Yes."

69  You will frequently find that high profile political contributors to the President's campaign land the more lucrative positions (England, France, Canada, etc), where career FSOs are normally assigned to the more challenging posts (from Azerbaijan to Zimbabwe).

Giving the Commander of CENTCOM, General Anthony Zinni, a tour of
Thumrait Oman in 1998.

Not to drag this story out either, but it did get ugly. My Headquarters
fought the good fight on my behalf, but they were doing so from back in
the U.S., while the deployed JTF commanding general caved. He folded
like a house of cards and completely deserted his troops in the field on this
issue. To be sure, the Ambassador was intimidating, and she had connections at the highest levels back home. It was her opinion that we needed to
acquiesce to the Government of Oman's demands. Notwithstanding our
security concerns, the Omani government felt they had security under control, and they would take care of us.

Again, I was the Director of Force Protection for the entire region the
previous year. I was sent there to fix everything after the Khobar Towers
bombing that had killed 19 Americans. When I left the desert, I had given
everyone my five pillars of force protection. One of which is to never let the
host nation seize control of your security; moreover, they should never have
control of who comes on to your compound. We were about to violate that
principle.[70]

70 My Five Pillars of Force Protection were (1) 100% US control of entry to your
facilities (2) 100% surveillance of your perimeter (3) adequate standoff distance for blast
protection (4) real-time intelligence (5) antiterrorism awareness training/education for
the troops.

What I'm about to describe I'm not, necessarily, proud of. Nor am I ashamed. I was, in fact, faced with a decision where I could roll over and comply with an order from someone who had authority, but was not in my chain of command. I could let her put my troops in jeopardy, or I could act on my own. I decided to act. This was clearly an expedient decision. It had, I felt at the time, life and death consequences attached to it. It had to be made quickly, and without the benefit of command assistance. Again, my bosses didn't order me to do anything. They just deferred to the Ambassador to make a call (cowards all).

My tent at Thumrait, Oman, in 1998.
"Home" for four months (on this deployment).

I called my senior staff together, to include my Security Director. I told them that, in appearance, we were going to comply with the Ambassador's order. There would no longer be any weapons in open view…but we were NOT going to disarm. I then instructed my Security Director to move all weapons to our security operations center at the very center of tent city[71]; we would secure at least most of them there. I then gave him two more actions. First, when I said secure the weapons, I meant guard them, don't lock them up. I wanted a quick issue plan and procedure. If we had a sudden fire fight in the middle of the night, I wanted to be able to quickly arm our response force. Second, I wanted several weapons placed in senior leader

---

71  As a force protection measure, we built our security operations center at the center of tent city to hopefully better withstand any adversarial penetration attempt of the camp.

tents throughout the camp. Give me a dispersal plan for whom and where those weapons would be placed.

At first, my security force members were outraged, and rightfully so. No cop on the beat, nor soldier in the field wants to be in a potential life-threatening situation without being properly equipped and armed. When they finally saw the action I was taking, and how I was handling a difficult and sensitive situation, they were relieved. Morale suddenly sored. If anything, they were now even more alert and aware on post.

The whole event subsided, things got back to semi-normal, and we sailed along for a few days…until one of our security force members was seen outside his tent with weapon in hand…and then things got really ugly. We had a security NCO who was having a problem with the sights on his M-4 rifle, so he took it to the guy that could fix it; at security control at the center of tent city.

The very next day I was on an airplane, on my way to the embassy in Muscat for a meeting with the Ambassador. When I entered her office, she was somewhat polite, but stern and visibly angry.[72] She wanted to know how the weapon was in open sight when she gave firm direction that they'd all be locked up. I gave some lame excuse about it all being a misunderstanding and that it wouldn't happen again. She threatened to have me sent home and asked if that's what I wanted. I told her I was certainly anxious to get back to my family, but that was completely her call. It wasn't a long meeting, because the only real purpose for it was to show me that she could summon me all the way to Muscat at her will. She did it because she could. That evening I flew back to Thumrait, never had another weapon incident while we were there, and never had to encounter her again.[73]

So what was the lesson to this story? Two-fold. First, as it pertains to duty, you have to do the right thing. I've tried to be consistent throughout my life and career about duty, honor, and integrity; and when I say the boss is the boss, I try to be consistent with that as well. Don't circumvent the boss unless you deem it to be immoral, unethical, or illegal. In this

---

72  I said earlier that Frances D. Cook was as mean as a junk yard dog. She was a physically intimidating woman. I'm not exactly a small man and she was bigger than me, with a booming voice.
73  I did have other issues, but not with the embassy. One of my aircrews decided on a little joy ride one afternoon. On their way back to Thumrait, following their mission, they descended their KC-10 tanker to about 200 feet and did a fly-by of the aircraft carrier USS Independence, violating countless flight rules (and I thought only cops screwed off on post). I caught hell for that one.

case I felt that it was, and I couldn't get anyone's attention to help rectify it quickly enough (given where I was, literally, in the world). Criticize me if you will, but I took control and did, I felt, the right thing. In the end, all turned out well.

Second, as it pertains to the art of decision-making, this is a lesson in thinking an issue through three steps ahead and two layers deep. This is a case of consequence management; the need to do a rapid cost-benefit analysis of the situation and the consequences you might face from your imminent decision. I thought this one through carefully. I considered all of the ramifications (or as many as I could come up with) on both me and the organization based on the decision I made. I was ultimately willing to pay the price of being sent home (fired).

Thumrait Oman in 1998. I'm third from the left. The Omani Base Commander, Brigadier General Abdul Wahab, is center and to his left is General Zinni.

In the end, we all survived this difficult situation. We concluded our mission four months later and we all returned home safely. Throughout the operation, we flew 190 sorties off-loading 8 million pounds of fuel to 1,239 strike fighters enforcing the no-fly zone over Iraq.

As I mentioned earlier, no one in the rated community ever wanted to talk again about the one non-rated officer that once had an aviation command in combat zone; and, I was okay with that.[74]

## Developing Your Decision-Making Skills

First off, you don't have to do it all by yourself. Every leader who's been hired into a senior leadership position has gotten the job because somewhere along the line someone thought they exercised good judgement. I think it's an unqualified fact; and, if you accept that as fact, then accept the fact that because you're now in a leadership position you already possess some level of skill at exercising good judgement, or in other words making good decisions. At this point you are smart, talented, and experienced enough to have gotten selected for a leadership job. So what's left? Learning how to put it all together, and doing that with the help of people around you.

I'm a decision maker. I've told various staff people over the years, don't give me a problem without also giving me a solution. If not, <u>I will definitely solve your problem</u>…but it may not be the solution you were hoping for. Those simple words have inspired and motivated countless people to think and act on their own. On some level it has empowered them, but it's also relieved me of the burden of having to be the smartest guy in the room. It's fostered an environment where we come up with team solutions to problems. Again, you can lay something on my desk. In which case, I'm like a raccoon with a shiny object; it won't take long for me to start playing with it. Then, suddenly, I've fixed it for you. I guarantee you, most senior leaders will do the same. Your job is to lead us down a path you want us to go.

The whole military decision making process is based on using decision trees (if yes go here, if no go there). Some would ask how you can do this in the heat of battle. The answer is that it's just ingrained. It's instinctive at this point. You realize quickly you need to think 3 steps ahead and 2 layers deep, and you need to do it right now or you might not survive. The commander that can anticipate the enemy's next move will be both successful in the mission while minimizing casualties. It's the same for business. The

---

74 Within Air Force culture, pilots have largely and historically run the Service. It is a union or fraternity that is hard to penetrate. Pilots promote pilots. Pilots select other pilots for major command jobs. They control the process. Historically, the Security Police/Security Forces field (the largest single career field in the Air Force) gets one Brigadier General promotion every four years. It's just the way it's always been. Although there have been a couple of out-of-cycle promotions in recent years.

leader that can quickly assess risk versus consequence, via several different decision routes, will be the successful executive.

I've been advocating a think "three steps ahead and two layers deep" decision-making approach to problem solving for years. In most cases it's simply the process of stopping to think; taking the time to figure out what's going on and what you need to do next. It's forcing yourself to resist making a knee-jerk decision based on partial information that hasn't adequately considered risk versus consequence for every possible alternative.

What about risk? I've heard many leaders and pundits say that a key to decision making is to understand risk. Should you be bold or risk-averse, or somewhere in between? I think it's more important to understand consequence; which, if you're adept enough, should be nothing more than a quick cost-benefit analysis on the fly. Think three steps ahead and two layers deep on any issue to determine what all the potential consequences of that decision might be. There's always risk to everything we do. A "consequence assessment" will often reveal what path to take. For instance, if you're exploring three alternatives, the consequences of one or two of those may be so potentially painful that it drives your decision to the more obvious choice. Just stop for a moment and ask the staff, and yourself (perhaps white board it), "what are all the possible ways this decision can go wrong, and what are the consequences for each?"

## The 100% Solution (or not)

I've said it before, success often comes down to your ability to <u>immediately</u> assess the consequences of the decision you are about to make, and the ramifications of it three steps ahead and two layers deep. If you equivocate, you could be safe but miss out on an opportunity. That said, don't over think things. While I don't necessarily advocate for the "Cortez approach" to decision-making, there are times you'll need to burn the ships to keep moving forward.[75] Nevertheless, make calculated risk/consequence decisions and then go for it and don't look back.

I once had a boss who liked to say "a C paper on time is much better than an A paper late." The context for this had to do with our time as staff officers in the Pentagon. We were constantly working against the clock. <u>Deadlines were</u> attached to everything and they were often extremely

[75] An interesting lesson in commitment. In 1519 Hernan Cortez landed in Veracruz in search of Aztec gold and burned his ships to prevent mutiny (some accounts say he scuttled them). He essentially told his men that the only path toward home was forward, not back.

(unnecessarily) short. However, in the world of operational field decisions you may not have the luxury of time to completely staff the perfect solution to a problem. There are times when you have to go with your instinct and accept the 80% solution.

I've worked for leaders who were slow and indecisive. I swear, at times it was excruciating to see us languish as the issue seemed to fester; all while we appeared to outsiders as being paralyzed. These are the times when you may need to step forward. Don't let the boss get mired in decision trees, flow charts, and a myriad of pros/cons/options/recommendation. Don't let the staff "overstaff." Make a damn decision and move forward!

In 1993 I was assigned to the Pentagon as a Military Assistant to an Assistant Secretary of Defense (it was my third assignment there). I can't even remember the issue we were working. It certainly had something to do with humanitarian relief or a peacekeeping mission in the Balkans, since those were the issues that consumed most of our attention during that timeframe. What I do remember vividly is the inordinate amount of time it took to staff the paper.

On a Friday afternoon, late in the day, we took the finally completed fully-coordinated Pentagon position paper to Secretary of Defense Les Aspin's office for his approval and signature. It was late in the day, and it had to be to the State Department by close of business.[76] Secretary Aspin's Military Assistant handed him the paper, gave him a quick overview of its contents, and explained the urgency and need for his immediate signature. After all, the State Department was waiting. What happened next? Call it an old-fashioned butt chewing, or perhaps a dagger through the heart. Secretary Aspin calmly put the paper down and looked up at everyone in the room and said "Gentlemen, I'm the Secretary of Defense." There was a collective "Yes sir." Then he said "The President hired me to be the Secretary of Defense because he was interested in my views on foreign policy in general and defense policy in particular. He's interested in my views, not necessarily your views. So next time, why don't we get this into me early enough for me to review it, make changes if necessary, and get it over to State with plenty of time. The last thing I want is to be reduced to nothing more than a signature. Sound good?" There was another collective "Yes sir."

The story about Les Aspin provided two lessons for all of us that day. First, perhaps sometimes the 80% solution might be the right approach (or

---

76 My Military Assistant counterpart (there were two of us in the office), now retired Vice Admiral Kevin Green, actually walked the paper in.

perhaps a C paper on time is better than an A paper late). You cannot over-staff issues to the point where it paralyzes you as an organization and you lose credibility with the boss, and others. Second, whether they'll admit it or not, leaders like to be (or will accept being) led down a logical path, but they will not accept being managed, or worse yet, marginalized.

It was a hard lesson learned.

> *"Don't manage – lead change before you have to"*
> —Jack Welch

## Innovation

In everything you do, work to be seen as decisive, as being right, but also as someone who seeks innovative approaches to problem solving. I once worked for a boss that coached me to always approach problems in-novatively; to train myself to always be both forward thinking and a person of great vision. He believed passionately that this was a learned skill, that you could teach yourself to do it, and that it was a major key to your suc-cess as a leader; and I agree. Again, it's nothing more than taking the time to think issues through three steps ahead and two layers deep, and then making a risk versus consequence decision. However, beyond that, you can never rest on your laurels!

Just because you are or have been successful at something (or a way of doing something) don't lull yourself into a state of contentment. Don't think that because it worked before, it'll work again and every time, or for-ever. Or worse yet, don't (or don't let your boss) allow the organization to just fall into complacency. You have to constantly fight the urge toward apa-thy, inactivity, and lethargy. Inertia is a killer in an organization. You have to keep your organization moving forward. Think of it as the "shark approach to leadership." Some species of sharks need to swim constantly in order to keep oxygen-rich water flowing over their gills. If they don't, they drown. They are in perpetual motion. It's the same for any organization. You have to keep the firm, its employees, and yes sometimes the boss, moving forward.

When I deployed to Thumrait, Oman for Operation Desert Thunder, we found ourselves suddenly in a "steady state" posture. That is, after a couple of weeks of saber rattling with Saddam Hussain, and the constant prospect of going to war, nothing happened. We spent the next four months waiting for the U.S. Government and the United Nations to decide what action it was going to take. In the meantime, we continued flying refueling missions, training, and preparing. Notwithstanding, daily life in tent city went on.

It wasn't long before I realized that for the sake of troop morale, something needed to change. For those of you that have never deployed to a harsh (bare base) environment, it may be a difficult concept to picture. We had nothing in place when we got there. Everything we had or needed we either brought with us, had shipped in later, or just did without. The heat, isolation, lack of regular mail, and absence any form of entertainment quickly took a toll on unit morale.

I realized not too far into the deployment that I needed to do something to enhance living conditions on at least a weekly basis. The organization needed to change constantly and frequently. Again, complacency and stagnation are two enemies that can challenge any leader. To combat both, I gathered my civil engineers, services personnel, and my senior leaders, and charged them to develop both short and long-term goals for bringing something new to the camp every week. We improved our dining facility (both in menu[77] and environment), shower tents, latrines, recreational tents, and living quarters[78]. As mundane as it may sound, the slightest improvement under conditions such as those we faced could/did have an impact on morale that was exponential. As in previous organizations, I also implemented an advisory group to provide particularly our younger personnel an opportunity to have an impact on the direction we were going with our constant improvement.

Again, keep your organization and its people moving forward, or they'll drown like a shark.

77  A lesson in the power of the situation report (SITREP). Every night I sent Headquarters our daily sitrep (missions flown, fuel off-loaded, personnel status, etc). At one point I started including our food status at the bottom of the report. When I got to the point of "we are now on day 55 of our 30-day supply of food" I got a call from the watch officer from the Air Mobility Command. He said Gen Robertson was having their butts every morning over my "food issue." If he promised that tomorrow morning a C-5 from Aviano, Italy will be there with eight pallets of food, would I drop this from my sitrep? I told him "Absolutely. But if it doesn't show up, future sitreps will include all the innovative recipes we've come up with on how to prepare chili and macaroni." The airplane arrived as promised.

78  I also took crap for buying food on the open market in the nearby port city of Salalah. The food nutrition geeks at Headquarters told me it may not be sanitary and hadn't been inspected by one of them. My reply? Well, the clean version is, first, we're combat airmen and we know how to take care of ourselves. Second, we're also Americans, so we know how to use bailing wire and chewing gum to fix things, and had done that a few times as well.

## Consistency

Consistency is arguably one of the most important attributes of any leader. I mentioned in the introduction to this book that you have to be a person "of your word." That means you are consistent, fair and predictable. They know what they are getting each and every time. Without that quality, employees are left guessing...can I trust that he'll be fair with me? You can be benevolent or you can be a butt kicker (or somewhere in between), but you have to be consistent in how you apply standards of conduct and discipline. Your employees need to know what to expect. If you rule on a decision, make sure you are consistent the next time you are faced with the same decision under similar circumstances. There are a couple of ways you can assure success in this area.

First, don't let "we" become "I." This is probably good advice in general but in the context of this discussion, standards of discipline should be those of the organization, not just yours. In most cases you didn't write or develop the standards. You probably inherited them, and for the most part they're probably the product of a government regulation, a corporate policy, or even a collectively-bargained union agreement. They were there when you got there; it's your job to enforce them. They are and should be "our" rules, not "my" rules. That said, a good leader is neither apologetic nor contemptuous of the standard ("Hey, I don't agree with any of this crap but I'm being required to enforce it"). Don't be THAT guy or gal! Your job is to support the organization; its rules and policies, or, get the hell out.

Second, don't take on too much yourself. Have someone (your assistant or the HR folks) keep track. You're likely to have a full plate already, and it's not unreasonable to rely on others to keep you straight on disciplinary and other HR issues. Again, use your assistant, the HR folks, the lawyers, EEO, and others to keep you on a consistent track. While we're at it, consistency doesn't only mean being consistent with what you've done in similar circumstances, but also what the agency has done. Throughout the agency, it takes a team effort to administer personnel policies fair and equitably across the entire employee population. Use your resources!

## Self Confidence

One of my favorite stories to illustrate self-confidence is one (perhaps not so famous) about Pete Rose. Pete was being interviewed in spring training the year he was about to break Ty Cobb's all-time hits record of 4,191 hits. One reporter blurted out, "Pete, you only need 78 hits to break the record. How many at-bats do you think it'll take to get the 78 hits?" Without hesitation, Pete told the reporter, very matter-of-factly, "78." The reporter yelled back, "Ah, come on Pete, you don't expect to get 78 hits in 78 at-bats, do you?" Pete then calmly shared his philosophy with all the reporters anxiously awaiting his reply to this seemingly boastful claim. "Every time I step up to the plate, I expect to get a hit! If I don't expect to get a hit, I have no right to step in the batter's box in the first place!" "If I go up hoping to get a hit," he continued, "then I probably don't have a prayer to get a hit. It is a positive expectation that has gotten me all of the hits in the first place."[79] Now that's self-confidence.

None of us are Pete Rose and, in fact, Pete Rose didn't go 78 for 78 on his way to breaking the record. He was, nevertheless, a bold guy who frequently made bold statements. He was a superb baseball player and a phenomenal hitter; but at least on some level he added to that Pete Rose mystique by promoting the legend; by being bold. That sense of self-confidence preceded him wherever he went and probably did as much to intimidate pitchers as his prowess with a bat.

My advice to new and emerging leaders? While I certainly don't suggest the arrogance of Pete Rose, I do encourage you to demonstrate self-confidence. Be bold and brave! Colin Powell said in his seminal piece on leadership, "You don't know what you can get away with until you've tried."[80] His philosophy was "If they haven't explicitly told me no, then I can do it." He always felt that it was much easier to beg for forgiveness than to seek permission. I think that's pretty good advice, but make prudent, not reckless decisions. I once worked for a boss that liked to say "every once in a while, you have to act a little audacious." Regardless, just don't be afraid to act.

When it comes to crisis situations, it's imperative that your decision-making process remain cool, calm, and collected. Don't let them see you sweat. As the leader, you want people to see you as their rock; you want them to rally around you; you want them to maintain trust and faith that you'll lead them through this crisis. If you get excited so does everyone else and soon, they lose confidence in you and themselves.

---

79 "What I learned from Pete Rose" by Anonymous, http://www.wowzone.com/pe-terose.htm

80 http://www.airpower.au.af.mil/apjinternational/apj-s/2011/2011-4/2011_4_02_powell_s_eng.pdf

## The "Process Leader" vs. the true "Servant Leader"

I read an article some time ago on how successful bosses run their meetings; and believe me, I've seen countless similar articles. It went on to suggest that in order to have a successful meeting and to at least be seen as a caring leader, you have to take into account everything from having a rock-solid agenda, to a comfy room, to bringing your employees snacks[81]. All of this is good stuff. But it's not leadership! It is process stuff. Don't get me wrong. I'm all in favor of taking care of employees. But don't let the concept of "Servant Leader" be sold to you as needing to be their servant; as the ultimate pathway to leadership success. It's not! Maybe it's just a matter of semantics, but I can't buy into the title of "servant leader" in that context[82]. While I subscribe to most of the basic tenets of the idea (mentoring, coaching, etc.), I'm not your servant, and a leader is either a servant or a leader…but not both. Stop calling yourselves servants; it, in some subliminal way, degrades and diminishes (if not undermines) your position.

Some of the most ineffective leaders I've ever seen are those that are too worried about, too focused on, what their employees think of them. Some have such a fixation on personal admiration (wanting to be liked by everyone) that it adversely affects their decision-making process. In some cases, they are either paralyzed by the thought that their popularity will decline, or worse yet, that someone might file a complaint. These leaders have an awful time having to say no to anything.

Again, don't get me wrong. I'm all for "process" as well. I'm almost a compulsive organizer; perhaps it's the military precision culture ingrained within me. I'm also in favor of employee social gatherings. I used to tell employees they could count on me to be at every cake-event (my personal favorite). Nevertheless, when your leadership approach revolves around planning an ice cream social every Thursday afternoon, it's time for a reality check.

There have been volumes written on the concept of Servant Leader. Again, I'm sorry to say, I'm not there to be their servant, nor even their friend. I'm there to be their leader. I used to tell my kids that I'm not your buddy or your friend and will never be. I am your Dad, and with that carries the awesome responsibility of parenting. I loved them deeply and

---

81  https://www.theladders.com/career-advice/
successful-bosses-run-their-most-effective-meetings-exactly-like-this
82  Not to be confused with the higher calling of "service" which I will continue to address throughout.

guided them as best I could as kids. From their Dad they always got fair and equitable discipline, and later in life, consistent advice…again, from their Dad. In some respects, it's the same concept for leadership; that awesome responsibility never ends.[83]

So, what is "servant leadership?" It's selfless leadership; you put everything (the mission and your employees) ahead of yourself. Every leader needs to be focused on the mission. Great leaders do that while tending to the needs of their troops (physical, mental, spiritual, health, financial, family…and the list goes on). A true leader is able to transcend the supervisor/subordinate relationship to develop a sort of loving family bond with those in his or her charge. The troops reach a point where they know that you care, and if you're genuine in this effort, in most cases, will follow you anywhere because they will have come to know that in addition to the mission, you have their best interests at heart as well. In most cases it's personality driven. It can't be forced. It has to be developed and earned.

I've said it countless times and I'll say it again. True leadership comes from taking care of your employees, as well as your willingness and ability to make quick, unequivocal, and hard decisions that are well-thought and based on a consequence versus risk; all with a focus on doing right and good things.

> *"No man will make a great leader who wants to do it all himself, or to get all the credit for doing it."*
> —Andrew Carnegie

**The "Art" Form of Leadership**

Just how do you lead the leader below you? Sure, they're your subordinate, but it's not like leading another one of the rank and file employees. These are people that have an awesome responsibility of their own to supervise, direct, guide, mold, and mentor employees below them. What do you do when you realize a manager a level or two below you is struggling? Honestly, I haven't seen much discussion on this aspect of leadership, but I do have some thoughts.

There are many people that I've worked for over my career that I admire and respect still today. Great leaders, all of them; people that have had a tremendous impact on my personal development as a leader. However,

---

83  Someone, I'm sure, will criticize me for using this example of subordinate employees and my kids.

my former boss and personal friend, retired General Art Lichte, was an extraordinary leader. I'll cut right to the chase…it takes a special skill to get people to do something by making them think it was their idea. This man was the Jedi Master. In fact, there were times it seemed like he would redirect a conversation as if to say "these are not the droids you're looking for."[84] Of course, he was neither clairvoyant nor even a manipulator of people. He just asked questions; often, asking enough questions that it led an individual through a full circle of decision options that sometimes resulted in a different conclusion.

My former boss and good friend, General Art Lichte, in 2001.

I was commander of the Security Forces Squadron at Fairchild AFB in 1995 when a newly pinned-on Brigadier General by the name of Art Lichte arrived as our new Wing Commander. I had been in command of the squadron for a little over a year. Our Main Gate entrance had a tricky

84   Many will immediately recognize this line as being spoken by Obi-Wan Kenobi in *Star Wars Episode IV – A New Hope*. With a wave of his hand, and a mystical power of persuasion, Obi-Wan was able to manipulate minds.

twist and turn to the road (which has since been corrected) where several lanes from different directions funneled into two as it approached the gate in the outbound direction. We (the collective we) had been concerned about the potential hazards of that situation for years; the potential of everything from congestion to an accident. Every evening, at the end of the duty day, it was a laborious (if not complicated) process of diverting patrols and detailing other people to the Main Gate in order to set out hundreds of orange traffic cones in order to create well-defined lanes for cars to follow as they left for the day. We did this every night!

After watching this process for several days, Gen Lichte called me (and selected members of the staff) into his office for a short discussion on traffic control at the Main Gate. I brought a few members of my staff along with charts and diagrams to aid in our discussion. The guys I brought along had been doing this for years and were clearly the experts.

Gen Lichte started the conversation by saying "you know, I've been watching this go on for a few days, and I think you guys are working too hard on a problem that doesn't exist." We were stunned. We tried to redirect the conversation back to what we'd always done because, for sure, if we did something else chaos would follow! We showed him our charts and presented empirical traffic data. Without doubt, he was the General and he could have ordered us right then and there to make a change. Instead, he just calmly kept turning the discussion by asking a series of "what if" questions. Have you tried this? Have you thought of that?

Certainly, my guys were very polite and respectful to the Wing Commander. Nevertheless, they dug their heels in and weren't about to budge unless directed to. They were absolutely convinced that without the system they'd been using for years we'd have cars piled in a heap at the Main Gate; it would be a calamity.

The meeting ended without any real resolution; which I thought was odd coming from a General officer that didn't just impose his will (which I had seen throughout my career). As it broke up, Gen Lichte asked me to stay behind for a minute. He then said, "Dennis, I know how your guys feel about it. But let's try, just for one evening, to go without the hundreds of traffic cones. Let's just let nature take its course and see what happens. If it's a disaster, then we'll continue on with your process and I won't bring it up again. Will you indulge me with this one-time experiment?" I agreed. After all, he was the boss; but I also thought it was a reasonable request.

As I left, he encouraged me to downplay this to the troops as any kind of directive from him.

I went back to the office, gathered the staff, and began a review of what we all went through during our meeting with Gen Lichte. Their reaction was, wow…we dodged a bullet there; we got the boss to see things our way. I, on the other hand, have always considered myself to be a fairly quick learner. I recognized the tactic the boss had used during the meeting, so I started a series of what if questions myself. What if we just tried it for one evening? What if we didn't put the cones out, but had them readily available, with all of our patrols standing by to spring into action when something certainly went wrong. Of course, it will all go wrong; then we can prove to the boss that we were right all along. They liked the idea, and I didn't even have to divulge the conversation I had with the boss.

So, what happened? You can guess. The next evening, we did nothing. No cones. No traffic control. No problem! Attribute it to human nature, or conditioned learning, or whatever…the traffic flowed smoothly out the gate. There was no congestion and certainly no chaos. Just like that, we were out of the traffic control business, and the troops took all the credit; it was their idea!

The real problem was that we were so myopically fixated on an issue that was handed down from generation to generation, that no one really understood the original problem or that an alternative approach should even be considered. It took an outsider's viewpoint and a very gentle nudge to get people moving in the right direction.

I worked for Gen Lichte on a couple of other occasions and saw him use this leadership technique countless times. He was a master at it and it was extremely effective for him. He had that special personality and tremendous skill necessary to motivate people in the direction he wanted them to go while convincing them that it was their idea all along. That, my friends, does take talent. It can also be learned. As talented and as adroit as he was at it, it was, nonetheless, nothing more than gentle per-suasion as opposed to direct confrontation. In addition to that, the mark of a good leader is to know how to balance the mission with people. But a better, more successful leader masters the art of knowing when there are times that the mission is more important, or times when people are more important. The trick is being able to swing one way or the other when appropriate, but being able to come back to that balance quickly. That skill, plus the ability to lead people through a decision-making process to undisputable conclusions, in my opinion, were Art Lichte's greatest strengths as a leader.

*"Leadership is the art of getting someone else to do something you want done because he wants to do it."*
—Dwight D. Eisenhower

# 5

# Run with the Bulls

## (Just Don't Get Trampled)

*"Nobody ever lives their life all the way up except bull-fighters"*
—Ernest Hemingway

If you've elected to enter the race to senior leadership, at some point (metaphorically) you've ceased being a young calf and now you're running (racing) with the bulls. Make no mistake, it's a race for a lot of reasons. First, life is short, and your career life is even shorter. You've got a lot to do; things you want to accomplish in a relatively short time. Trust me, it'll be over faster than you can imagine and you'll be wondering what happened. Second, there are plenty of others racing to the top as well. The field is crowded, and you want to take every opportunity you can to make yourself stand out. If you're going to make it to or near the top, you'll need to keep up.

My first bit of advice here is (and I've already said it elsewhere) <u>be bold and brave</u>. How bold? Let me give you another one of my personal experiences to illustrate.

In 1974, I was a young enlisted Airman assigned to the base hospital at March AFB, in Riverside, California. I'd been there a year and had both recently graduated from college[85] and had applied and been rejected for Officer Training School (OTS). I wanted desperately to get a commission and become an Air Force officer. By this time, I'd been married for almost three years and had a young son; we were well on our way to starting a young family and I saw life as an Air Force officer as the best opportunity to provide for my family, and as a stepping stone for when I finally separated from the Air Force. The only problem was, the war in Viet Nam had just ended and the entire U.S. defense department was drawing down. Within the Air Force there was a massive reduction in force (RIF) underway. They <u>were putting m</u>ore officers out of the Air Force than they were taking in.

85  Upon arriving at March AFB in August 1973, I immediately enrolled in night school at Chapman University, doubled-up some classes, tested out of others, and finished my degree within a year (I had about two years of college under my belt when I enlisted).

More than just wanting to be an officer, I also wanted to fly, but new accessions for pilot and navigator training were virtually non-existent at the time. Nevertheless, I had applied for OTS anyway, and was promptly turned down.

A young Airman First Class Dennis Hunsinger graduating from tech school at Shepard AFB, TX, in 1973

I don't know what caused me to do it. Call it an act of courage or perhaps one of desperation. I was taking a lunch time course (at this point, enrolled in graduate school) and was driving back to work from the base education office. As I drove down the road, I glanced to my left and noticed the office building for 15th Air Force Headquarters. I'd driven past that building probably a hundred times without ever giving it a second thought. For some reason, at this moment (in the flash of a moment), my thought was "I wonder if there's anything they can do for me", and then it was "Oh, what the hell." I made a sudden left turn into the parking lot, and the next thing I knew, I was standing at the desk of some Captain who, as it turned out, was the 15th Air Force commander's executive officer. The Captain was very cool, very polite; but at this point I was very nervous. Good Lord! What have I done? I'm an Airman and I'm standing in the General's office! Oh well, I'm committed now.

I explained to the Captain who I was and why I was there. I told him that I was a good troop, had a great performance record, was a recent college graduate, and was having trouble getting into OTS. I told him, in so many words, that I knew it was highly unusual for a junior Airman to be doing what I was there doing, but I was determined to get a commission and saw few avenues open for me. Since I was (at least in my view) such a worthy member of the commander's team, perhaps he'd consider sponsoring me for admission to OTS. Honestly, at this point I thought I'd get thrown out of their office; worse yet, that someone would call my squadron commander and make a complaint against me. How dare I have the audacity to think I could walk into the commander's office and expect to be treated with respect, dignity and compassion! To my surprise…that's exactly what I got.

As it turns out, I was the first person to have ever attempted something like that. No one had ever walked into their office seeking the boss's help. They were overjoyed! I think I was, in some small way, an answer to their prayers; a break from the monotony of daily headquarters life. They had a pet airman they could take under their wing. I don't mean at all to be flippant about it; but I do think there is a grain of truth to it. More importantly, they were genuinely pleased and anxious to help a young guy succeed. As they got deeper into it (a review of my records, transcripts, and interviews of me) they realized they had a candidate worth supporting. I also believe they fully embraced their leadership responsibility to mentor and develop the next generation of leadership. They were doing what they saw as the right thing.

The next few steps went rather quickly. The Captain introduced me to the Chief of Staff, a Colonel, who interviewed me and then turned me over to a civilian who was the command's director of educational services (he had a direct link to OTS). The civilian helped me put my next OTS application together which, this time, would include a letter of recommendation from the boss right on top. About a week later, dressed in my service dress blue uniform, I found myself entering the commander's office.

Lieutenant General William F. Pitts was an allusive figure that very few of us airmen had ever seen. He was the commander of virtually all of the Strategic Air Command west of the Mississippi. Needless to say, he was a busy man…but he found time for me. When I stepped into his office I saluted smartly and he shook my hand and told me to have a seat next to his desk. I tried as hard as I could to sit up straight, at attention; but the chair next to his desk was an over-stuffed easy chair. As I sat down, and slumped into the chair, I lost all military bearing. He just laughed, put me at complete ease, and then just started a very casual conversation about what my life goals were. I'm sure I was only there for about 15 minutes, but that short meeting with him was an extremely valuable lesson in leadership that I've carried with me the rest of my life. I saw in him a man that was kind, gentle, and genuinely caring for the welfare of his troop. After talking for a while, he turned around to this (I swear) giant phone bank behind his desk, pushed one button and a guy came on the line. He said "Jim, this is Bill. I've got a great troop here that wants to go to OTS. I'm signing a letter of recommendation and hope you can get him into the next class." After a few other pleasantries, he hung up, turned around and signed the cover letter, handed me the package, and said "enjoy OTS." The rest, as they say, is history. I never saw Gen Pitts again, and regretted over the years having never reached out to him to report how well I had succeeded (to validate his support of me), and to just say thanks. He died in 2008.

Lt Gen William F. Pitts, Commander of 15th Air Force in 1974.
(Official U.S. Air Force photo)

This whole experience was a lesson in boldness. It was my first attempt to run with the bulls. It was fraught with danger at every step; but this one proved to be a case where sometimes you have to cast caution to the wind and just go for it.

A still young 2nd Lt Dennis Hunsinger graduating from
Officer Training School at Lackland AFB, TX, in 1975.

## *Keep the Bulls Focused on the Big Picture*

I said earlier in Chapter 4 that senior leaders generally bristle at the word
no. My experience has been (believe me, via hard lessons) they'd rather
hear an answer along the lines of "boss, we can do that, but here is what
that decision will cost you." Despite your disdain for the boss's idea, it
might not be politically wise to tell him or her that the idea sucks. You
need to be a little more discreet about it, and perhaps provide the boss
with alternative options and a recommended course of action. You may

still lose, but at least your views will have been considered. If you're skilled enough, more often than not, you should be able to steer the boss in another direction.

In doing so; in trying to dissuade (or persuade) the boss regarding a certain action, try to always consider this: Some leaders are far too focused on only the things they can control, not the things they can influence. In other words, there are times when the boss is so mired in the weeds of an issue that he doesn't take time to step back and see the bigger picture. For instance, maybe we shouldn't just go after a <u>piece</u> of the pie. Perhaps we should go for the <u>whole</u> pie.

To give somewhat of an illustration, in 1990, during the months immediately preceding Desert Storm (our first war with Iraq), I was still working in the Secretary of Defense's counterterrorism office.[86] My duty title was Assistant for Combatting Terrorism, working in the Office of the Assistant Secretary of Defense for Special Operations and Low Intensity Conflict (ASD-SOLIC).

I had recently authored a DOD Directive that gave our office and our Assistant Secretary authority and responsibility for setting antiterrorism and force protection policy for the entire Department of Defense. As Desert Shield was ramping up, we were working with all DOD agencies that were dispersed throughout the desert to tighten their procedures. For those months preceding Desert Storm, we were deploying forces, building infrastructure, and establishing bases for operation. Our job in SOLIC was to ensure everything from guard force requirements to armored cars. We set policy on what needed to be done and how to protect people and assets; the Joint Staff implemented the policy.

As weeks and months passed, and the war was looking to be more likely, we began to notice a marked increase in threat intelligence directed toward Americans abroad in general, but more specifically toward official Americans. There was certainly support from certain sectors of the world for what Saddam Hussain had done to Kuwait, and for what he was now doing to the U.S. and the rest of the non-Islamic world (a sort of poke in the eye by not acceding to our demands to withdraw from Kuwait). By fall, there were reports of planned suicide bombings and other assassination preparations being made by sympathetic terrorist groups.

---

86 I was there from 1988 to 1991. Desert Storm was the actual prosecution of the war; January 17, 1991 when we actually crossed the border into Kuwait. Leading up to the war was Operation Desert Shield, which included the entire build-up for the war.

By late October, our Combatting Terrorism office had convinced DOD senior leadership (our bosses, the Joint Staff, and the Secretary) that it was time to start moving non-essential (noncombatant) people back to the US. We had at the time, a large number of family members assigned in what could/would quickly become "harm's way" if we didn't act soon. There were U.S. military compounds in Saudi Arabia and elsewhere that had been there for years to accomplish a military assistance mission.[87] Most of these facilities had significant numbers of military and other U.S families residing there. In short, it was time to draw down and send both family members and other noncombatants home.

It was an arduous process to convince senior leadership to do it. Were there political consequences to this action? Yes, but we argued that, as the Department of Defense, this is what we do and how we think. Our job is to defend. We take care of the nation, and our people, in the process. Let's leave it to other Agencies to have a different focus (which I'll get to in a moment). So, following a flurry of position papers and briefings, we had the boss convinced; it was time to act.

It began as a low-profile initiative, and I think in the beginning the media hadn't caught on, or at least it hadn't made the nightly news. As the weeks went on, the intelligence threat reporting increased. We had reached, by December, a critical phase where protests were springing up in various parts of the (mostly Islamic) world. It was sometime in mid-December that I was home one evening watching CNN and noticed reporting on some of the protests. They were interviewing an embassy employee in Malaysia (as I recall) who indicated that they weren't very concerned about it, and that no unusual activity by the embassy was being taken. I sat there thunderstruck as I realized we hadn't coordinated with the State Department on all the actions we had taken. To be clear, they were certainly aware, and had access to the same intelligence we had, but we hadn't met with them for any joint planning. We were going one direction and they were going a different direction.

I went to work the next day, briefed my boss, and then called a contact over at State. "Nope. We're not doing anything. We're diplomats and we need to remain at our posts for diplomatic reasons. That includes our families. For us to pack up and leave sends a message that we don't trust the host

---

87   Joint U.S. Military Assistance and Advisory Groups (JUSMAG) are located in various countries worldwide to facilitate military equipment transfers and some training activities.

nation to take care of our security concerns." My response? "You gotta be sh***in me! The threat is almost critical worldwide, it's getting higher every day, and we're about to go to war!" What I just described illustrates what I mentioned earlier (and I think rather clearly) the differences in cultures from one Department to the other. We defend; they conduct diplomacy (and in this case, naïvely).

I immediately got to work. This was a case of not focusing on just what you can control (DOD response) but what you can also influence (US Government worldwide response). Throughout the next several weeks (the war started on January 17, 1991), I pushed the interagency community to consider previously overlooked force protection measures. I wrote and staffed the initiative that led to the drawdown of non-essential embassy personnel in the Middle East, as well as an increase in worldwide threat conditions by the joint staff. Our Assistant Secretary pushed for an immediate meeting of the Deputies Committee[88] that finally got the issue, the threat picture, and the proposed course of action on the table for a U.S. Government-wide, fully coordinated plan. When it was all over, the Deputy Assistant Secretary of Defense wrote in my performance report, "...his well thought-out and clearly articulated initiatives to enhance U.S. worldwide force protection posture undoubtedly saved lives during desert shield/desert storm." Yeah, well, who knows? Maybe. But at least I sleep well at night for having done the right thing.

I have to tell you, I lost a couple of friends at State over this one. This was a case where the bulls (or at least one...the State Department) could have turned and gored me to death. I learned a long time ago that it's easy to get crushed between two pachyderms (or bulls) if you're not careful. In this case it could have been a fight between DOD and State with me in the middle. It was a risk worth taking.

The point to this whole story is that I could have easily "minded my own business." I could have hunkered down in the Pentagon, done my own thing within DOD, and let State muddle along. But I had an opportunity to reach beyond my narrow scope (which was pretty broad in itself) to a wider sphere of influence. I had the track record and reputation for making the correct calls, the accurate threat picture in hand, and <u>right</u> on my side. I made a bold move to influence what all of government was doing in this time of crisis, and it worked.

---

88  A sub-Cabinet meeting of all of the Deputy Secretaries of the major Departments of U.S. Government.

*"Surrounded yourself with {people} who concentrate on the possibilities, not the difficulties"*
—George C. Marshall

## Things not to do Around the Bulls

You need to assume that senior leaders are always short on time and generally on patience. <u>Develop what's been called an "elevator speech."</u> If you're riding in an elevator with the boss and you need to get a point across, how can you articulate your argument in 45 seconds? Same goes for the first time you meet a senior leader. Whether it's in a meeting or a social setting, you may only get 30-45 seconds to make that first impression. What do you want that person to walk away with as it relates to who you are, what you value, and what you feel you can accomplish?

<u>Please don't whine</u>…about anything. It is unbecoming and very bad form, if not pathetic. Try to offer only constructive comments. I've said it before, if you see a problem don't just dump the problem on your boss without also presenting a well-thought solution; or you might get a solution and it's not the one you wanted.

Senior leaders <u>don't want to hear your excuses, or hear you throw someone else (especially your boss) under the bus</u> just to save yourself. Throwing anyone under the bus, especially your boss is both disloyal and dangerous. There's an old saying; if you're going to attack the king, you better make sure you kill him. If the boss has done something illegal, unethical, or immoral, then by all means take it to the appropriate authority. But make damn sure you're right.

<u>Be careful about being candid</u>. I once worked for a boss that often asked employees to be candid during meetings. "You can trust me. It'll stay in this room." It never did. When the information got back to intermediate supervisors, there was often hell to pay. Don't let a senior leader bait you into that situation. If you're the senior leader that is doing just that…then stop! No one should ever say anything in those meetings they wouldn't want their boss to hear; and that includes you. Don't run your boss down in front of the troops, ever! Don't expect your employees to divulge candid information to you. Certainly, you should be open to hearing from them, but don't cajole. Otherwise, again, it is disloyal and dangerous, both ways.

What you say and, for that matter, what you write will eventually come back to you, and could come back to haunt you.

Don't fret too much about what the bulls think of you, or particularly about what they think of your leadership decisions. You won't always make the right decision, and who's to say they would have done anything different or better? Just make a decision and don't look back. However, I've always stressed that any good leader should stay on top of things without appearing to micro-manage. Follow up, follow up, and follow up some more. You need to "trust, but verify" as Ronald Reagan said. Do spot checks.

Finally, and you've seen me say it couple of times now, senior leaders rarely want a "no" answer (at least at the beginning). They want some assurance (demonstrate to them) that you've done your homework and that you've explored all the options. Even then, if it has to be a no answer, I'd take the tactic of providing them background information, options for consideration, and then a recommended option that leads them down your desired path. Even then, don't be surprised (or worse yet, become obstructive) if the boss launches in a different, yet moral/legal/ethical direction.

As damaging as the "no" answer can be, the "I don't know" answer can harm your reputation just as easily. Learn better responses than "I don't know" to the boss's very direct and tough questions. If you truly don't know, then come up with an interim response. For certain, DON'T LIE or make stuff up! But there are other things you can say that will buy you some time, and hopefully ensure a continued level of confidence from the boss. Perhaps, something on the order of "Based on what we know right now, here are my thoughts (or the actions I've taken)", or even "I'll get an answer for you immediately after the meeting" is better than saying I don't know. What follows is a personal story on how I prepared for such an event.

In the summer of 2008, while serving as FEMA Acting Regional Administrator, I was sitting on a national hurricane video teleconference. There was a hurricane approaching the southeast that was potentially impacting several states up the eastern seaboard. Being a west coast region, and in a support role, our participation on the call was silent. In other words, we had no formal briefing or speaking role and would only speak if a specific question was directed at us. The call was facilitated by the FEMA Administrator, with all of his regional administrators, NOAA Weather, US Coast Guard, US Army Corps of Engineers, US Northern Command, many other agencies, DHS Headquarters, and the White House[89].

---

89  Usually, the Chief of Staff represented the White House on the call.

As the call got underway, there was an interruption from the White House to announce that President Bush would be joining the call. He came on the phone, said a few pleasantries about how well we were all doing in planning and preparing for this hurricane and then settled in for the remainder of the briefing. At this point, the "pucker factor" went up by a factor of ten. You could hear it in the voices of briefers, and I sat there thanking God that I was a silent participant and praying that I wouldn't be asked a question.

At a point in the briefing where the affected FEMA Regional Administrators were supposed to brief on actions they were taking, the President began asking questions. They weren't very hard questions; in my view, pretty simple innocuous questions that any FEMA RA should be able to answer like "what actions are the states taking to preposition commodities in advance of the storm?" To my shock, one of the east coast RAs struggled for answers and, in fact, there were a couple of times of "I don't know." I was embarrassed for him and the Agency. I turned to my staff and said that will never happen to us.

I lost a lot of sleep for the next couple of weeks trying to figure out how to tackle the issue of being prepared…not just prepared for a major disaster, but prepared for the likely 4AM national video teleconference after a major event with, potentially, the President asking me questions. I started to backward plan the event to the critical moment in my decision-making process; the actual phone call I might get from my operations center notifying me of a catastrophic incident in my region. The answer was simple, I needed a playbook, not a checklist, but a playbook.

I used NFL football coach Bill Walsh's West Coast Offense as a model for what I wanted to get done. The West Coast Offense was designed to spread the field and get downfield as quickly as possible using a short passing scheme. More importantly, it employed a scripted set of plays (25-30) to start the game. As they came out of the locker room, they intended to run a specific set of plays to open the game regardless of what the defense was doing. That's what I wanted! Go big and fast; and script all of my actions for the first couple of hours leading up to that video teleconference. In addition to all of that, I asked the staff to run the computer models on the top three likely catastrophic scenarios in each of our four states. Tell me what the likely computer-generated damages would be for each scenario (9.0 earthquake in Anchorage, Lucky Peak Dam breach above Boise, and so on), and then plan on "push-packages" for each (food, water, power generation, and other commodities to be pushed forward to the state). I then formatted that information, to include contact information for Governors and their staff in all four states, and key members of the FEMA staff. I then added questions I would ask the state and questions that Headquarters might ask me. I now had something that, when I rolled out of bed for a 2 AM phone call, I wouldn't be fumbling for what to say or what my first action might be.

This example was how I prepared for what former Secretary of Defense Donald Rumsfeld called a known known.[90] It was how I'd deal with the potential "I don't know" question I knew I could get. For those questions that you can anticipate, I'd suggest preparing for it as best as you can. For the others (the known unknowns and the unknown unknowns)[91] I'd recommend, again, a few key phrases to deflect and perhaps placate the boss for the time being.

In the end, I had Hunsinger's West Coast Offense; a small loose-leaf binder that was near my night stand every night, and something that I took with me everywhere I went. Like the President's nuclear "football" it never left my side. I felt, as confidently as I could be, that when the big event happened in my region, when damages were so severe that communication was cut off from the state and the President asked me what they (or I) were doing, I could say: "Mr. President, we are still trying to reach the state. But we have run the computer model for a similar type event and based on that, these are the damages we think they are facing. Based on that information, these are the actions I have taken to forward deploy response assets and commodities into the state. We will continue to contact the state and adjust as their needs become known." That statement was scripted as well. Was it a perfect system? No. But I think you might agree it was better than answering… "Uhhh, I don't know."

## Ethics (and Sometimes Explaining Them to the Bulls)

In my view, ethics and integrity go hand-in-hand; they are inextricably linked. They both involve basic standards of right and wrong. However, to distinguish between the two, I'd characterize one as being mostly extrinsic while the other as mostly intrinsic. That is, on the one hand, ethics are

---

90  https://en.m.wikipedia.org/wiki/There_are_known_knowns
91  Yeah, I know. Another Rumsfeld-ism. Scratch your head over that one.

more outwardly influenced on an individual. They are generally a set of codified rules of appropriate behavior; some (most) grounded in law, while others are based on what, both, society culturally accepts as organizational standards as well as personal standards of conduct. They are, nevertheless, more formally enforced. On the other hand, integrity (to be covered next) is more intrinsic in the sense they are personal values of how you (and others) measure your character. In short, the difference between the two is in <u>what you do</u> as opposed to <u>who you are</u>.

Ethics are also governed by the rules of morality (again, either your rules or what you've allowed society to dictate to you). But even deeper than what society has dictated to you, what's moral to you…your personal sense of morality… drives what's ethical to you. That, in turn, drives your personal sense of integrity (how well you uphold your personal standard of conduct, or society's). For example, in determining whether you are a vegan or a meat eater, the vegan will say, morally, that meat eating adds exponentially to the earth's carbon footprint. Conversely, the meat eater will say that being a vegan still hurts the earth by purchasing products that never break down and that take a lot of energy to make. So who's moral standard is right? In many cases, it's a personal choice and a personal standard.

So once again, ethics are guidelines. You need to set your own standard of morality. You have to determine in your mind and heart what's right and wrong.

Almost every organization has some formal code of ethics; a set of rules by which your behavior is governed. The federal government is no exception. Almost every Department and Agency has an office of lawyers and other personnel devoted to full-time ethics issues. Many of the rules are clear. You can't cheat on your travel voucher; you can't take your family with you on a government plane headed to a conference in Italy for the week (or anywhere for that matter); and, you can't spend tens of thousands of taxpayer dollars redecorating your office. Yet, some of the rules are not so intuitive; the rules on political activity by government employees almost certainly requires a lawyer to advise you.

Notwithstanding well-established rules of conduct, or even what should be intuitive, there are frequently too many people (particularly more senior political appointees), that come into government without understanding the rules. I say senior political appointees because those are the folks that have been (in some cases, a long time) entrenched in the corporate world where the rules of conduct are completely different.

1992, while working as Mort Halperin's military assistant, was a time when the Clinton Administration had a penchant for hiring younger people. I was already over 40 and was one of the old men of the office. Don't misunderstand me, the people they hired for senior leadership positions were smart, well-educated, and very talented. In most cases, I think they were the right people for the job. But they were also very young and some very inexperienced; and worse yet, some lacking in good old fashion common sense. Within our Directorate, Mort and the Administration had hired three 32-year olds, coming from the private sector, to fill three Deputy Assistant Secretary of Defense (DASD) positions. Again, I had great respect for all three, and, all three have gone on to impressive careers. Nevertheless, it takes years of government experience to understand all the nuances of the ethics rules. It's very easy to be doing what you think is the right thing, only to find out suddenly you're in trouble.

I was sitting at my desk one day when the secretary for one of my DASDs walked into my office and sat down next to my desk. She was visibly distraught and said she was on her way to the Equal Employment Opportunity (EEO) office to register a race and gender complaint against her boss. I did a double-take and said "Wait, what? You're both black women!" She said yes, but that she was tired of being abused on a daily basis by her boss; she had all she could take of being "treated like her personal slave." She was, in fact, a federal employee and had been one for some years. Her duties where governed by an approved (and appropriate) job description. Notwithstanding that, her boss was having her, on a daily basis, do some combination of the following; take clothes to the laundry, pickup personal mail, do grocery shopping, make personal doctor's appointments, have the car serviced, and other things as needed. Of course, her right was to go to EEO any time she wanted. But I asked her, and she agreed, to let me have a talk with her boss first. I knew instantly what the problem was.

I went down to the DASD's office, closed the door, and said "we've got to talk." She was mortified! She was completely blind-sided by the complaint, and had no idea of anything being wrong or that her employee was even upset. The problem? This 32 year old political appointee had come out of the private sector. She had been a well-established, highly-respected lawyer in New York City; she made big bucks and had a personal staff where, under their rules, they could be detailed to do the things she was having her federal employee do.[92] Her genuinely naïve response to me was "You mean I can't do this?" We quickly resolved the complaint without it going to EEO. The DASD happily complied, and the employee was satisfied. I spent the next several days getting her the training help she needed from the Pentagon ethics lawyers, as well as one-on-one mentoring sessions with her on how to operate within the Pentagon. There was just so much of that culture she didn't know and had never been exposed to.

The lesson here? Don't assume the Bulls know how to run the race on their own. Just because they've come into the organization as a senior leader doesn't mean they're versed in every aspect of the operation. Again, there are times you'll need to step up and lead from below. I've seen too many intermediate leaders who will stand back and apply the big boy theory. "Oh well, he's a big boy, he'll figure it out." No, they won't, and you could be setting them up for failure.

## Integrity (and Sometimes Convincing the Bulls to Show Some)

I've tried to weave throughout this book the concept of integrity as something I hold dear, perhaps dearest to my heart and character than anything else. I said earlier that your integrity and your sense of honor are paramount as a leader; if you're an honorable person with great integrity, and you're loyal, then little else should matter.

My advice to every leader (everyone for that matter) is keep your honor, and that of your agency, clean and pure. Don't get talked into doing dumb stuff, especially by the bulls. Make no mistake, at some point in your career you'll run into the senior leader that has no morals, scruples or integrity. They'll come up with an idea that you know, on its face, is a bad idea. It may not be illegal. It may not even be a direct violation of any rule or regulation. But in your heart, you know that it's wrong and you shouldn't do it.

The entire Pacific Northwest is dotted with tribal casinos. In no leadership situation where I had some control, did I ever allow the organization

92   Honestly, I don't know what the attraction is for some of these folks. She was seriously making huge money in New York. She took at least a 75% pay cut to take this job. I suppose it could be an impressive sense of altruism, or more likely, a desire to punch her political ticket for some other role later in life. As far as I know, she ultimately went back to the private sector and stayed.

to hold conferences at tribal casinos. I was accused at times of being too conservative on the issue, but I could see nothing good coming out of that situation. As public employees we're an open book, and through the Freedom of Information Act, anyone can request copies of our budget, calendars, agendas, or almost any other document. I just wanted to make sure we were squeaky clean at all times. Besides, it just looked bad. I also resisted attending conferences in Las Vegas and Reno (at least in large numbers…and I definitely didn't go). There were times that I failed to convince FEMA Headquarters that this was bad policy. Nevertheless, they continued to hold meetings and conferences at these venues.

Everywhere I've been I've successfully prevented us, as an organization, from doing anything that would get us in trouble (although, without doubt, I've had individual employees do some pretty dumb things). The standard I always used, and would encourage any leader to consider, is what has been called the 60 Minutes Test. If one of the 60 Minutes TV show anchors knocked on your door and started asking you questions with a camera in your face, could you adequately defend what you're about to do? If not, you better not do it.

I also never once took a dime of award or bonus money while at FEMA. In the military it was non-existent. However, in federal civil service an organization typically gets about 1% of its salaries and benefits budget for senior leadership to distribute as they see fit at the end of the year. That includes bonuses for the senior leader. While I mostly turned that process over to an employee committee, I kept final decision authority to arbitrate any disagreements. I always felt extremely uncomfortable carving any of that money out for myself. I avoided anything and everything that would call my integrity into question. I never wanted to take the chance that someone might complain about a self-serving decision I might make about award money. I know plenty of other leaders that don't share my concerns or philosophy on this issue. They have no reservation about giving themselves a nice bonus at the end of the year. I always told the committee to divide it up among the troops; it was their money, not mine.

These are just a few of my personal approaches to the integrity issue. As I said, I hold my integrity as dear to me as I do my name; it's who I am. Each leader will have to decide or define what the concept means to them, and where they intend to draw that bright line. I can sleep well at night because of my approach to issues surrounding integrity. Did I make the right call every time? Probably not. Again, no leader is perfect. But I didn't step on anyone. I didn't climb over anybody to get to the top. I did my job and focused on trying to do right and good things, always.

## Outside Actors (Who Are Not Bulls…Just Bullies)

Here's a Hunsinger maxim for you; it's easy to get crushed by outside bulls when they're vested with more power than they should have.

It was about 1992, and I don't even recall the circumstances within the Air Force that caused the Chief of Staff to bring all field commanders to Headquarters for a short commander's summit. However, during that meeting, he was quoted with a line that has stayed with me ever since; it has guided my outlook on lawyers, headquarters staff-assistance teams, HR climate assessment teams, the Inspector General, the General Accounting Office (GAO), the Joint Services Integrated Vulnerability Assessment (JSIVA) team, and countless others like them. He simply told commanders in the room, "Lawyers advise and Commanders command. Don't let the lawyers ever run your command."

I took the Chief's advice to heart and have practiced that maxim religiously ever since. As I've continued to process his statement over the years I've come to realize that all these outside influences have absolutely nothing to gain or lose in neither the outcomes of my organization, nor from the results of their inspection and recommendations they want me to implement. They have no stake in the outcome! Yet, they have opinions and, more often than not, theirs are supposed to (and often do) count more than mine? They're quick to declare themselves the authority, to criticize, and to make recommendations. Just who are these guys? What makes them so smart?

Let me just say this…when the "big one" occurs in your region… when the you-know-what hits the fan…and you're all standing in front of a Senate Accountability Review Board and they ask who is responsible and accountable…watch all these experts take one giant step backwards, leaving you standing alone.

Everyone comes from a different point of view, and there's an old saying that addresses that: "Opinions are like {rear ends}; everyone has one, and yours probably stinks." When these guys finally demonstrate their stake in the outcome, only then will I pay deference to their opinions.

Call me militant if you want, but let me provide just a short story to illustrate this issue. In 1996, as the CENTCOM Director of Force

Protection, I was in my office one afternoon when the American Vice Wing Commander at Prince Sultan Air Base (PSAB)[93] called me. He was frantic, but probably more pissed, that the Joint Staff had sent a special team to Saudi Arabia to assess the security posture of U.S. forces now bedded-down at PSAB. By this time, I had been in country for about 4-5 months and "assessments" were in my portfolio; to be done on behalf of the CENTCOM commander, not some headquarters element out of the Pentagon. Moreover, the move from Dhahran had just occurred within the previous few weeks and we were far from being finished with building our security posture.

What had the Vice Wing Commander tied in knots was a critical comment made by the assessment team about the Wing Commander's "questionable priorities." He had made the, apparently unforgiveable, decision to place troop morale and recreation high on his list of items to address. He placed them equally with his security concerns.

For the record, I was completely aware of what the Wing Commander was doing, and fully endorsed it. I had been to PSAB numerous times, had seen what their plan was, had observed their progress, and was totally content with the state of security as it was unfolding.

The commander's cardinal sin? Notwithstanding the fact that he had established a formidable perimeter, placed guards at key locations, established roving patrols and a backup force, implemented sound entry control procedures, built machinegun over-watches at his entry control points, set up an alert warning system, and began an antiterrorism education process with his troops...besides all that...he built a swimming pool.

The team was critical of the Commander's action and was about to file a report that, if they had, the consequences would have been cataclysmic; and I can't over state that. We were in the throes of regrouping after one of the worst attacks on American service members since the bombing of the Marine barracks in Lebanon. All eyes were on us. If an independent agency wrote such a scathing report, the Wing Commander would probably be relieved; all of this because of a team that had no real business being there, had no stake in the outcome, and just had an opinion like a thousand other guys.

I jumped in my car and drove to PSAB. When I got there, I met with the team; they knew who I was and courteously offered a brief on

---

93 Following the Khobar Towers bombing we moved all allied forces from Dhahran on the east coast of Saudi Arabia to PSAB. PSAB was a secure Saudi air base located in the central part of the country.

their findings. In short, I convinced them to drop the critical language. I reasoned that none of them were commanders, but if they were, they could easily sympathize with a guy that was undergoing a massive move, it was a remote location, there was significant emotional trauma remaining from the bombing, there were no other services available on base, and a commander's job in that environment is to balance operational issues with morale issues. So, what! He built a swimming pool to give the troops something to do.[94] In fact, what the swimming pool turned out to be was a couple of extra water bladders they put together to provide some depth to it. It was very rudimentary, but effective.

Truth be told all these years later…I threatened the team chief. This team was new; a new concept that the Joint Staff was rolling out to accomplish vulnerability assessments worldwide. We were their first assessment anywhere. The CENTCOM Theater was a target rich environment for their type of work; we were where the action was and where all teams wanted to come. I told the guy if he published that finding, I would ensure that they'd never set foot in that part of the world again. And yes, I can sleep well at night over that one too.

## *Customer Service*

*"It is amazing what you can accomplish if you do not care who gets the credit"*
—Harry Truman

I am, without question, an avid promoter of an open and friendly customer service approach. I'm the guy that always wants to do good things, and have always stressed to the staff that doing good things often comes at the expense of who gets credit for it.

I worked for an Air Force Colonel by the name of Sam Stocks, who I revered as probably the most visionary person I've ever encountered. He had an uncanny genius for being able to see multiple layers of an issue and project the results of multiple approaches to it…and to do that quickly; again, three steps ahead and two layers deep. He was a master at thinking outside the box.

---

94   PSAB in those early days was a tent city for all of the allies. The Saudis had control of all of the buildings on base, so tent city was relegated to one corner that the Americans could control.

Colonel Stocks was also savvy enough to recognize that security police officers, as non-flyers, were at a disadvantage when it came to promotion rates. The flyers always seemed to be in the forefront; support officers to the rear.[95] So as he stressed to us his customer service approach to the field, it was never a surprise that our first charge as a headquarters staff was to make the cops in the field look good, by all means necessary. His guidance to us as a staff assistance team was, whenever visiting a base, do everything we can to fix issues on the spot; coach, mentor and correct informally, but don't inspect. In fact, he wouldn't allow us to put anything derogatory in a written report or to brief anything negative to the Wing Staff.

That's not to suggest that Stocks covered for any one of the SP commanders in the field that might be under-performing. If at the end of the day, at the end of one of our visits, we discovered performance and/or procedures that were a serious breach, we were to write that on a separate sheet and give it to Stocks. He would then have a private conversation with the Wing Commander. This was always after we had already briefed the Wing Staff on how great the SP Squadron was doing. Internally, they always knew from us if they had problems. Nevertheless, by all outward appearances, they were doing great.

I guess in his own way, Stocks was always trying to protect the honor and reputation of the career field first; perhaps the individual commander second. When it was time for the commander to go, he didn't hesitate to give the Wing Commander his opinion. Conversely, if the SP Squadron commander was doing well, he fought like hell with Wing Commanders to get that person promoted.

The lesson to this short story is, while Stocks' customer service approach to the field was legendary, it also sometimes takes a bull to do battle with the other bulls to protect the heard.

Nevertheless, there are pitfalls of customer service. No matter how hard you try to do the right thing, sometimes the other bulls will take the opportunity to protect themselves by goring you in the back. Here's just one example.

When I took over the FEMA region in 2008, actually long before that, I told my four State Emergency Management partners that I would always

---

95  I have always found the term "support officer" offensive, if not derogatory. Ironically, throughout the wars in Iraq and Afghanistan, there hasn't been a single Air Force aerial combat casualty, while (sadly) "support" people have suffered virtually all the combat related deaths and injuries. So tell me, who are the real warriors in the Air Force?

do everything I could to protect their interests. I told them (I suppose naively) that I would always strive to arrive at "yes" on most issues; but, where I couldn't get to yes on an issue, I would stand in front of them at take the goring from their Governor.

In the spring of 2009, after a torrential rainfall (the same event involving the Howard Hanson dam issue), the Washington Governor and her staff gathered at Boeing Field in Seattle for a helicopter tour of some of the areas affected by flooding. I was invited to attend. We assembled in a conference room at Boeing Field for a quick briefing on damages, and an update on response activities. As the briefing unfolded, her staff (specifically, the Adjutant General briefing with his subordinate Emergency Manager looking on) told her that response was going well; people were being evacuated and shelters were established. However, when she asked a question about preliminary damage assessments, he said they were going slowly because they were only able to field one assessment team. When pressed as to why, he said (with his Emergency Manager saying nothing) "Well, that's all that FEMA could support."

At this point, with the two U.S. Senators on each side of her, the Governor launched into a scathing rebuke of FEMA and me. Her message to me and everyone in the room was that she was disappointed in me and the federal government for not doing their job. After all, our job was to support the state by being the cavalry that rides over the hill to save the day. Again, neither the Adjutant General nor his Emergency Manager said anything in my defense. I sat there, took the brunt, and said nothing…for a little while.

When the tirade was over, the Governor began to go around the table to see if anyone had any items for the larger group. She first asked the two Senators who, of course, had to add their two-bits on their FEMA expectations (and disappointment) and then she went to the Adjutant General and his Emergency Manager, who still said nothing. Then she got to me.

I took a moment to brief her on some of the good things that FEMA was doing for the response (we assist with sheltering, coordinate Coast Guard search and rescue, and other things). Then I said "Governor, I want to circle back to something you said a few minutes ago about FEMA's lack of support for field teams. FEMA's policy is that we follow our state partner's lead. We never get out in front unless the Governor asks. I have the capability to literally put a hundred teams in the field, and, I have an endless pot of money with which to do it. But again, I follow the state's lead, and your staff told me they could only handle <u>one team</u> for the next couple of days; that it would take that long for them to be up and running at full strength. However, if you want me in the field now at <u>my</u> full strength, just say the word. I'm here to help."

You could have heard a pin drop, yet, still nothing from her staff. They sat there looking like the cat that ate the canary. She was stunned for a moment and then just said "OK, thanks" and moved on around the table.[96]

I patched things up with the state guys later; we were all fine. However, a lesson learned for me was to be careful about offering to take spears for someone. More often than not, they'll accept the offer.

## *I'm King and You're Not*

Elected and appointed political folks are, in my view, a different breed. Yet, for me, military people and career civil servants were pretty predictable. For some of them, it was a sense of duty, honor, and integrity. For others, it might be that altruistic sense of service or even just the security of having a job with a virtually guaranteed pension. Regardless, I could almost always size up career people pretty quickly and figure out what motivates them.

Politicals, however, are different. Yet, they really shouldn't be. Like the rest of us, they all want to take care of their families, and they want to succeed in what they do. But as you might imagine, most of them are driven by political ambition. They worry more than the average employee about their image, and consequently, many of them invoke a decision-making process that is often self-promotion based. Also, consequently, I've seen many of them (not all) duck in the face of adversity. To be fair, I've seen career people do the same. Then, there are those that carry on as though they're oblivious to the real world around them. For instance, here's an example:

One of the primary missions at Andrews AFB is to provide Presidential security as he and his entourage transit in and out of the base. Of course, Andrews is also the home of Air Force One, and the entire fleet of other Presidential support aircraft. When I was assigned to Andrews as the Support Group (Base) Commander, we had countless occasions where the

---

96  Governor Christine Gregoire and I had a solid relationship after that. When Secretary Napolitano came to town, the Governor sang praise for me and the FEMA region.

President would helicopter over from the White House, land adjacent to Air Force One, get off the helicopter and make the short walk (less than a hundred yards) to the airplane. The whole process took just a couple of minutes from aircraft to aircraft. During inclement weather, someone (usually a protocol officer) would walk alongside holding an umbrella.

President Bill Clinton and me at the golf Course, Andrews AFB, in 1999.

It was a cold and rainy night.[97] The President had been somewhere in the country, doing whatever President's do. This time, it was late in the evening; about 9 PM as I recall, and it was raining hard. To set the stage, there is a logistics piece to any Presidential movement that is huge and often unseen by the public. Even on a closed base like Andrews, the security detail is more than tripled just prior to his landing, and it's held in place until he leaves. Base Operations is held open, and the Distinguished Visitor lounge is fully staffed just in case he suddenly needs to use the facilities. There is a convoy of backup vehicles standing by in the event that the weather conditions prohibit the helicopter from flying. Most important, at least to

---

97 I know, it sounds like the beginning of a cheap dime store novel.

me, there are additional guards (both Air Force and Secret Service) posted around the base, the flight line, Base Operations, and the aircraft. This is always a manpower intensive operation, and it was no less that evening.

On this particular evening, the troops were all posted approximately 30 minutes before Air Force One landed (as they usually are), and then suddenly the rain started. By the time the aircraft landed it was pouring rain. The aircraft taxied to its normal spot right in front of Base Operations and then…nothing. We waited and waited, and no one came out (no one dare go up and knock on the aircraft door to see what's going on). After a few minutes, word filtered down from the Presidential Pilot to those of us on the flight line; it was raining hard, and since the President was in the middle of a movie, he has decided to stay on the aircraft for a while.

As minutes turned into more than an hour, I (and others) were furious over the insensitivity. Sure, it's our job to provide security and other services. But it was pouring outside, the troops were drenched, and it was their sacrifice so that one clueless leader wouldn't unnecessarily suffer. After a while, the rain slowed considerably and (I guess) the movie ended. He finally descended from Air Force One, flew off in his Marine helicopter, and the troops were released from their posts.

Not to quibble about this incident. In the grand scheme of things, it was a minor nuisance, at worst. But it highlighted a leadership flaw in an individual. He was oblivious to the events going on around him (and perhaps I'm just giving him the benefit of the doubt for that); at least that's what I want to believe. Nevertheless, senior leaders need to make it a priority to be situationally aware at all times. As a senior leader, you may be shocked to learn what some intermediate leaders are demanding of their people in order to satisfy or impress you. When that's done, do you think the troops are pissed at their intermediate leader for it? No! They resent you! I think what really upset me the most about that incident was this; the President may or may not have been aware of the troops standing in the pouring rain, but his handlers certainly were. Someone on that airplane and close to the President could have stepped up and said "hey boss, are you aware…?"

Simply put, as a senior leader your radar needs to up at all times. That is, unless you truly don't care.

I wish I could say stories like the one above were a rarity, but they weren't. On another occasion at Andrews AFB, I was at home, in my base house, enjoying the Sunday morning just after Christmas. I suddenly got a call from the Wing Commander, Brigadier General Art Lichte, saying he was on his way and would pick me up in just a few minutes. My immediate thought? Sunday morning, Christmas week, he's in a hurry, this can't be good.

While serving as commander of the Support Group
(base commander) at Andrews AFB in 1999.

Earlier that week, General Ralph Eberhart, Vice Chief of Staff of the Air Force, had called Gen Lichte seeking a place where he could play tennis over the Christmas break. When Gen Lichte approached me, I said the indoor tennis facility would be closed for the Christmas holidays (Dec 20-Jan 4), but I could easily make arrangements for it to be opened the morning of Sunday the 28th so the General could play. After a couple of calls back and forth, General Eberhart said yes, that would work fine.

On our way to the fitness center, Gen Lichte gave me a quick brief. It seems that Eberhart had unloaded on Lichte about the condition (cleanliness) of the tennis center and demanded to see Lichte immediately. Me? "If he wants to see you, what am I doing here?" Lichte? With a chuckle…"Oh, you're not getting out of this one."

When we walked into to the fitness center, Eberhart was lobbing tennis balls back and forth with his guest, while the young troop, who was probably "voluntold" to come in on his Sunday morning to open the facility, was pushing a broom across the tennis court. Gen Lichte approached Eberhart to hear his complaints and immediately got an ear full. It was loud and disturbing. Eberhart expressed his embarrassment to have brought a guest into the facility with it "looking like it did." Honestly, it wasn't that bad, but did need sweeping. We had closed it on the 20th, no one had been in there since, and it would have been completely spotless when it reopened on the 5th. While Gen Lichte was getting his rear end handed to him by a four-star, I was over talking to the troop. He said the General had his ass too, and then ordered him to empty the trash, and to sweep and mop the floors.

After thanking the troop (as well as apologizing for taking the heat, and having to do work that was not his to do), I walked over to where Eberhart and Lichte were; by this time, they were totally engaged in a one way shouting match. Eberhart took one look at me and said "who the hell are you?" My good friend, Art Lichte…never one to miss an opportunity to give his troop credit…pushed me between him and Eberhart and said "oh, sir, this is Dennis Hunsinger; he's the Support Group Commander." Eberhart then turned to me and went right to work on my rear end. I've since thanked the boss countless times for that one.

It was ugly, it was uncalled for, it was disrespectful, it was embarrassing (maybe to Eberhart, but certainly so to Lichte and me), it was insensitive (as it related to the troop), and it was extremely ungrateful behavior on the part of a senior leader who had concessions made for him that others probably wouldn't have gotten. The facility was closed, and hadn't been properly cleaned for a reason; after all, it was a Sunday between Christmas and New Year's! By the next regular business day, January 5th, it would have been (in fact, it was) clean and ready to go.

Gen Lichte and I still laugh about that incident to this day; almost how comical Eberhart was as a jerk. He was a spoiled brat! Nevertheless, at least I came away from that incident scarred. It was/is disturbing to me that a leader can be that callous and insensitive to junior troops, or be so oblivious and show such lack of grace and appreciation to the people around him that are only trying to accommodate. That day I saw everything in a leader that I never wanted to be.

## Don't Poke the Bull

There are times when you have an employee that pokes the bull just to see what happens. Those are the ones that really scare me. Others, however, are well-intentioned employees, trying to do good things that end up unnecessarily causing a full-on stampede!

Mark Smart was a young Staff Sergeant law enforcement patrolman working for me at Peterson AFB in the 1983–1984 time frame[98]. He was a sharp, young, aggressive NCO; but, if anything at the time, a little inexperienced and a lot naïve.

SSgt Smart had gone to work one evening as a base patrolman working the midnight shift. Peterson AFB, at least in those days was a quiet little base without an active operational mission (we had recently transferred from the Strategic Air Command to the new Space Command). The base population was nothing in those days like it is today, so there was little real (in other words, exciting) law enforcement activity for a young troop of Mark's ambition.[99] On this particular night, after providing relief to the gates and doing all of his required building checks, Mark decided to find something to do to occupy his time.

Peterson's base housing was, at the time, some of the nicest I had seen and certainly the nicest we had lived in. But it did have one particular flaw. The curbing throughout the housing area was not discernable. That is to say, if you tried to parallel park and weren't careful in doing so, you could easily get out of your car and learn that you'd parked on part of the sidewalk (again, there was no obvious rise to the curb edging that you could "feel" when trying to park your car). Nobody liked that, but everybody accepted it as just one of those things. Some people would get back in their car and try to re-park; most others just shrugged and walked away.

Mark came into the law enforcement desk that night sometime after midnight and started going through the base traffic regulations. After a little while of reading he finally had his "Ah ha!" moment. He found an obscure line in the regulation that prohibited any vehicle from parking on any

---

98  Mark worked for me again, as a Senior Master Sergeant, in 2001 at Scott AFB when I was the Air Mobility Command Director of Security Forces.

99  Today, Peterson AFB is a sprawling headquarters base. NORAD/Space Command (now NORTHCOM) has since moved from downtown Colorado Springs to Peterson, and the base population (and associated buildings) has increased significantly.

portion of the sidewalk. With chapter and verse in hand, Mark launched out on patrol once more.

1001st Security Police Squadron, Peterson AFB, CO, 1984. While not the entire squadron in this picture, I'm in the front center and Steve Ross is to the right of me. Not sure if Mark Smart is in this picture.

I came into the office that morning at about 7:30, my normal time. As I passed my secretary, she said there were four messages from angry senior officers on base, one was still on the phone (on hold), and there was a pile of tickets on my desk, and the Chief was waiting to talk with me. The problem? You can probably guess…Mark had gone back out to base housing and had written 37 tickets for illegally parking on the sidewalk.

After getting a quick brief from the Chief, reviewing the tickets, and returning all the phone calls to offer my apologies and vowing to fix the problem, I asked that Mark come in and see me that afternoon after getting some sleep. When he came in, I first told Mark how proud I was for his initiative and his adroit, if not aggressive style of enforcing base regulations. However, this was a regulation that had NEVER been enforced. As right (technically) as he may have been, there was, really, a better softer way of tackling the problem. What we could have/should have done was, after getting approval from our senior leadership, run an article in the base newspaper citing the problem with an implementation date for compliance, and then enforce the regulation. As sorry as I was for him, I had to void all of the tickets. It was just the wrong way to approach the issue.

Mark was obviously disappointed, but seemed to understand. Besides, all was forgiven and it all worked out. He was a hero with the other troops and I smoothed it over with everyone else.

As for everyone else, particularly the bulls, I got to the Wing Commander quickly. He understood and laughed the whole thing off. The rest were pretty put off by the whole incident. It's amazing how many of them would use either their personal relationship with me, or just outright pull rank to weasel out of a ticket. I worked at lightning speed to end this conflict fast in order to save us all from the awkwardness.

Years later, we laughed often (and still do) over that incident. Mark went on to a very successful Air Force career in his own right, and then retired and became a lawyer (I haven't forgiven him for that).

Mark Smart and me at Peterson AFB in 1984. "Mark, raise your right hand and swear you'll never write another ticket."

I said at the start of this that sometimes you have employees that are well-intentioned. They certainly mean to do right and good things, but the actual execution sometimes also leaves you with unintended consequences. As long as their heart's in the right spot, do your best to applaud initiative and innovation (as opposed to stifling it), and then try to move forward from it. It does little good to overly chastise, when the employee was trying, was perhaps technically correct, but just a little messy in the delivery. Try your best to make a teachable moment out of it all.

# 6

# Organizational Guerilla Warfare

## *(The Things Employees Will Do)*[100]

*"A man who wants to lead the orchestra must turn his back on the crowd."*
—Max Lucado

Many years ago, I heard a colleague coin the term Institutional Guerilla Warfare. At the time, he jokingly claimed, the first rule of the office is to "never piss off the boss's secretary; that's the person that really has the most power over you. He or she can make your life pleasant or they can make it a living hell, all based on what they do (or don't do) on your behalf." As I started to think about it over the years, and as I became more senior in my leadership roles, I began to observe more and more the nuances of these types of social-professional hybrid relationships within an organizational setting. They were formal and informal and often transcended the various supervisory levels. I haven't seen much written on this issue, but I've come to realize it's real; it happens every day in almost every organization, on some level. Whether it's everything from water cooler gossip to cliques with nefarious intent, someone is always out to get (or get head of) someone else.

You don't necessarily need to be paranoid about who might be out there lurking in the bushes. In most cases, there are very few sinister employees that are out to conspire against you; but it does happen. You just need to be aware of your surroundings, some of the issues that can arise, some of the tactics they might employ, and some thoughts on how to deal with them.

## *What They Will Try to Do to You*

I read an article not long ago, written by Brian Fielkow, a former executive with Waste Management, which described the 20/60/20 rule. I've heard

---

100 Admittedly, this is the most negative chapter in the book. It describes (calls into question) some of the darkest, more insidious, sides of human nature; at least as it applies to what some employees and some of their bosses will do. I apologize at the outset. But this book is about leadership (in all its forms), and some times it just doesn't go as well as you'd like.

of the concept before, and it was a great reminder of some of the other axioms of leadership that I'd heard throughout my career; for instance the 80/20 rule, where a leader spends 80% of his or her time with 20% of their employees. However, his 20/60/20 rule suggests that when a new manager enters an organization (particularly one that needs change), there are always 20% of the people that recognize the need, the problem, and are on board immediately to assist the new boss. There are about 60% in the middle that are aware of the need for change, but are either reluctant or are skeptical that you are the right person to bring it about. Then, there are 20% of that are not on board, refuse to change, and in some cases will actively work against you. Some of this bottom 20% of employees will even recruit other employees to assist them in working against you. [101]

On the one hand, Fielkow's approach is to focus on the 60%; to convince them that he is the guy to lead them through troubled waters. On the other hand, he is quick to cast aside the bottom 20%. In fact, he says of them "My commitment is to ensure you a fast and graceful exit." My approach (perhaps to a fault) is to be much less cynical or quick to give up on that bottom 20%; but nor will I ever take my eye off of them.

Any new leader facing a hostile work force (of any percentage) needs to immediately identify both the extent and the root of the problem. I've found that, most often, the troubles you have with employees are culturally based. That is to say, respect for authority, work ethic, and loyalty are based on the environment (and in some respects, again, based on their formative years). How bad was the leadership before you? Did employees always get what they wanted? Is there a history of disciplinary problems (to include race, gender, ethnic, or other issues)? Is this organization military, civil service, or private sector; is it unionized? Notwithstanding all of this, as a newly arrived leader you'll have to deal with whatever baggage you're handed. Similarly, very few of us get to choose our team. Most of us walk into a new organization and are introduced to people that have been there for years. You might even face some that resent your presence; upset that you got the job and one of them didn't. I've faced that situation before. Whatever the circumstances, you'll need to muster all of your experience and skill as a leader and begin to start winning their hearts and minds; you'll need to start building a team that is committed to the organization, the mission, each other, and to you. Despite your best efforts, and depending on the size of your span of control, if you're not pissing someone off

101  https://www.entrepreneur.com/article/316461

then you're probably not doing your job. You can't possibly make everyone happy all of the time.

Here is a list of just some of the antics you'll face over a career of more than 40 years.

### They will call you a racist.

I don't intend to marginalize an issue that is both serious and has been with us since well before the founding of this nation. But in today's world, the term is so casually thrown around that it loses its potency; leading to the saying that if everyone is a racist, then no one is a racist. Nevertheless, for some it can be a career-ending label. In many cases it's justified and, perhaps, that person should lose their job. But in other cases, it ends in a wicked perversion of justice…it should never have happened.

In 1999, as the base commander of Andrews AFB, I was quietly sitting in my office one day when I heard my secretary, Marlene, laughing out loud. When I say laughing out loud, I mean it was a belly laugh that could be heard from one end of the building to the other. I got up from my desk and walked out to the outer office to see what was going on. There was an African American civilian employee standing at her desk. Marlene looked at me, hardly able to keep a straight faced, and said "this gentleman is from Civilian Personnel, Race Relations. He's doing an investigation and he thinks you're a racist!" She then started laughing again. By this time, I was mortified. First, that I was under investigation, and second, that Marlene was taking it so casually (by this time I didn't think that was helping at all!). That's when she said, "Mister, I'm black. His Deputy, both a woman and black, sits in that office. His Administrative Assistant, who sits over there is also black. The Chief Master Sergeant that sits in that office over there is black. These are all people he hired, and if you think he's a racist just look around this office."

I ushered the guy into my office as quickly as I could, sat him down, and asked him what the heck this was all about. He began to tell a story about a black family that I had kicked out of base housing. They had a son that had gotten into a fight at the bus stop, he was a model student, had never gotten into trouble before, and I summarily, if not callously, ordered the family out of base housing…only because they were black; and, I had done it without even the courtesy of discussing it with them. The family had now filed a formal complaint with the Air Force, and was considering a civil rights suit against me and the Air Force.

Now it was my turn to talk. I gave it a minute or two for it to all sink in, I sat back in my chair, and asked just three questions. "I suppose they didn't tell you that their son had beat up this neighbor kid four times at the bus stop, did they?" He replied no, they hadn't. "Then I suppose they also didn't tell you that after three times, we served them a letter signed by me that warned them they could lose their housing privileges if it continued, did they?" Again, he replied no, they hadn't. "Well, then I suppose they also didn't tell you that on the fourth occasion these parents held the neighbor kid down while their son beat the hell out of him and sent him to the hospital. Did they tell you that?"

The guy didn't even take time to reflect on it. He opened his briefcase, shoved his notes inside, got up and told me he was sorry for wasting my time. I escorted him out of the office and right past Marlene. She was still laughing because she had her ear to the door and heard everything I said. She also knew the circumstances of the case and knew, going in, just exactly how this was going to play out.

While this story didn't specifically involve an employee issue the lesson is, nevertheless, if you're true to policy, the law, morality, and you're consistent in your decisions, you should have no problems. However, there are societal issues where, in practice, some people will indict a person's character and reputation before they even make an attempt to discover the facts. Unfortunately, there's little you can do to defend against that; except to be honest and forthright with yourself and others. Again, just do right and good things; and, it helps to document your actions.

**They will write anonymous letters about you.**

By the time you've been around for 40 plus years, you've just about seen it all. Sooner or later, you'll encounter an employee or two that will stoop to "whatever means necessary" to disrupt your rhythm as a leader and to impugn your character. To me, it's the coward's way; it's the lowest of the low. I've said several times here that every boss, from the highest rung of politically elected office to the corporate mid-level supervisor, has the right to implement their policy and/or procedure. That's what they were elected for, or that's why they were hired. If you, as a subordinate, are unable to support their position, then either have the courage to confront them directly or get the hell out! It's NEVER acceptable to fabricate false and salacious stories that puts someone in a position to awkwardly (and embarrassingly) have to defend themselves. It takes a sick mind to do that;

similar to an arsonist who sets a fire and then stands across the street to watch the fire department try to put it out. There's an infamous story about the time Lyndon Johnson was running for office in Texas. As the race was getting close, he turned to his campaign manager and told him to plant a story in the press about his rival's penchant for having sex with barnyard animals. "Christ, we can't get away with calling him a pig-f****r," the campaign manager protested. "Nobody's going to believe a thing like that." "I know," Johnson replied. "But let's make the sonofabitch deny it."[102]

There's an old saying in the special operations community; "No shot too cheap, no blow too low." What follows is my own personal account with what an employee will do, as well as what you may or may not expect in the way of support from your senior leadership. There are times you'll find yourself hanging out there on your own.

In the spring of 2011, three unsigned, anonymous letters attacking me personally and professionally were passed down from FEMA Headquarters to the Region Administrator "for action."[103] All three letters were either addressed to the FEMA Administrator, the Inspector General, the media, or all three. I can't begin to tell you the hurt, anguish, and embarrassment I felt then and still feel today. It was devastating; and like LBJ's Texas rival, I was forced to deny the accusations while others watched me squirm. In short, the author(s)[104] accused me of exploiting my position by, among several things, hiring my personal friends into vacant government positions. The letters also characterized my leadership style as intimidating. One letter claimed I "ran amok"; "He rules like a third-world nation despot by whim and decree, ignoring all standards of ethical conduct and daring his subordinates to do anything about it." The letters go on with outlandish charges that almost anyone who knows me, or has ever worked with or for me, would know to be completely out of character; and they were, in fact, simply untrue (countless others would, and did, vouch for that).

Because of the nature of my position, as Deputy Regional Administrator in Region 10, the number of employees I supervised, and the nature of the accusations made, FEMA's Office of Chief Counsel was notified to make them aware of the unfounded accusations. The matter was referred to the

---

102 https://masscommons.wordpress.com/2012/03/15/
fear-loathing-on-the-campaign-trail-make-them-deny-it/amp/
103 By this time, I was no longer the Acting RA, but had resumed my role as the Deputy.
104 Both the IG and General Counsel believed it was the work of one person since there were some similarities across all three letters.

Office of Inspector General. While they declined to investigate the matter, I did sit with the General Counsel and categorically, line by line, addressed each allegation with written documentation. For instance, my rebuttal to the charge of hiring friends into jobs was supported by several emails that first, confirmed they were acquaintances and not friends; and second, I was nowhere near the hiring decision. In fact, in one instance, when the hiring decision had been made by someone else, I played devil's advocate providing reasons why it might not be the best fit. Again, categorically, each allegation was demonstrated, proven, to be false. Notwithstanding, there was nevertheless a stain now on my unblemished reputation.

What I can't guarantee is how people (all people) will always perceive you. Clearly, someone felt wronged by me and felt the need to lash out. I said earlier that as an effective, successful leader you can't please everyone all the time. If you're trying to please everyone you won't be an effective leader, and you'll eventually fail. Somewhere along the line I'd made a decision that adversely affected this or these employees, and for the adverse effect I'm sorry. Had I known that it would upset them so, would I have taken the action? Almost certainly yes! If it was the right thing to do (and I'm sure it probably was or I wouldn't have done it), then yes, I would make the same call as the right call each and every time. Nevertheless, I am sorry it had an adverse effect on them, and they felt no other recourse but to take the action they took. But the fact is, you sometimes have to say <u>no</u> to someone!

Following the "unofficial" resolution of the incident (unofficial because it was dropped without action by the IG and General Counsel) I requested that my Regional Administrator, and the Chief Counsel of FEMA, launch an official investigation to exonerate me of any improper, illegal or unprofessional conduct. Some might argue that was an act of retribution on my part. But I argued that, to do nothing, to just completely drop it without explanation, would look even worse for the Agency. To the rank and file the appearance would be that leadership was rallying around one of their own and accepting my side of things without a thorough inquiry. To be honest here? Yes! I was egregiously slandered and wanted to set the record straight.

No investigation ever occurred; nor did I even get an official response to my official request. My record with FEMA was unblemished until the arrival of these letters. After that, I felt that my position had been compromised, my credibility with my subordinates had been undermined, and I felt I'd lost the faith and confidence of many. Perhaps an over-reaction on my part. But I had an otherwise exemplary career with FEMA had been damaged by the cowardly actions of a person (or persons) who lacked the character, integrity and maturity to sit down with me and discuss our differences, or file a legitimate grievance with me or my superiors. To make matters worse, the entire incident had gone unaddressed by senior FEMA leadership. It was the darkest moment of my more than 40 years in government. I retired (resigned) from FEMA effective July of 2011. I'd had enough of the lack of honor, integrity, and loyalty by some in the federal civil service.

The lesson here…I tell this story for two reasons. First, I'm not nor have I ever claimed to be the perfect leader. I've made plenty of mistakes over the course of my 42-year career. But my heart and my intentions have always been pure. I was always out to do right and good things…always. Could I have prevented some of this? Absolutely. Again, as I always told my kids, there was some action along the line that I could have taken that could've/would've/might've led to a different outcome. Hindsight is always 20/20, but nevertheless, there are things I wish I would have handled differently.

Second, this story highlights the fact that if your integrity remains intact at all times; if you are honest, forthright, consistent, fair, and true to what's right and good, you should prevail. People make mistakes, but mistakes in a well-intentioned decision-making process are rarely fatal (at least in my observations). But then again, a lapse in your integrity is more often a career-ender. If you're out to seek either personal gain, or some mean-spirited act of vengeance, then your integrity is quickly compromised; you've demonstrated to yourself and others that you are no longer true to the more noble ideal of always doing what is right and good.

## Some will attempt to sue you.

I mentioned earlier that during my FEMA years I had a young GS-15 Division Director working for me whose sense of loyalty was to himself and to his immediate family, and to no one else. I said it earlier and I'll say it again, he was the biggest disappointment of my entire leadership career. My inability to successfully mentor this young man…to turn him from the dark side…is something I take as a personal failure; it haunts me still today. This man was so loyal to only himself, that he, in fact, successfully sued a previous agency and his boss because a hiring decision affecting his wife that didn't go his way. He also sued FEMA and me under similar circumstances.

There is something about senior leaders suing senior leaders that is just plain wrong. Nevertheless, it happens. Sometime in the 2009-2010 timeframe we were advertising and hiring for a new branch chief (GS-14 position) within our Preparedness Division. It was a position overseeing several programs, some of which required at least some level of technical knowledge and expertise. As was customary, I was not involved in the hiring process. I, generally, set the guidance and direction for how we would conduct a panel and selection process, and then at the end of all of that I would ask a number of questions to ensure that my policy had been followed correctly; all in an effort to ensure a fair and consistent process. In the end, as Acting Regional Administrator, I signed all selection documents as the formal "selecting official" for the region.

I have to say, in all of my years in government, this hiring action was the smoothest, cleanest, and "by the book" I had ever seen. My Preparedness Division Director was in charge of organizing (selecting) the hiring panel; he was/is probably the most meticulous person I've ever known. He set up the panel, provided the scoring system with copious instructions, and developed standard questions that each panel member would ask and in which order (to ensure consistency). Nevertheless, there were two women and one man vying for the job; they ultimately selected the man. That's when all hell broke loose.

Of the two women candidates being considered, one of them was the wife of my young GS-15 Division Director. She was already an employee within our region, and had impeccable qualifications and enjoyed tremendous respect across the board from her FEMA peers, the leadership, as well as her customers in the field; as did both of the other candidates. Nevertheless, her husband decided she was clearly the worthier candidate for the job, and that she had been egregiously wronged during this process…so he filed a complaint with the Inspector General that led to a lawsuit.

To the point, we demonstrated that we had done everything correctly. Besides my Preparedness Division Director chairing the hiring process (a white male), the other two members comprising the panel where our regional Senior Policy Advisor (a white female GS-14) and a FEMA headquarters senior staff director (a black female member of the Senior Executive Service). When the tabulations were finished, both females picked the man who eventually got the job as their first choice, and the other woman candidate as their second choice. The panel chair, picked the other woman as his first choice and the man as his second choice. All three picked my young GS-15's spouse as their third choice!

The IG and legal proceedings were both ugly and a lesson for me; a lesson in trust (who you think you can trust) and a lesson in integrity. Throughout the ordeal I kept my integrity intact. My young leader did not. In addition to fabricating a story, an accusation to fit his narrative, his ever-eroding reputation as well as any remaining respect I had for him was completely lost. At that point, we were done. I personally had to sit through a deposition with a FEMA lawyer at my side, a court recorder, and this young man grilling me with questions in a failed effort to perjure myself. It was one of the more disappointing moments of my career.

I didn't then, nor do I want to now, walk away from the event with an overly cynical outlook on leadership. I don't want to keep looking over my shoulder for the knife that might be pointed at my back; nor should you! But what I did learn, and what you should know, is that if you're in the leadership business long enough, you'll eventually see EVERYTHING there is to see. That includes those employees (and yes, other leaders) that possess a level of narcissism and self-indulgence (an evilness) that will motivate them to do almost anything to continue their climb to the top. Just beware.

**Your Boss Will Undermine You**

Face it, there are few senior leaders (hardly anyone for that matter) that like confrontation. It's human nature to do what you can to avoid looking someone in the eye when it's time to deliver bad news (performance, discipline, you name it). It takes a strong leader to gather the courage to hold people accountable for their actions when it's needed. Far too often, and countless times in my career, I've seen senior leaders pass the "dirty work" off to someone else (usually me).

I'm not a psychologist, but I really do think it's on the lower end of the spectrum for the fight or flight reflex to danger. In some cases, senior leaders will avoid it to the extent they just naturally gravitate to the path of least resistance. Take the case, for instance, of the employee A who is a type A personality (with high energy and high maintenance; who will raise hell and pitch a fit whenever he or she doesn't get their way), and you have employee B who may also be a strong personality as well, but is calmer, more pragmatic, rational, may not roll over but at the end of the day would probably acquiesce for the good of the organization. I've seen time and again where leaders are so averse to confrontation that (without even recognizing they're doing it) they'll default the tough decision in favor of employee A at the expense of employee B as <u>the path of least resistance</u>. Is that fair? Absolutely not. But it happens, and the responsible leader has to make a concerted effort to recognize the tendency ahead of time. Employee A may well pitch a fit. But if it's the right call, then make it. Anything less is unfair to employee B and the rest of your organization.

My counsel to all senior leaders is…grow a pair! Step up and make the tough decisions without passing it off to one of your subordinates; that's not leadership! Resist any and all temptations to be only the "good cop" and never the "bad cop." While most leaders would prefer to avoid confrontation, almost every leader, at every level, embraces the hope that they'll be wildly popular with their troops. But your integrity is on the line here. Your employees want to see leadership out of you. That includes a demonstration from time to time of your ability to make hard, tough calls. They want to see a caring, compassionate leader, but also someone who will impose fair and equitable standards of performance, conduct, and discipline. Be that leader! Be the leader you'd want to work for.

Here are just a few other examples of where senior leaders can inadvertently (or will overtly) undermine their own leadership team:

1. Most likely of these is the boss is inexperienced. I've given tips earlier on how to lead from below (to lead or mentor up). Frequently, in government (or perhaps even in business), people are given the top job because someone has recognized their potential (that's the less cynical view). Others are given the job out of some sense of loyalty, reciprocity, or political favor (that's the more cynical view). Regardless, it happens, and your duty is to mentor and develop your (hopefully receptive) boss and to keep the organization moving smoothly forward.

2. The boss might be deliberately practicing Organizational Guerilla Warfare. This could be an interesting situation; you may never know what is motivating him or her to do such a thing. You might see deliberate acts of intimidation and bullying. He or she could be playing favorites, which sometimes leads to the interesting phenomenon of stoking petty jealousies to gain favor with the boss. These situations breed

insidious conduct by some members of the rank and file; it can and will promote subordinate back stabbing to get the boss's attention.

3. The less cynical view from just above is the Boss could be deliberately playing one side against the other in an effort to keep people focused on something other than adversity (I've done that). If your team is facing or recently faced severe hardship, you might try the tactic of diverting their attention toward something more productive (I'll discuss an example of this later). The bottom line here is to keep them focused on things they can control and away from things they have no influence over. In some cases, your senior leadership team may be oblivious to what you're doing, which might be a good thing. Again, if your senior leader does some of this it may not be for nefarious reasons.

4. The boss could be suffering from some pathological disorder (like being a first-class jerk with no people skills). I've seen this. Usually it's someone that is only interested in furthering their career and sees the current job as nothing more than a stepping stone. These are the saddest, most destructive and difficult situations. If it happens, again, your job is to hopefully mentor and develop your boss and to keep the organization moving smoothly forward. At no time should you ever compromise your integrity. Remember, as long as what he or she wants to do is moral, ethical, and legal, the boss is the boss. There is never an acceptable basis for leading anything that amounts to an insurrection, coup, or mutiny unless an objective moral/ethical/legal standard (not yours) is violated.

5. The boss might be jealous of your relationship with the troops. This happens a lot. If you've been around for some time, or especially if you've been filling in as the acting senior leader, there is a tendency for a newly appointed senior leader to be concerned about existing relationships. I mentioned earlier that, in military tradition, you can only have one commander at a time. If the deputy remains in position after a

senior leader has been hired, there can (and often is) confusion among everyone where their loyalties should lie. It's your job, not the new guy's, to resolve any and all confusion. If for no other reason, it's wrong (a breach of your integrity) to allow such jealousies to develop. Moreover, don't give your new boss a reason to marginalize your role within the organization.

6.  The boss might be oblivious to the fact he's done or is doing it; probably a less likely scenario. More likely it's a case of an inexperienced leader; someone who lacks the background to recognize the nuances of leadership. If you feel that you're being marginalized, or that your role is being diminished, it may be time to have a closed-door discussion. Don't be afraid to say what's on your mind. Nevertheless, you're likely to continue a mentoring role for that inexperienced senior leader. Just deal with it without letting your own ego get in the way.

*"No passion in the world is equal to the passion to alter someone else's draft."*
—H. G. Wells

## A Meddling Headquarters Will Undermine You

Oh man! I've got so much to say about this one…but I won't. I will tell you that over my career I've been micro-managed countless times by (I suppose) a well-intentioned headquarters; staffed with pencil-necked geeks that thought they knew all the answers. That said, I was one of those geeks on a few occasions. But having the opportunity to move from the field to headquarters and back again several times gave me a rare insight (and appreciation) for what field leaders go through almost daily. Because of that, and when I ascended into headquarters leadership positions, I took an approach that put service back into "customer service." In doing so, I would ask the staff this basic question…"Do we exist to support them, or do they exist to support us?" You might (or might not) be surprised at some of the responses I got. Nevertheless, I quickly turned our focus on the very appropriate headquarters role of support. My belief has always been that headquarters (or the home office…or the mother ship, as we used to call FEMA headquarters) exists to provide policy direction, standards, and resources (funding, supplies and equipment). I've often said, give me all of those things, hold me accountable though monthly metrics, and then get the hell out of my way!

I mentioned in Chapter 5, Running with the Bulls, that outside actors can often be a source of frustration. I also mentioned that years ago, the Air Force Chief of Staff assembled all of his commanders and reinforced his firmly held belief that "commanders command and lawyers advise; don't let the lawyers run your command." I've had a number of opportunities to deal with headquarters lawyers on a variety of issues. I've always taken pleasure in telling the lawyers that, on the one hand, if it means I might get criticized by an auditor (or anyone else) then I'll seek your advice; but I've got the last vote. On the other hand, if I stand a chance of going to jail over this decision, then I'll almost always defer to your advice. That outlook on leadership has served me well over the years. I've seen countless occasions where leaders have been so swayed by some lawyer's legal opinion that it's completely paralyzed the organization's ability to do good and right things. Don't misunderstand me on this. Lawyers have opinions, and often they are good, sound, and scholarly opinions. But they should always be based on legal fact, leaving judgement to the senior leader whose obligation, responsibility, and accountability it is. That's why we hire senior leaders! Otherwise we might as well just hire lawyers to run our organizations.

Lawyers will almost always take the conservative (cautious) approach. But if we were always conservative and cautious, we'd never get any of the bold and courageous things done. Your decisions should be based on a spectrum of input, lawyers included. However, when a decision is needed, don't be bullied or intimidated into failing to act decisively by those who have opinions, but are not accountable.

As with a lawyer's advice, I'm equally guarded when it comes to someone from outside my organization suggesting that what we need is a "climate survey." I understand completely that our human relations folks have an extremely important role to play. When an employee is, or feels they've been, aggrieved, it's important we have an outside party that can serve to champion their interests. That said, I refuse to be (once again) bullied or intimidated by an outside agency that wants to "get to the root of the problem" by doing a morale survey of the organization. Make no mistake, I have never had anything to hide. However, I've done my share of empirical survey research; because of that, I'm skeptical (if not suspicious) of how outsiders frame their questions and then interpret the results. Moreover, if you're a new leader (new to the organization), until you can define who it is you are as an organization, and it resonates with your employees, you won't get off the bottom. This takes time, and I don't need outside help to accomplish it. That also said, it does help if the larger organization (your government agency for instance) has achieved some fundamental progress in establishing an identity. Two very good examples are what the U.S. Marine Corps and FEMA have done. Years ago, the Marines laid their foundation by announcing that everyone in the Corps is a rifleman first. FEMA did the same shortly after Hurricane Katrina by announcing that everyone in the agency is an emergency responder first. That kind of identity is crucial in inspiring employees.

Then there's the larger problem of field versus headquarters culture and perspective. Within a military context, the problem of headquarters being constantly in your business is somewhat mitigated by an ongoing process of rotation. That is, and much like what I experienced, those in headquarter will soon find themselves in the field eventually.[105] Because of this, there's a natural affinity for those you're supporting; you're naturally less likely to "meddle" because the roles will soon be reversed. This is not the case within Federal Civil Service or probably any business enterprise that is governed by a corporate office. But at least in government, many (I would say most) employees within Washington DC have never been in the field. Many of the people sitting inside the beltway are either local hires (are from northern Virginia or southern Maryland) or are recruited from other regions of the country without any real hands-on experience within that region.[106]

In my case, when I did return to the field, I was so happy to be on the opposite coast (in my FEMA years), and overseas in my military years in places like Saudi Arabia, Turkey, and Oman. It was relatively relaxing to be as far as you could possibly be from a 3000-mile-long headquarters screwdriver that would otherwise constantly be trying to tweak my every move. I've often felt that (of headquarters people) if they want in on the operation, then by all means get in. But don't sit back and criticize from the comfort of the supply room!

One of my favorite stories, one that I've used several times to illustrate my frustration with headquarters meddling, comes from a letter the Duke of Wellington wrote to the British Foreign Office in August of 1812:

---

105 In a military career, not all officers and NCOs will serve a tour in a headquarters position, but all headquarters people will have come from the field and most will eventually return to the field.

106 Particularly noticeable among political appointees. With few exceptions, they come from academia or industry with little practical government experience.

"Gentlemen:

Whilst marching to Portugal to a position which commands the approach to Madrid and the French forces, my officers have been diligently complying with your request which has been sent to H.M. ship from London to Lisbon and then by dispatch rider to our headquarters.

We have enumerated our saddles, bridles, tents and tent poles, and all manner of sundry items for which His Majesty's Government holds me accountable. I have dispatched reports on the character, wit, and spleen of every officer. Each item and every farthing has been accounted for, with two regrettable exceptions for which I beg your indulgence.

Unfortunately, the sum of one shilling and nine pence remains unaccounted for in one infantry battalion's petty cash, and there has been a hideous confusion as to the number of jars of raspberry jam issued to one cavalry regiment during a sandstorm in western Spain. This reprehensive carelessness may be related to the pressure of circumstances since we are at war with France, a fact which may have come as a bit of a surprise to you gentlemen in Whitehall.

This brings me to my present purpose, which is to request elucidation of my instructions from His Majesty's Government so that I may better understand why I am dragging an army over these barren plains. I construe that perforce it must be one of two alternative duties, as given below. I shall pursue one with the best of my ability, but I cannot do both.

1. To train an army of uniformed British clerks in Spain for the benefit of the accountants and copy-boys in London, or, perchance,

2. To see to it that the forces of Napoleon are driven out of Spain.

Your most obedient servant,
Wellington"[107]

There's no way I could have put that any better!

---

107 https://ssi.armywarcollege.edu/pubs/parameters/articles/04spring/archives.pdf

## They Have Their Own Personal Agenda (certainly not yours)

I loved the last job I was in; just before retirement. I was the Regional Director for Headquarters DHS's Office of Infrastructure Protection. For the most part, these were my kind of people. They were older, a little more conservative, and came from either a military background or from law enforcement. Unfortunately, a significant percentage of the force (more than a hundred Protective Security Advisors around the country ) was also white and male.[108] There were many of us (I'd say almost all of us) were aware of this and worked the entire time I was there to reverse the trend. It happened in 2003 when the Department of Homeland Security was established and Secretary Tom Ridge decided he wanted a cadre of professional security experts to begin mapping and assessing all of the critical infrastructure around the nation. The problem was…there was hardly anyone in the civilian sector that had the experience in accomplishing vulnerability assessments. Most of that experience resided in the military. Consequently, recruitment and hiring rules were waived in order to quickly build a DHS capability, and most of those folks were recently retired military security/law enforcement or special operations professionals.

While attending our 2015 annual Protective Security Advisor (PSA) conference, the Assistant Secretary for Infrastructure Protection announced to the audience that she wanted the hiring position description (PD) for PSAs rewritten. Her vision was to change the PD to reflect a major shift in roles and functions, and to devise a new recruitment program that would significantly increase agency diversity. Then, she announced to the audience that she was assigning this project to Regional Director Hunsinger; a surprise to me, and at that point she had my undivided attention. What happened next was the entire audience of 102 PSAs from across the nation making a collective turn in my direction and giving me a cold stare, as if I had colluded with the Assistant Secretary on an attempt to undermine the safety and security of their world; and it would soon be confirmed, they all believed this new initiative to be a direct threat to their standing with federal, state and local partners, as well as how they

---

108   Each state had at least one PSA, and larger states had more than two. The PSA was the security expert. He or she, since 2003, had mapped and assessed most of the critical infrastructure in his or her respective area. They were, and still are, the <u>only</u> people in this nation that can give a picture of interdependencies and cascading effects if one were to fail. It is critical information for FEMA, state, and locals to know, following a major disaster, what is down, how that affects everything else, and what order things should come back up.

felt about themselves. Yikes! I was suddenly the bad guy, and had nothing to do with it.

Not one to shy away from a challenge, and immediately recognizing an opportunity to influence the outcome that would bridge both sides of this emotional and controversial issue, I went straight to work. In follow-on private conversations, the Assistant Secretary confided that she felt the PSA of-the-day was very different than when the program was first conceived. In fact, the federal career series for the job had been established early on as an 1801-series (law enforcement) function. Her belief was that "law enforcement" was too narrowly focused for a function that evolved into more of a referral agency (referring customers to other elements of DHS that could provide other law enforcement and security services that we didn't provide directly); in a sense, it was now more focused (at least in her eyes) on marketing and salesmanship than ever before, and she wanted an employee that better fit that profile and, less so, someone who was a security technician. [109] The PSAs, on the other hand, felt that without the security technician qualification they would lose credibility with many of their established customers. They believed that law enforcement experience was critical for the mission, and added credibility that opened doors for them.

I know that to the novice, this all sounds a little too much like "inside baseball." The crux of the story is that there was an element at work on the senior staff that was conniving, manipulative, and to the point of being almost nefarious. They were driving the Assistant Secretary to make precipitous decisions about the future of our organization. Yes, some of them needed to be made; most appropriately were changes that would make us a more diverse workforce. But not to the point that we would neutralize some of our critical skill sets, and thereby lose the confidence of our customer base. That was the road we were headed down! Several of the people surrounding (and had the ear of) the Assistant Secretary were there with a political, and to a large extent, social, agenda. In short, they were there to take down the organization as we knew it. [110]

My job was to get through the mess without both side killing each other; to bring both parties together to find common ground. Regardless of my personal feelings on the issue, my job was also to support the legitimate

---

109   Given the footnote on the previous page, I'll leave it up to you to judge.

110   Frankly, for them, it was too white and too male. In their view, the only way to fix that was a complete blow-up of the organization.

demands of my boss while trying to preserve the integrity of at least parts of the original program that were still relevant, as well as the interests of the legacy employees still involved with it. As well, my job seemed to be clearly defined for me; build coalitions and lead the organization through a significant (emotional) change.

In the end, we got it done. I worked formal and informal leaders collectively and individually to build trust in the process. Along the way, I was able to convince the rank and file that change was necessary and the right thing to do; they finally realized that while the original recruiting effort was essential to initially establish the organization, it had the unintended consequence of hiring a work force that was far too under represented by minority employees. We began the process of building an apprenticeship program, bringing junior-grade employees into the program so that we could grow diverse senior leadership candidates from within. We changed the job series, broadened roles and functions, and developed a position description that would lead to a more generalized employee.

Not all parties were satisfied. Nevertheless, their concerns were addressed. While not completely happy, together as a group, we came to a relative consensus on most issues in a way that mitigated any potential hostility. As an organization we were better for it, and in 2016 the agency became the most diverse in its history with the hiring of 21 new positions.

While all of that sounds like we had a kumbaya moment, there were plenty of hard feelings after it was all over. I returned home to the Northwest and began my retirement out-processing. But as my parting bit of advice to senior leadership I sent a detailed email to my immediate boss laying out my observations and those of others that were shared with me while at the conference.

I told my supervisor that he needed to be aware, and observant, of people in influential positions (particularly low-level political sycophants) that were unnecessarily spinning up the boss; making their priorities the boss's. While their primary role should have been to provide the boss with well-staffed and unbiased advice, they were out there trying to work the system (and the boss) for their own personal agenda and benefit; all while they should have been doing good and right things. They have a responsibility to take care of the boss's interests, NOT theirs! Often times (as was in this case) the boss is oblivious to what's going on around him or her.

All of this relates back to my role as an Exec Officer, or to the first paragraph of this chapter about the boss's secretary. If you're in one of those positions, you have tremendous power to sway or influence the boss's actions. <u>Use that power carefully.</u> If not, you could be setting your boss up for failure.

## Some Will Constantly Test Your Resolve

I can't begin to tell you how many times in my career I've made a decision on a policy, procedure, or some operational issue, only to be challenged continually over it. My leadership style, moreover, my decision-making process, is one where I seek a variety of diverse opinions. I don't act spontaneously very often unless it's a crisis situation where immediate action is required. But if there's time to staff a well-thought position on an issue, I'll gather the senior staff and conduct a brainstorming session around the conference table. Even then, there are times (I swear!) when it's all said and done and you've all come to an agreement, you'll look around the room and see them nod their heads up and down, when really, they meant side to side. As hard as you try to get them to have an honest exchange, some will pay lip service and then do what they can later to undermine the effort. Or, when they don't like what you're doing, they may comply once but then hope you forget so they can go back to doing what they wanted to do in the first place. Problem for them is…I never forget.

In 1999, while serving as the Director of Security Forces for the Air Mobility Command, one of my major security programs, the Air Force's Raven program, had suddenly come under scrutiny for being "too hard." Ravens are a special-skilled cadre of security forces members that receive unique training in hand-to-hand non-lethal defensive skills, as well as close-in and on-board aircraft security techniques. They are the Air Force's version of the Department of Homeland Security's Sky Marshall Program. It's a very intensive three-week program that also contains very rigid physical prerequisites, as well as physical training throughout the course. In the early fall of 1999, all twelve of the security forces squadron commanders from within the Air Mobility Command were complaining to me that the failure rate for Raven school was too high; that the physical standards required for entry were too tough, and that the physical demands throughout the course exceeded what was reasonable for a standard Air Force course. To facilitate the debate, and to appease all sides, I conducted "hearings" on the issue by assembling squadron commanders, current Ravens, and members of the training staff from the Raven School at Ft. Dix, New Jersey. While some (many of the squadron commanders) wanted entry and course standards relaxed, others (to include current Ravens and the instructor cadre) wanted the standards to remain. Before rendering a decision, I listened to all sides, consulted with professional health officials, and then with Air Force training and doctrine professionals at the Air Education and Training Command.

Raven training in 2001. I'm still feeling the pain from that one.

Ultimately, I decided to continue the course with the rigorous standards already in place. I thought the decision was based on sound reasoning (not to mention empirical data and countless recommendations). When we left the room, I thought we were now unified in our approach. Notwithstanding, within a few days, I began receiving calls from a few Wing Commanders from AMC bases, echoing their security forces commander's concerns. By this time, I'd had enough...enough of (1) testing my resolve on the issue, but more importantly, (2) an attempt to weaken a program (an element of our security force) that needed to be at the top of their game; they needed to be fit, highly trained and capable, and yes, they needed to be elite.

In a move that surprised everyone, I told commanders at all levels that I would do one last thing before rendering my final judgment; I would personally enter and finish the Raven course and then decide for myself. In doing so, I risked considerable humiliation. If I were unable to pass the physical requirements (push-ups, sit-ups, and run time) on the morning of the first day, I would be sent home with approximately 30 percent of the students that wash out on that first day (the basis for their complaint). Nevertheless, I accepted the challenge and proceeded to Raven School. Result? I was the first and only active duty Colonel to attend and pass the Raven program. I did every push-up, ran every mile, took every baton strike, and participated in every aircraft security scenario presented, and graduated as Raven #23 (every Raven is given an assigned number). Upon my return from Raven School I pronounced both the course and standards fair and sound. I also challenged the 12 squadron commanders of the Air Mobility Command (and all security forces commanders throughout the Air Force) to attend Raven training as well. A few even accepted the challenge. Leadership by example? Absolutely. To this day I don't know if I was being obstinate about the issue. It wasn't so much that my resolve was challenged and I wasn't going to concede. It was more the case that I'd made what I considered an informed decision, had done the right thing, and gained the respect of the troops in the process.

There are times when paranoia will completely supplant any semblance of reasonable thought in some people, particularly senior leaders. In Chapter 1, under *Your Sense of Honor*, I mentioned my time on the Arabian Peninsula following the Khobar Towers bombing. It was a bizarre time in my career that, in some sense, still haunts me today. For the entire year I was there, I saw seemingly countless after-action review studies, Senate fact-finding trips, Congressional delegations, the Air Force Inspector General, the Downing Commission, US Marine Corps Red Team, and too many more to list here. Nineteen Americans died, and it seemed somebody needed to be held accountable. Consequently, an organizational guerrilla warfare environment emerged throughout the region. No one wanted to be held accountable; everyone did what they could to displace responsibility (or pass the buck), or certainly to avoid scrutiny. I found out, at a point not too far into my tour, that I was the most feared (perhaps hated) person in the region. If I showed up at your deployed base, did a vulnerability assessment, and then left you with a laundry list of things to accomplish, you were then on the hook to get it fixed ASAP. The clock was ticking. If an attack were to occur with that list in your hand, and no action taken, you were in serious trouble. Commanders knew this, and hated me for it.

On one occasion I flew into Sheikh Isa Air Base in Bahrain where we had a deployed fighter wing. As I landed and got off the airplane, I was met by a young Captain who was the security forces deployed squadron commander. We spent a few moments getting to know each other and then loaded into his truck and began a tour of their security posts, fence line, and fighting positions. After being in the vehicle for about an hour I told the Captain that it was time for me to check in with the Wing Commander. It's common courtesy anywhere in the Air Force for a visiting senior officer to make an office call with the installation commander. At this point, the already nervous Captain suddenly became very quiet for a minute or two and then said "Sir, I'm sorry to say, the Wing Commander is not interested in seeing you." I told him that was OK, I guessed, but I was definitely interested in seeing him…so let's go.

What my security forces hero told me next just completely blew my mind. He told me that as my airplane was on final approach, he, the Wing Commander and Vice Wing Commander were all standing at base operations waiting for the airplane to land. The Wing Commander's plan was to meet me at the airplane and conduct the tour himself. But according to the Captain, his boss became agitated as he stood there waiting for me to land. In fact, he was downright pissed that I was coming. From his point of view, they had only been deployed to that base for about a week, and Wing leadership had yet to implement a comprehensive security posture (something I had noticed already at that point of the tour). It seems the boss was so upset by my arrival that he ordered the Captain to place guards on my airplane to prevent me from disembarking. My security forces Captain assembled his troops and had them ready to deploy around the airplane. As we touched down on the runway, apparently the Wing Commander thought better of the idea, threw his hands in the air and said "Awe, f**k it!" He turned around, got into his staff car and drove off, telling the Captain that he needed to keep me out of his sight for my entire time on the ground.

I'm straddling the perimeter fence at Al Jaber Air Base, Kuwait, in 1996.
This is an 8-foot-high chain link fence with outriggers and an excellent
example of what I think deployed commanders feared I'd find on their
installations. This fence hadn't been attended to in years.

There are two good things that came out of that experience. First, the
Wing Commander gained control of his emotions and made the right call
at the last second. I spent 29 years in the Air Force. I'm a pragmatic guy
and know where support officers (of which a security forces officer is one)
fall within the spectrum of importance. Given a pissing-contest between
two Colonels, most senior Air Force leaders will always side with a Wing
Commander; that's the ways it's always been, and that's the way it'll always
be. But this was different. There were two Colonels in the entire theater
that had the two primary missions; a Director of Operations back at Joint
Task Force headquarters that was busy fighting a daily air war over Iraq,
and a Director of Force Protection (me) who was working to keep deployed
forces safe and secure in order to accomplish that operational mission.[111]

111  The Ops guy and I both worked for an Air Force two-star who was the overall Joint Task Force Commander. Frankly, there were many times where the JTF
Commander was more focused on what I was doing than the air campaign over Iraq. It
was the only time in my career where security was a (the) primary mission.

We were in an environment where home station culture didn't apply. Had the Wing Commander followed through with his poorly conceived plan, he would never have survived. Emotions were raw at the time, and there were commanders in the field (in command at the time of the bombing) that were now "lawyering up." It was an environment <u>that</u> intense. While I had to be extremely careful of what opinions I rendered and where and how I expressed them, an unflattering assessment by me could have sent the Wing Commander home…and he knew that.

The second good thing to come out of the episode was that I didn't allow emotion to rule my behavior. I gathered my thoughts, composed myself, and had the Captain drive me to the Wing Commander's office. I walked into his office as though nothing had happened, extended my hand, greeted him with a smile on my face, and proceeded to have a cordial conversation with every intention of putting his fears and concerns at ease. By the time I was done, he had an appreciation for the gravity of my burden and (I think) a sense that I wasn't there to make his life miserable. We parted amicably and nothing was ever said of the incident again (I never reported it to my boss).

I had a mission. I was sent to the desert with one charge…fix everything! And in this (and every) case, my resolve was unwavering.

## Some will Pull Out Their Union Card

In 2009, while serving as the Acting Regional Administrator for FEMA in the northwest, I had a Division Director who brazenly (defiantly!) announced one day that he was turning all of his program funding back to headquarters. This was a time when FEMA, still recovering from the aftermath of Hurricane Katrina, was trying to instill sound business practices throughout the agency. One of those was to implement a fiscal year programming/budget cycle consistent with other departments and agencies within the Executive Branch. As I mentioned in a previous chapter, there was no organization and maintenance (daily operating) budget process in FEMA up until 2009. There were some funding streams that were "fenced" by Congress; all of these were for specific programs like flood mapping, assistance to firefighters, and some planning funds that couldn't be used for anything else. Otherwise, FEMA managed a budget line called the Disaster Relief Fund, which, Congress kept filled with up to $3B on any given day. Up to this point, if FEMA needed new computers, they would order them and charge it to a current disaster. That's how they funded themselves for years. The Post-Katrina Emergency Management Reform Act of 2006 changed all that.

Throughout the conversation (weeks and months of how to implement the Reform Act's budgeting mandate), I'd given all five of my Division Directors the headquarters guidance on how to implement a planning, programming, and budgeting system, and we seemed to be well on our way as headquarters functional offices began telling each of my Division Directors what their funding streams would be for the coming year. During one of those conversations I made a casual reference jokingly to my time at Andrews AFB where I used to "tax" each subordinate organization for 10% of their budget as a sort of reserve fund. As I was explaining this to my five heroes, you could see the looks in their eyes and feel the tension in the room, so I decided to end the discussion right there. Nevertheless, as you can probably imagine it wasn't long before, once again, all hell broke loose.

I guess it was probably about an hour before the first of the five walked into my office and announced that he was giving all of his program money back to headquarters. I said "Wait, what!?" He said yes, he couldn't allow me to take any of his program money to be used anywhere else in the region that was un-related to any of his programs. In good conscience, he felt duty-bound to turn 100% of it back; if he couldn't have it all he didn't want any of it. He thought it should go to some other region that would spend it for the program for which it was intended. I guess it was probably another hour or so before I got a call from his headquarters program director who demanded that I cease and desist, and informed me that I was not to spend a dime of <u>his</u> program money.

At this point I hadn't done anything; I'd just told a story in a staff meeting! I quickly got the situation under control; talked my Division Director off the ledge, and assured his functional counterpart at headquarters that I would gladly comply with whatever fiscal guidance comes out of their office. But the whole episode highlighted a problem then (and I'm sure continues today); one that I have often euphemistically referred to as "pulling one's union card."

I've seen it time and again, mostly within the civilian side of government. Nevertheless, it prevails to at least some extent with the military as well. It's a form of tribalism; where one tends to identify with, and perhaps holds greater allegiance to, a cohort other than the larger unit to which they're assigned. In my situation with my Division Director, he saw himself not so much as part of the regional organization as he saw himself as part of his functional group. He was my Mitigation Division Director. I saw him as a key senior leader on my staff and within our larger regional structure. He, however, saw himself as one of ten Mitigation Directors from across ten regions throughout the country subordinate to the Mitigation program lead at headquarters. That's who and where he identified with; where his loyalty was. Not to the region!

One of my all-time favorite "union card" lessons goes back decades and reinforces the theory that flawed paradigms can be inherently human and thereby persist for generations. My step-dad worked on the Washington State ferry system. He was a deck hand on the ferry run between Mukilteo (on the mainland) and Clinton (on Whidbey Island). He used to tell me about "how it was in the old days." Fifty years ago (and probably more recent than that) the deck hands did everything on that boat. They operated the boat, parked the cars, performed all the minor (and even some major) maintenance. He told me about his memory of being on a gang plank, painting the side of the boat, while underway. They were in three shifts with each one having responsibility for part of the boat. It was a competition to keep the boat clean. Nowadays, no one touches a paint brush. The deck hand parks cars, and that's it. The ticket booth guy sells tickets, and that's it. When maintenance needs to be done they take the boat off line, put it in dry-dock, and spend millions on it because no one has touched it in the past couple of years. Consequently, the system is going broke and the boats look like crap. You can blame union cards (and unions) on that. Not the type of organization I want to run, or the type of customer service I want to provide. Yet, it seems to be the corporate climate that we've evolved (or devolved) into; one of tribalism.

More to the issue regarding union cards is that I don't want to hear about it…I don't want to hear about your union card. I don't want to hear, when I ask for either your personal help or that of your subordinate unit, that it's not your job. When I need something done for the greater good of the team, I don't want to hear that you have your responsibility and can't be bothered with someone else's. In every organization to which I've been assigned, I tried to instill a total team concept when it came to accomplishing the unit's mission. I'd stress at every opportunity that we're in this business together, as a team, and, especially in a customer service environment, you have to learn to back the other guy up. Put away the union card and join the team!

*"No shot too cheap; no blow too low"*
—Old Special Operations motto

## Yes, Some Will Even Wish You Harm

I've seen it all! Just like the Farmers Insurance Company commercial… I know a thing or two because I've seen a thing or two.

As mentioned earlier, I've had an employee sue me over a frivolous personnel issue, I had one gentleman order guards around my airplane in an effort to keep me from doing a vulnerability assessment of his base, I've been called a racist, and I had my Air Force career summarily ended (I believe still today) by a General officer over the stance I took on what I considered at the time to be the right side of an issue.[112] All of that notwithstanding, the fact that I had a FEMA employee wish out loud that I was dead was probably the lowest of lows.

In 2009, at FEMA Region 10, we were in the process of hiring a new Geospatial Information System (GIS) technician. As with all of our hiring practices, I instructed my Operations Division Director to form a panel, develop interview questions, and so on, in order to legally and ethically hire the best qualified GIS person available. When it was all said and done, the panel presented me with a ranked list that had one of our reserve employees at the top.

Now, as I saw it, there were a number of things wrong with their selection for the job. In my opinion, the experience level of this individual was modest at best. Moreover, while he was somewhat proficient, he had virtually no formal GIS education or certifications; all of his qualifications were derived from on the job training. While age cannot be a hiring factor, and personal appearance perhaps should not be a disqualifier, the individual in question was nevertheless very young (which meant, also, inexperienced) and wore long matted dreadlocks. He had been deployed to the Southeast (Region 4) earlier that summer for a hurricane response and the Alabama Director of Emergency Management had been embarrassed at a meeting he attended; he sent word back to us of his disappointment and asked that we never deploy to him or his state again. While not a huge factor for me personally, things like that do reflect negatively on the Agency. So given all that I described, would it be wise for me to hire the guy (given also that there were other more qualified people on the list)? As it turned out, the

---

112  To be covered in detail in Chapter 7.

staff wanted him because he was their pet employee; he was part of the "klick." There were just so many things wrong with this choice, almost all of them having to do with qualifications, that I finally just said no!

It wasn't long after my decision that I heard from a couple of other employees that one of the supervisors in the Operations Directorate was heard at a water cooler (literally) commiserating with others about my decision. She (a GS-13 supervisor) was heard saying to others (including the employee I had denied the promotion to) "I wish Hunsinger were dead. Someone ought to take him out."

For a while, I thought about what had been reported to me. I mulled it over, talked to a couple of my trusted advisors in the regional office (to include both our staff lawyer and personnel specialist) and decided against their advice to take action. I just decided to let it go as a "heat of the moment" venting of an unpopular decision. In hindsight, after reflecting on it over time, and certainly given what's become a national trend in workplace violence, that was a mistake. I should never have let that issue slide; I should have confronted it swiftly and compellingly. Here's why…

Any leadership position carries with it some level of influence and power (of persuasion) over other employees. In her case, she was seen as the more senior, wise and sage mentor to her band of minions on the lower floor. They almost worshiped her. She had more daily contact with them than anyone. They were loyal to her, and it would only take one of them to decide he wants to do anything he can to please her. "If she wants Hunsinger dead, then I need to deliver!" What are the odds of that happening? Probably extremely low (as it turned out). But who really knows, and it was irresponsible and careless of her to utter the wish. Again, the correct action for me at the time would have been to confront it, and to deal with it swiftly and decisively.

As a leader, be careful of what you ask for! Simply uttering the words "I wish I had…" may surprise you when you show up the next day and it's sitting on your desk. People want to support and please you. Some are either so loyal (bless their hearts), or so eager to ingratiate themselves to you, they will do almost anything to help; sometimes without understanding the consequences of their actions. Choose your words wisely.

## *What They Will Do to Each Other*

### Friends

I guess the first subject to discuss here is the concept of friendship. How many times in your life have you sat back and really thought about who your friends are? Have you really taken stock, done an assessment, of who the people are in your life that, when the chips are down, will come to your aid? I'm not talking about acquaintances; not people in your life that you'd have a beer or go see a ball game with. I'm referring to people that <u>have your back</u>. When you are at the lowest point in your life, and you truly need help, will these people put aside their personal lives in order to be at your side?

How do you define friendship? Well, let me tell you how I define it. In an earlier chapter I discussed my buddy Steve. Steve and I worked together a few of times in our careers, and on at least two of those occasions he worked for me. But in 1994, when we lost my oldest son Don in a horrendous accident, without doubt the darkest moment of my entire life, Steve and his wife Julie (and their kids) were at our sides. Steve had just happened to call my office the day after the accident and was informed by my secretary that Don had died. When he called me at home, we both cried, and then he said he was on his way from Florida to help out (we were in Virginia at the time). I insisted he not come; that everything would be OK and that he should stay home and hug and take care of his kids. The next morning the doorbell rang and Steve, Julie, and their two kids Sherry and David were standing at the door. They had driven all night. They barged right in and literally took over the place. They weren't guests, they were there to help and took charge. That's friendship! There's no way that we would have survived the ensuing memorial service and countless other details without their help. They put their lives on hold to be there for us! Again, that's friendship. I've never forgotten and never will forget what they did for us. Steve knows that I will always have his back. The big question here is how many of the people around you, that you call friends, would do something like that?

So, if you do an assessment of your life, and of those people who you think are close to you, what do you think you'd come up with? My guess is that you can count the number of "Steves" in your life with probably three fingers. Of ten people that you think are your friends, maybe only two really are. The others will look you in the eye and tell you what you want to hear, but when the time comes, they probably won't be there for you. I could be wrong. Maybe I'm cynical about this too. I hope I'm wrong; I truly hope that when you take an accounting, you're able to come up with many more than that. But I'm doubtful that you will.

Another of my closest friends in life, Joe Markin and me in 1996.

Here's the thing about friends (and not to be cynical, but to be pragmatic). First, don't be naive about this critical (maybe the most critical) aspect of your personal life; that is, who you've picked as your friends, who you associate with, who your allies are, and who are and are not loyal to you. Certainly, within the context of this chapter, and inter-office alliances, you should be extremely careful. In many cases, the old adage there's no honor among thieves rings true. In other words, among the people you count as true and loyal, you have to ask yourself is there a certain professional and personal courtesy among each other where there's a sort of moral code of conduct? If things get ugly, or at least tense, how many of them will turn opportunistic at your expense? Who among the group will turn disreputable and unethical and will sell you out for their own personal gain? I'm just sayin. Again, don't be naive, choose wisely, and then be prepared to live with that choice.

Second, it's said that who you choose as your friends (who you associate with) will define who you are and what you will become in life. Entrepreneur and author Tim Ferriss has said, "You are the average of the 5 people you associate with most."[113] Think about that for a second. Not the people you most admire in this world. No, the people that you've chosen to be your friends and daily associates are the ones who shape who you are. Think about the people you've allowed to surround you and the impact, the influence, they've had on your life. Is it always positive? Are their motives always in the right place (at least when it comes to your interests)? I happen to believe it's not just the average of the 5 as Ferriss suggests, but the average of all of those you consider to be close. That could be one, three, or ten. Some of us have had a friend throughout life that needs constant care, and we're not about to abandon them. That too is a major aspect of our character. But continue to be aware and vigilant of those occupying the space around you. Never lose sight of the potential that, if you're not careful, that one particular person you care so much about may be skewing the average in a direction that is detrimental to your best interests. The question becomes are you happy with who you've become? If not, perhaps it's time for a change?

Andrew Ferebee (who I know little about) wrote an article entitled "Here are the 7 rules of success." What struck me most about that article was rule #3 where he states "show me your friends and I'll show you your future. If you spend time with great people who are on a mission and regularly achieve big goals, you'll become one of them. If you spend time with losers who have no work ethic, motivation, or ambition, you will become one of them"[114] I can't say it any better than that, and as Ferebee goes on to say…the choice is yours; you need to choose wisely.

Nevertheless, here's Hunsinger's take on the issue of friendship. First, just remember that with very few exceptions your co-workers are NOT your friends. They have no interest in being your friend and, again, are only "friendly" as a relationship of convenience. Second, if your allies are the bitchers and complainers of the organization, then you're probably going to be a bitcher and complainer as well. Don't be that guy.

## The Toxic Culture

So, what about the bitchers and complainers? Fighting, bickering, backstabbing, conspiratorial rumors, and (my favorite) water cooler gossip are

---

113  https://amp.businessinsider.com/tim-ferriss-average-of-five-people-2017-1
114  https://www.theladders.com/career-advice/here-are-the-7-rules-of-success

all elements of what I've described as "the cesspool of venom and discontent." I've done everything I can over the years to stamp it out. I'm afraid to say that it's a losing cause; it'll always be there. I've had one employee refer to it as "the 7th grade culture" and another refer to it as "mean girls"; with it being almost a zero-sum game to them ("I may lose. But just as long as you lose too, I'm okay with that"). How's <u>that</u> good for an organization?!!!

What you need to do as a leader is draw discernable bright lines, set standards, and continue to enforce them fairly across the board. There will always be people that are disgruntled. You can't completely mitigate that. But what you can also do is start recognizing what causes it, and then take steps to minimize it. Most of employee dissatisfaction is derived from poor communication, pure and simple. In most cases, leadership has done an inadequate job of keeping employees informed and/or providing opportunities for employees to be engaged. Believe me, employees want to be invited in; they want to participate and to be engaged. But at the very least, they want to know what the hell is going on! Even then, either driven by competition, greed, envy, or petty jealousies, some employees will turn on each other; if you're not careful they'll turn on you as well.

In 1975, as a young, recently commissioned Lieutenant at McChord AFB, I was part of a program the Air Force implemented to flood the security police career field with additional officers. Until that point, and throughout the brief history of the Air Force, a typical security police squadron had a commander, an operations officer, and perhaps one other (training officer, administration and other duties). Almost all of the leadership positions throughout the squadron, particularly those on shift duty, were filled by noncommissioned officers (NCOs). It was in 1975, the Air Force decided that at bases with a nuclear mission (a weapons storage area and/or a nuclear-capable aircraft alert area) an officer needed to be present on-duty at all times. Consequently, there was an accession effort to bring on over 700 officers, almost overnight, into a career field that only had about 200.

When I came into the program in 1975, like many of us, there was no technical training slot available for me. In fact, I didn't go to the Security Police Academy until the spring of 1976. Instead, I reported directly to the squadron for duty and almost immediately went to work on midnight shifts as one of the newly appointed Shift Commanders. At McChord, with no training or experience, and at the age of 23, I was suddenly in charge of a security flight of about 60 troops (with a Master Sergeant flight chief reporting to me) and a law enforcement flight of about 15 troops (with a Technical Sergeant flight chief reporting to me).

By now you've probably gotten the picture. I was young, untrained, inexperienced, and now in charge; thrown into an environment where the NCOs had always been in charge, and where suddenly they had an unnecessary (in their view) layer of additional supervision forced on them. It was not a good situation for anyone, and ill-prepared for as a career field. To say the least, there was resentment, if not open animosity, among some in the NCO ranks. So now to the story…

On one particular day in 1976, I was getting ready for work. The troops had assembled, the flight chiefs had their respective formations gathered and ready for my inspection. I gave an order for open ranks, and then proceeded down each file in the formation, checking each troop to ensure they were neat and trim, properly equipped, and otherwise ready to go to work. Off to the side, were two senior NCOs from the squadron, one of which was the squadron Chief (the ranking NCO for the entire squadron).

When the inspection was over and guardmount[115] broke, Chief "O" (as I'll call him) stepped up to me and began to complain that several of the troops were not in compliance with dress and appearance standards; certain troops needed, in his opinion, haircuts. I was polite to the Chief and told him that I had it under control. As I started to walk away, the Chief grabbed a couple of airmen and stood them in front of me. "See, this guy needs a haircut!" the Chief shouted. Again, I told him I had it under control, I had identified the discrepancies with my inspection and they would be corrected. Once again, the Chief grabbed another guy and did the same thing. By this time, I just walked away as the Chief was heard shouting at me.

I let things slide for about ten minutes (time enough for me to cool off as well). Then, I walked into the administrative part of the building and back to where the Chief, Commander, and Operations Officer all had their offices. I walked into the Chief's office, pointed my finger at him[116], and in a low but stern voice told him that I never wanted him embarrassing me

---

115 Guardmount is an official term for formation that security police (now security forces) uses prior to each shift. It is an open-ranks inspection, accompanied by a safety briefing and any other posting order for the day. We are the only career field in the Air Force that begins their duty day in this way.

116 I'm told that's one of my flaws, or at least a characteristic of mine. When I get pissed I'll point at someone when I'm talking to them. I've even been known to leave an indentation in a few chests.

like that again in front of my troops. That's when things got ugly! To my shock (as well as everyone else in the building), the Chief sprang from his chair and began screaming at me at the top of his lungs. All I remember to this day were a couple of phrases, like "I'm not taking this shit from some snot-nosed little Lieutenant." I turned around and walked out of his office, got into my truck and left for a check of the troops on post. As I learned later, the Chief turned around, walked into the Commander's office and said "Well, I guess you heard our little spat." The Commander replied "Yup. Sure did. You f**ked up, and you're fired."

Inspecting guardmount at McChord AFB in 1977.

Now, firing a Chief Master Sergeant in the Air Force is a big deal. At least in 1976, as I found out, it was a huge deal. But the commander had no choice. The Chief chose to make it public. Everyone saw and heard it. The commander was forced to choose sides and, in the interests of good order and discipline, had to support his officer. There was an Inspector General investigation that followed, as well as judicial action against the Chief for insubordination. I really had nothing to do with any of that, except to testify as to what happened. It was a case that reverberated throughout the

Air Force. In fact, some 20 years later, I was in a briefing given by the head-quarters Judge Advocate (JAG) for new commanders on a variety of legal issues they might face. When the JAG began briefing that case, I stood up and introduced myself to him. I think he was shocked that the Lieutenant was still around and had done so well in his career.

The point to this story is to highlight the petty jealousy and desperate hold on power the Chief was trying exercise. NCOs seemed to always have the power within the squadron. Now some "snot-nosed Lieutenant" had supplanted their authority and relegated them to administrative duties. They didn't like that and, in this case, one of them turned viciously on a fellow employee. In this case, it was a very toxic culture, and it took a long time to change old habits.

The other aspect to this story, as I believe to this day, was a very poor effort by the Air Force to introduce the officer Shift Commander program. The NCO corps was left out of the decision, and ultimately the implementation process. I said earlier that employees want to be engaged (have their opinion heard), but at least they want to know what the hell is going on! None of that was done with the implementation of this program. It was a higher headquarters edict that was forced on everyone concerned. Consequently, there was plenty of resentment to go around.

The long and the short of it is that life is chocked full of resentment and petty jealousies, particularly in the workplace. You see it everywhere, in every organization. Unfortunately, it's probably most visible in how Congress conducts its business and, consequently, their conduct probably adds some twisted sense of legitimacy on how the rest of the world behaves. For them, it's not what's good for the country. It's what's good for their political party. It's all about staying in power (as it was for the Chief).

When he left office, George Washington warned about the rise of tribalism (my word, not his), but more importantly the ever-increasing prevalence if not dominance of political parties.[117]

117  In speaking of our differences (at the time he was referring mostly to geographical differences), he urged Americans to remain united. "...your union ought to be considered as a main prop of your liberty, and that the love of the one ought to endear to you the preservation of the other." With respect to political parties he said, "To the efficacy and permanency of Your Union, a Government for the whole is indispensable. No Alliances however strict between the parts can be an adequate substitute." "The alternate domination of one faction over another, sharpened by the spirit of revenge natural to party dissension, which in different ages & countries has perpetrated the most horrid enormities, is itself a frightful despotism." http://gwpapers.virginia.edu/documents_gw/farewell/transcript.html

Nothing has changed, or perhaps everything has changed. Within FEMA it wasn't about what's good for the Agency or the regional team, it was about what's good for the Ops Division, or what's good for my branch, or what's good for me. When you have that prevailing attitude it's no wonder there's no sense of greater community. It's all about tribalism. And that appears to be human nature; something we seem to be unable to escape.

## A Few More Words

As it relates to what employees will do to each other, think about the entire concept of team work. Throughout, I've discussed various aspects of friendship, tribalism, loyalty, and others. They all relate. They all conjure (at least for me) images of troops dying in battle for one another. Many studies have suggested that soldiers don't die for motherhood, apple pie, flag or country. They fight, risk their lives, and some ultimately die for their buddies. Combat fosters a sense of brotherhood, if not family, like no other environment. You can't let your buddy down. Yet, in other sectors of society, you'd think we'd be able to instill some (albeit lessor) sense of comradeship. After all, in the "battles" of daily corporate life some of us have survived our own version of hell, perhaps many times with the same comrades.

If being part of "the team" is too touchy-feely for you, then at least be respectful of the team for others. You can start by simply following the rules. More specifically, follow the law as it relates to your job. Failure to do so disrespects your profession and your team (as well as yourself). To illustrate, I've used the example of professional athletes who are frequent and shameless substance abusers. It's cheating!! To do so, demonstrates to all that you have complete disrespect for yourself and the profession, and flagrantly breaking the rules demonstrates the team just wasn't important enough. Don't be that guy either.

Email Blasts: They're often a cheap, inappropriate, and coward's way of trying to defend your point without having to do it in person. It's the wrong forum for gracious, if not chivalrous, conduct. I don't know how else to better describe it. Be very aware that anything and everything you put in print (especially anything internet-based) is there forever and is likely to end up in the public realm at some point. Just ask yourself before you push send…would my grandmother be proud of this?[118]

Politics: Leave your politics in the parking lot on the bumper of your car where they belong! Within federal government, we're all governed

---

118 I have a few more words about emails in Chapter 8.

by the Hatch Act[119]. Federal employees are, with certain few exceptions, prohibited from campaigning and raising money for partisan political elections. Nor can an employee run for a partisan political office. My direction to all employees has been there will be no displays of affection (posters, signs, or water-cooler discussions) of a political nature within our federal building. For us Feds, the law demands it. But in other environments it's probably sound advice to preserve good order and discipline and to prevent animosity in the work place.

Frequent Supervisory Checks: If you're a supervisor, do it. If you're the supervised, don't be offended or worse, resentful, if your boss comes down stairs to see what everyone's up to. It's part of a credible leader's job. Embrace it. Take the opportunity to demonstrate something you're proud of, or perhaps that's the time to roll out that great idea you've been thinking about while you have his or her attention. If you're the boss, don't be like the flight chief I once had (we all had them) who, during a heavy rainfall would drive up to his troops walking a post, roll down the window of his vehicle (just a crack), and ask "how's it going?" Then he'd drive on. How do you think the troop felt it was going? If he had enough time to even respond, what four letter word would he have chosen followed by the word "you?" Definitely don't be that guy.

How do you motivate the unmotivated? If you ever figure this one out, I'll be happy to fund your book for 50% of the profits. I was on a post check once and came up to a guard that was walking the taxi gap of the fighter alert area. His job was to cover a patch of ground about 50 yards long. It was an area surrounded by fencing, except the gap where aircraft taxied in and out. As I approached, he hadn't seen me coming. But I noticed that as he was walking along, with his weapon slung over his shoulder, he was looking down (not out and vigilant as he should be). As I got up to him, he was startled to see me, but pulled himself together and reported his post. I asked him what he was doing and to my surprise he was completely honest. "Well sir, I'm playing golf." I said something like "Wait, what?" As it turns out, it's such a boring job that he'd found a way to entertain himself. He built (within that 50 yards and off to the side of the tarmac) and 18-hole golf course complete with fairways, sand traps, water hazards, and putting greens. It was beautiful! He'd been working on it for weeks. Every evening when he took his post he walked along kicking a pebble playing

---

119 The Hatch Act of 1993, titled "An Act to Prevent Pernicious Political Activities" (Pub. L. 76-252).

golf. As amazed as I was, this was clearly a violation of his post orders and a dereliction of his duties. But I was so impressed, and I had to give him credit for innovation and ingenuity. I gave him a very slight admonishment, told him to get back to work, and let it slide. At least I had a troop that was trying to find something that motivated him to come to work every day. I suppose one might cynically argue the best practice here isn't to motivate the unmotivated with money, time off, or other perks, but rather teach them how to be self-motivated.

## What You Have to Do to Them

*"Don't argue with an idiot. People watching may not be able to tell the difference."*
—Anonymous

I guess the title to this section is a little deceiving. I'm not advocating that you "do" anything to your employees other than <u>lead</u> them. To suggest anything else probably carries with it some sinister undertone. Nevertheless, I've got plenty of advice on just how to lead them, with perhaps a trick or two in the bag for the times that call for something special.

I was in command four times. Six, if you add Regional Director and Acting Regional Administrator. For that long, and that many people, you can't make everyone happy and will eventually get complaints...about something; like the time I was accused of covering up a sex crime while at Fairchild AFB. Did I tell that story? I don't think so. So here it is; and I'll try to keep this one short.

We had a young woman come into our investigations section one day to file a complaint against a senior NCO on base that had sexually assaulted her. Remember, I was the Chief of Police on base, so the investigators worked for me. As it turns out, the senior NCO in question also worked for me. Now, some might say right away "conflict of interest." But throughout my career in law enforcement, whether one of my organizations or in other civilian police departments, it's not uncommon for law enforcement to investigate one of their own. We took the case and ran with it as hard as we could.

Just as we were about to file charges on this senior NCO, the young woman came back into our investigator and recanted her story. She, with vigor, commitment, and sincerity, asserted that she was just angry with him at the time and had made the whole thing up. This stunned us; partly because she had originally come in and asserted the charge with the same vigor, commitment, and sincerity. It also stunned us because we had heard bits and pieces previously about other abusive relationships he'd been in, but we couldn't get anyone to come forward. The case was dropped.

About 4-5 months later I left Fairchild AFB for my assignment to the Arabian Desert. Within a month or two of my departure. The young woman that made the original charge came back into the investigators and refiled her original charge. However, this time there were other women willing to come forward. The long and the short of this story is that my successor (Steve Ross, by the way) and the base Judge Advocate made a successful prosecution, putting the perpetrator of these crimes in prison for years.

Throughout the trial, it became a sensational news story in the local Spokane press and TV media. At one point, based on a spurious report (a fabricated story) from a woman that had no real knowledge and was completely unrelated to the case, KREM 2 (ABC) News in Spokane ran a story that I had the information on this guy for months and sat on it because he was one of my employees. In the desert at the time, and unable to defend myself, the base Judge Advocate called KREM 2 and demanded a retraction and an apology. True to their profession, they did neither. They just dropped the story after the first day and moved on. Nevertheless, the damage was done to my local reputation, and I had to defend myself a few times over the years. In fact, the woman who promoted the story dogged me for years. I, and others, believe she's certifiably crazy. She called one day while I was working for FEMA and demanded that I resign that position or she would be calling the FEMA Administrator. I immediately reported the entire story to FEMA lawyers so that everyone was aware.

All is well. Years have gone by now and I've never heard from her again. Despite a lack of cooperation from KREM 2 News, the story died on its own. But again, the media did me no favors. I sure wish the Pulitzer Prize was given for media ethics. Oh wait, there wouldn't be anyone to give it to.

So the point to this story? If you're in charge, you're in the line of fire... always. As I said, despite your best intentions, you can't please everyone.

If you've been in leadership positions as often and for as long as me, you're bound to come out on someone's hate list.[120]

## Set Standards

I've said it several times now. Whether in government or industry, you have to draw a line in the sand and advise (okay, yes, warn) employees to not step over it. You have to tell them, repeatedly, what is and is not acceptable behavior; explicitly discuss issues of conduct, performance, and discipline. If you don't address disruptive employees, or poor performance for that matter, what kind of message about accountability does that send?

My common practice was to address one or more of these issues at every commander's call (in the military), or "all-hands" meetings in the civilian world. Depending on the season, I might discuss the Hatch Act and the federal government policy on political activities. But at nearly every meeting I'd say a few words about the others (sex, drugs, and rock-n-roll). You don't have make it a theme, nor do you have to kill the mood of what might also be an otherwise joyous occasion (an awards ceremony, for instance). Just sandwich it in there somewhere and then move on. They'll hear it, and moreover, they'll always know where you stand.

The types of things that are (or are not) acceptable conduct can differ depending on the environment. What is acceptable in the private sector may not be within government. During my times as a Security Forces Squadron Commander, for instance, I'd draw the line at stealing, and drugs. As members of the law enforcement community my expectations of employees were straight forward and simple. If you use drugs, I'll discharge you from the Air Force. If you steal or are engaged in any type of theft activity while on duty, I'll put you in prison. Everyone knew where that bright line was drawn.

Later, during my FEMA years, I made sure that employees knew where they could potentially come into serious conflict with me. I held (still do) a very strong opinion that going outside the building and spreading rumor, innuendo, or even disparaging remarks about the regional office, FEMA headquarters, the Administration (particularly the President, no matter who he was), or any one individual to outside partners; especially state and

---

120 That reminds me, I'm on some guy's list as one of the Ten Kings of the Apocalypse mentioned in Revelations 17. Seriously!! Look up this web site and you'll find his conspiracy theory that the 10 FEMA Regional Administrators (at the time his article was written) are proof of the end of times, and on and on and on. https://forum.prisonplanet.com/index.php?topic=167164.0

local government partners was a gross breach of their trust as government employees. It was unforgiveable. I had a couple of employees (one who had been appointed to be our liaison to the state emergency management offices) violate this principle, and was pulled from that job. It's inexcusable to have an employee behave with such blatant disloyalty.

When you do experience a serious breach of conduct within the ranks, you have to act! Take action with lightning speed in issues of sexual misconduct, race, or almost anything else. You want to preserve individual rights and due process, but in today's viral social media world, not to mention a culture of wanting someone's head, don't let it be yours. Our society's new blood sport is holding leaders accountable via Twitter and Facebook. It's shameful, but it's the world we live in.

If you don't act, and act decisively in those situations, you'll lose the rest of your employees long before you lose your job. You have to be the enforcer of standards, and then you have to live by example. Over and over again, in your daily life and routine, you have to be the leader. That's not an easy thing to do, but it has to be done or you won't last along. Never forget that the culture of the organization is a reflection of <u>your culture;</u> <u>your value system,</u> and how you carry yourself.

## Take Care of Them

Within a military context, a commander should never eat until his troops have been fed. Not all commanders have ingrained that into their value system, but I did. Whether I was with troops in the field or running the FEMA Region, I always hovered near the end of the line trying to maneuver my way to the back without being too obvious. That's just me (and a lot of other commanders I knew). Again, while somewhat common in a military environment, it's also metaphorically relevant in a civilian leadership context as well. It simply means take care of your troops. Their health and welfare are paramount; yours should be secondary to theirs. I guess on some level you can attribute it to the servant leader concept (that I've already addressed). In a very visceral sense you are being a servant leader by eating last. More importantly, you're showing respect and a genuine concern for their welfare.

Jack Welch said "When you were made a leader you weren't given a crown, you were given the responsibility to bring out the best in others." That means your job is that awesome responsibility of the health and welfare, as well as the development, of your employees. They know, they can sense, when you are or aren't genuinely concerned about their interests.

*"I have to get my way once in a while or I wouldn't be leading."*
—Margaret Thatcher

## Encourage Participation

I've heard it said there are two ways to listen. You can listen to understand or you can listen to respond. I like to listen to people to get a sense of who they are, not just what they're saying. I want to understand them completely; to hear the content as well as the context. I think most people listen to respond. I can't begin to tell you how many times I've sat across someone, presenting my opinion, while I'm almost literally watching their mind work. You can see it in their eyes. You can watch the body language; watch them shift their weight as though they're getting ready to say something. You can see their head go up and down as you're talking, but their lips are already starting to form words long before you're even finished with your thought. These people are watching your lips move but they're really not hearing what you're saying. They spend the whole time that you're talking, thinking about how they'll respond to you; what they're going to say when you shut up. And Lord, they wish that would be soon. Then, more often than I can count, for many of them, it's not a discussion but an attack. I hate these conversations!

I believe in a participatory style of management, but not always consensus management (or a democracy). Nevertheless, my approach is to encourage participation, as well as to also encourage discord. Discord can be good. It can also be bad if you're not careful. Every good leader should seek as much input as time will reasonably allow, but then make the decision and move on. I'm a firm believer that creativity is fueled by discord; that too much harmony in an organization can stifle it. But there is a tipping point where too much discord is destructive. You have to find the balance, and never let that tip happen.

Encourage your team to close the door and as I used to say "cuss and discuss." As you sit in that conference room, pouring over an issue, encourage everyone to get their opinion out and on the table. I also believed fervently that my team should speak openly and candidly about issues; but bring solutions and be prepared to withstand the scrutiny. Defend your position; and the rest of you need to pick it apart. I demanded decorum, or it would devolve into a bitter fight. Again, let's get it on the table. Cuss and discuss. Afterward, we walk out of the meeting in unison, reinforcing with the larger team that it's really been a team decision. It's only then, when you have everyone nodding in the right direction, that you open the door, walk out, and move on as a team. It worked often. While I've been very successful with that approach, I've also seen failure with it. Nevertheless, on balance I'd use it every time. You have to realize there are petty jealousies that'll never go away; there might even be reprehensible forces within your staff that'll never accept defeat, and will later do what they can to undermine you and your decision (that was unacceptable to me).

All of this said, don't let "cuss and discuss" devolve into just cussing. While it seemed to work well while I was there, and in control, there were times that I couldn't be there. If you're in a job that requires you to travel frequently, you better have someone left behind, in charge, that is capable (by position and personality) to keep things under control. While running the FEMA Region, I hadn't designated a Deputy to "take charge" of the Region while I was gone. We did have a line of succession, and the most senior Division Director did proctor the meetings. However, that official charge was something less than really being in charge. While out of the office, I was still in charge of the Region, I just wasn't present at the meetings. Consequently, during those times that I was gone I found out later that some of the meetings devolved into just a lot of screaming and yelling. Certainly not a good situation and something I would've, should've done differently by wisely choosing and formally naming an Acting Deputy. I should've delegated the power and authority to take charge. Lesson learned.

*"Bravery is being the only one who knows you're afraid"*
—Col David Hackworth

## Display Leadership!

Do so with both humility and empathy, always. I mentioned before that I learned a long time ago that you never have to remind anyone that you're the commander (or CEO, or whatever the title might be). When you walk into a room, or when conducting a staff meeting (or in any other venue), you don't need to remind people that you're in charge. They know that. Be humble. If for no other reason than you're extremely grateful for having been given the opportunity to lead. Show that! If you find that you're having problems connecting with employees, or that at some point you seem to be losing them, the first thing you should probably do is check your ego; how am I coming across to these folks?

There should never be public displays of anger. As a leader you should always strive to maintain your composure. As Hackworth says about bravery, the same goes for anger (or for excitement, confusion, uncertainty, or a variety of countless other human emotions). You want those emotions to be concealed from others. At times of great stress, people want to look to their leader as their rock, their anchor; someone that will exude confidence, poise, and calm under the most extreme conditions. That said, you may be on the verge of distress yourself. Don't succumb to it! If you get excited, flustered, or yes, angry, others will as well. If you're ever in a response situation or some other type of high tempo operation, look around the room. All eyes are on you. Be the leader they need in that situation. Let others get excited; you remain calm and in control (or at least seem that way).

As for Public displays of anger, it's egregious to publicly scold employees; especially a junior leader, if in the presence of his or her subordinates. There is no faster or more effective way to undermine their position and authority with their troops. The long term implications to their standing (and perhaps your reputation) could be ruinous. Don't do it!

Why, then, wouldn't you want to yell at someone when they've screwed up? Most of us have been on the receiving end of a good old fashion butt chewing at some point in our life. It's a fact of life; it happens. But I've learned over the years that the most powerful word in the English language (or any language for that matter) is "disappointment." You don't need to say you're angry with anyone. To say, instead, you are disappointed with someone or that they let you down cuts very deeply. It hurts and is far more effective; especially if it's coming from someone you respect and admire. Think about that for a second. Have you ever stood in front of a boss and had him or her say rather solemnly "I'm really disappointed in you; you let me down on that one." I have. Not very many times; but I have, and it hurts. The couple of times that did happen in my career I walked away thinking "holy crap, I wish he'd have just chewed my butt!" In an earlier chapter I mentioned the Colonel I worked for and the time that I left him standing at the air passenger terminal without a ride. He came in the next morning, walked past my desk, pointed at me and said "that's one." I wanted to run into his office and throw myself on the floor, volunteering to be flogged. As I said before, I never let him get to "two."

The more you use words like disappointment and the less you use yelling, the more they'll respect you (and the more they'll respond to you).

They don't want to disappoint you or let you down. The first time you're in a staff meeting and things just aren't going right, close your notebook and say you guys really disappointed me…you let me down. That will cut to the bone and will be far more effective than anything else you could do. After that, from time to time, just close your notebook and pause…then get up and walk out. You won't need to say a word. The effect of that can be devastating; but use it sparingly.

There are plenty of other ways to display leadership. As the boss of the organization, you have to be able to operate from the board room to the shop floor and back. That doesn't mean you need to be technically fluent in all aspects of the operation. You have skilled employees to handle the details. You're the boss. You're the senior leader responsible for big picture issues. Notwithstanding, you do need to be conversant with your employees is some of the intricacies of their jobs. Show interest! Take the time to learn. When I was deployed as commander of an Air Expeditionary Group to Oman in 1998, I took the time to learn what my maintenance guys were doing. I'd go out onto the flight line and watch them turn wrenches on the jets. I'd spend time with civil engineers, my supply folks, and my chow hall workers; all in an effort to both get to know them a little more personally and to learn what challenges they faced daily.

Bottom line here? Get down on the shop floor. Manage by walking around, or you stand the risk of being seen as aloof or out of touch with employees. But the caution here? If you're the captain of the ship and you keep going down to the engine room to make sure the boiler is fired up, you're likely to run the ship into an ice berg. Stay focused!

### Delegation, and Then Your Veto

My advice has always been to delegate as much as you can, as often as you can. Abraham Lincoln talked about "…the better angels of our nature." I, for one, believe in the better angels of our nature; so I guess that makes me the eternal optimist. I also believe it's that better angels of our nature that move employees and management to come together for their mutual self-interests, and those of the organization. Call me idealistic, but it's in my nature to encourage (to perhaps compel) employees to take an active role. I've said it many times, and I'll say it here once more, I believe in leaders being leaders. Someone has to be in charge, and someone has to be accountable and responsible for the conduct and performance of the organization; at the end of the day someone has to make the tough decisions.

But encourage creativity, and let others flourish. How do you do that? By delegating responsibility and authority when and where you can.

When you do delegate, try to delegate as much of the task, authority, responsibility, accountability, consequence or reward as you can. It won't always be easy, but if you don't, your junior leaders (your rank and file for that matter) won't otherwise mature and grow. Your job, as much as anything, is to develop and mentor future leadership. You can't do that unless you let them spread their wings, and you can't do that unless you share. Again, employee engagement and delegation are key to both a creative organization and a stronger decision-making process.

All this leads me to an important subject; the power of your veto over their decisions. This is the slippery slope to delegation that you need to be cautious of. If you do choose to delegate whenever or wherever you can, you need to understand there are risks. You need to make it clear to employees where the parameters are to their authority, and under what circumstances they can act on final decisions without your approval, as well as those situations where you may over-rule them.

A favorite concept used by countless organizations is the "employee advisory council."[121] Be wary! If you don't lay the ground rules for such meetings, they'll soon misunderstand their charter, authority, and limits of power. I've seen it time and again, where an employee advisory council quickly assumes that because we formed one, they are now making the policy on behalf of the boss. They'll come to the boss with a policy proposal assuming that senior leadership will rubber stamp it and it then becomes promulgated policy. If they're over-ruled by the boss, they become resentful; insisting the whole council effort was a sham. If not handled correctly, it can have a ripple effect within the organization, and a negative effect on morale. One of the worst things a leader can do is dangle the carrot and then yank the rug (mixed metaphors, I know, but you get the point).

The best use for an advisory council is to form one for a specific issue; a well-defined, well-scoped subject (a problem within the organization) for which you want a small group's focused attention. Then, give them explicit

---

121 When I was with FEMA, I turned our annual performance award (cash awards) program over to an employee panel. They racked and stacked nominations and came to me with a "draft" list of who should get what. I was very clear about their charter and the ground rules, as well as the possibility that I may rearrange their draft. Even then, on the occasions I'd do that, there was some resentment that I didn't appear to trust their judgement.

instructions, a timeline, expectations for frequency of progress reports, and what you expect to see in a final recommendation. Finally, ensure they understand how you intend to use their work (probably the most important piece as it relates to potential misunderstandings).

## Find Things to Occupy Their Time

There comes a time in a career (if you've been around long enough) that tragedy may strike and then you're faced with a dramatic, if not emotional, setback. If you're one of the lucky leaders, you'll get through a long and distinguished career without ever experiencing the heartbreak of death and destruction. But for some of us, it happens. There's hardly any way to really prepare for it, except to rely on your training, experience, and instincts to get you through. But there are some tips on how to recover from it. Probably my biggest piece of advice, in the weeks and months following a traumatic event, is to keep or re-direct the focus of your employees on efforts and things that you want them focused on. Don't allow them to idly find issues to dwell on; certainly, don't let their lives be consumed by the "event."

I've previously mentioned (glossed over really) the active shooter event we experienced at the Fairchild AFB hospital on June 20, 1994. I did cover the B-52 crash that occurred on base later that week, June 24, but saved the hospital shooting until now since it was an all-encompassing event for our squadron. The aircraft crash was horrendous in its own right. But we were the squadron on base that provided for the safety and security of Fairchild AFB; we were responsible for base law enforcement and security. Accordingly, that singular event impacted every person in my 440-person squadron like none other I had ever experienced in my life. The response was heroic, the aftermath chaotic, and the long-term adjustments were difficult and painful.

It was the first day of command for our new support group (base) commander, Colonel Rich Wirth. It was a Monday. The base was buzzing and excited about the upcoming air show the following weekend, as well as the fact that we'd just had a base-wide change of command and retirement ceremony for the outgoing support group commander that morning. All in all, it was a pretty festive mood. Rich had settled into his office, trying to make sense of all the incoming and outgoing paperwork, and receiving briefings on a variety of issues; he hadn't even been to the base hospital or even met many of the commanders on base. Yet, fairly soon, his command presence and critical decision-making skills were about to be tested under fire, literally.

Dean Mellberg was a now-discharged Airman who had been assigned to the Precision Measurement Equipment Laboratory (PMEL) on base. He had been assigned to Fairchild AFB from April until September of 1993. He was also a very disturbed young man. In the short time he had been assigned to Fairchild, he had been accused by his roommate of making threatening overtures. His supervisors and co-workers had reported fits of rage and anger and, consequently, he had been referred to the mental health clinic at Fairchild's base hospital for an evaluation. Through a series of events, as well as unfortunate missteps attributed to systemic (if not leadership) failure, Mellberg had been passed from Fairchild to Wilford Hall Medical Center at Lackland AFB, where an Air Force Medical Evaluation Board reviewed his case and found him fit for service. He was then sent to Cannon AFB in New Mexico, where he continued his pattern of hostile, aggressive, and bizarre behavior. By May of 1994, Airman Dean Mellberg was discharged from the Air Force with a diagnosis of paranoid personality disorder.

On June 20th, 1994, Mellberg, with his recently purchased MAK 90 semi-automatic rifle and 80-round drum, arrived at the Fairchild AFB hospital via taxi. There are varying theories about why Mellberg did it. Regardless, he was angry with almost everyone; from his previous roommate at Fairchild to his commanders to the two mental health doctors who originally recommended his evaluation and eventual discharge. Notwithstanding any of that, the results of his actions left five people dead (to include an 8-year-old girl and an unborn child), 22 wounded, and an Air Force Base and larger community in complete devastation.

As Mellberg arrived at the hospital, he carried a large duffle bag from the taxi into the Mental Health Clinic first floor restroom, where he assembled and loaded his weapon. From there he proceeded down the hallway of the first floor, fatally shooting his first two victims, the doctors (a psychiatrist and a psychologist) who had originally referred him to Wilford Hall Medical Center for evaluation. From there he left the mental health clinic, walked across the parking lot to the main hospital building, and continued his killing spree until he was confronted outside by one of our responding patrolmen, Senior Airman Andy Brown.[122]

---

122 For a more in-depth account of events of June 20-24, 1994, I recommend Andy Brown's book "Warnings Unheeded."

As for me? I was off base at the time of the shooting. I had gone home to Virginia[123] to attend my daughter's high school graduation. By the time I got back to Spokane on Wednesday the 22nd, the crime scene was well under law enforcement control, while the rest of the base was certainly in an emotional crisis. When I got there, I went straight to the office, was briefed, and then went straight to the hospital. While again, the crime scene was secure, we still had an active investigation on-going, and by the time I got there, nothing had been cleaned up; there was still blood and debris everywhere.

Aerial view of the Fairchild base hospital with mental health annex. The yellow line shows Mellberg's route of travel. 1 – Where Mellberg was dropped off by the taxi. 2 – The mental health clinic's ground floor restroom. 3 – Where Mellberg's first two victims were sitting, across the hall from each other in their respective offices. 4 – Additional fatalities and wounded. 5 – Where Mellberg left the building. There were additional fatalities and wounded in the parking lot. 6 – Where Mellberg was fatally shot by our responding patrolman. 7 – Where Senior Airman Andy Brown had ridden his bicycle from the East Gate (approximately a quarter mile), dropped his bike, took aim, warned Mellberg to drop his weapon, and then ended the carnage firing four shots from his 9mm pistol, with two hitting Mellberg from approximately 70 yards away. (crime scene photo)

---

123 My youngest son, Matt, and I had left home in mid-February for my assignment to Fairchild. The rest of the family (Jeanne, Don and Joanne) stayed behind in Virginia to allow Joanne to finish high school and for Jeanne to sell the house.

I will readily admit, that in the aftermath of a horrendous shooting, a mass casualty incident, the largest crime scene in the history of Spokane County, with carnage and destruction on a large scale, and countless lives impacted, I could've/should've done some things differently.[124]

In his book, *Warnings Unheeded*, Andy Brown alludes to the notion that he was mistreated by his command chain; that he unnecessarily had his weapon seized, and was humiliated by being relieved of duty, following the shooting. While I've never claimed to be the perfect commander, or to have done everything perfectly during the week of 20-24 June 1994, I do want to set the record straight on a couple of issues. Andy's recollection of some events highlighted in the Trauma and Recovery section of his book are completely without context.[125]

At the time, Fairchild AFB was home to a B-52 Wing with an associate KC-135 Group. It was, in fact, a bomber base with a nuclear mission. I was in command of a Security Police Squadron of 440 personnel. Most of those were security troops responsible for the protection of aircraft on the flight line, but moreover, the security of a nuclear weapons storage area (WSA) we had on base.[126]

Beyond the daily posting requirements for a WSA, the Department of Defense also mandated we establish a back-up or reserve force. The idea is that if your on-duty forces become engaged in a fire fight, and potentially overwhelmed, you've made the necessary arrangements for their reinforcement. The mandate? At all cost, not a single nuclear weapon would leave our possession. Accordingly, we'd made a decision years ago to PRP-certify (more on this) all of our law enforcement personnel, those that patrol the base and man our gates, in an effort to fulfill this requirement. They were after all, security policemen, armed and trained, on duty, and members of our unit.

The Air Force has a program called the Personnel Reliability Program (PRP) which is associated with any activity in support of nuclear weapons. Its primary purpose is to create an administrative apparatus (thereby forcing deliberate leadership intervention…some would say intrusion) where anyone associated with nukes is monitored for strange and unusual

---

124  Particularly as you take into account the PTSD exponentiality of multiple such events in the same week.

125  *Warnings Unheeded: Twin Tragedies at Fairchild Air Force Base* by Andy Brown, 2016, WU Press, Spokane, pages 299-307.

126  Both the B-52 Wing and the WSA are long gone now. Fairchild is, today, a tanker base and the Security Forces Squadron is roughly 150 personnel in size.

behavior that might pose a threat to the safety and security of the weapons. For instance, the commander must consider anything and everything from a domestic dispute to mood- or mind-altering drugs that may cause a person to lose rational thought and could potentially cause harm to themselves, others, or the weapons. Something as simple as drinking the over-the-counter cold/flu medication NyQuil prior to reporting for duty, required the leaders to temporarily suspend the individual from duty.

Senior Airman Andy Brown
(photo from 1994 edition of *Airman Magazine*)

Yes, botching the administrative rules of the PRP was deemed to have a potential impact on the safety and security of nukes. But to a lesser degree, yet still extremely important, the program and its administration where (are) pass/fail items in a DOD nuclear surety inspection. Believe me when I say, the slightest administrative oversight could sink the entire Wing in an inspection, potentially causing the base to lose its nuclear mission.

If they were to go through my paperwork and find that someone had been prescribed Vicodin to relieve pain for a broken toe, but I hadn't made a deliberate and documented "commander's assessment" that the individual was still able and capable of performing his duties…the Wing fails.

In Andy Brown's case, my hands were tied. The fact is, that across the nation, it's standard practice for any police officer involved in a shooting to be relieved and weapon seized pending an investigation. The officer and his/her weapon are, after all, "elements" of a crime scene, whether the shooting is justifiable or not; they are now part of the investigation. When our incident occurred on base, the Spokane County Sheriff's Department wanted the weapon for that purpose.[127] Moreover, Andy, along with all other members of the law enforcement flight, had been PRP-certified as members of the WSA's back-up force. Again, I was bound by Department of Defense Directives with no exception to policy. Whether he needed it or not, for a short period where I was required to assess (with the help of professionals) his mental and emotional state following a very traumatic event, he had to remain on the PRP-suspended list. Pure and simple. It wasn't punitive, as he or others might suggest. It was a requirement with which I had to comply.[128]

I know this too sounds like a little too much "inside baseball" for the casual reader, but it serves to illustrate an important point. There are times when a leader must do certain things as well as times when he should do certain things. The hospital shooting and B-52 crash (four days apart) were more than anyone should have to face in their professional life. But it happens! The challenge for any leader is to plow through all that, keeping both his people and himself moving forward. It was an extremely emotional and heart-wrenching time for everyone on base; more so for those families who lost loved ones, but almost as much for those first responders involved. Following both incidents, I had several people come forward requesting

127  It took several months for the weapon to be returned to us via the Air Force Office of Special Investigations.
128  I'll let Andy's account of his eventual mental health counseling stand. Although I did implore him several times to seek help.

counselling assistance. The challenge then and now, is to identify those that aren't identifying the need themselves. Years later I'm hearing stories of people who were on duty then that are experiencing issues today. I personally lost four friends, to include my boss, in the B-52 crash. As the second person on scene, while standing in the middle of fire, smoke, debris, and charred bodies around me, that scene has come back to haunt me over and over years later. If you watch the video of the crash you can see (on some of the wider angled shots) our weapons storage area posting bus. The aircraft just missed coming down on top of our swing shift going to work. I had one troop on that bus, so distraught, that he refused to immediately go to work. The rest jumped off the bus and rushed to the scene, being posted as a cordon around the crash site. While a functional necessity, was that wise on my part? All these years later I've come to second guess that. Notwithstanding, the spirit, courage, and dedication involved by all was/ is inspirational.

Throughout the entire week, my troops did great without me during the initial point where I wasn't there (particularly the actual shooting event). Did they need me? They may have been more comfortable with me there; probably depending on who you ask. But no, they didn't need me. I've always been a proponent of picking the right people, giving them sound procedures, training and drilling them, and then trusting them. As a leader, you can't be everywhere at once, and there will be (as luck would have it) times where things happen at the worst time. Despite the chaos, which will always occur in a situation like that, my folks excelled at response, recovery, and restoration. They were professionals from top to bottom, and I couldn't have been prouder.

At the end of the week Rich Wirth and I were standing near the B-52 crash site as the sun was setting and things were getting quiet. He turned to me and said "In the last five days I've faced more than most commanders will ever face in a career. I'm exhausted. I can't even imagine what the next two years[129] will bring." Then with a little smile he said, "Can I go home now?"

I began this segment with the title "Find Things to Occupy Their Time." Now that I've given a little of the back story, <u>what can go horribly wrong</u>, it's important to focus a little on what you can do to get people back on track. It's pretty simple really. It's important that you get back to the number one

---

129 At the time, and I think still today, the standard length for anyone in command was two years and then it was time to rotate.

priority at hand. If you're a corporate or private business, it's what you're in business to do; it's what you're in business to make or the service you provide. In my case, I was dealing with a military unit that was responsible for security and law enforcement on an Air Force base. Whether it's a military mission or manufacturing and selling widgets, just going back to the daily grind may not be enough for most people. Often, you'll find (perhaps you'll have to search for) something else to occupy their attention beyond the mission. They had the mission before the incident and they have the mission again, but perhaps something different is needed.

Following the events of late June 1994, we spent the better part of fall, on into winter, trying to determine whether the troops wanted to wear berets or ball caps. Yes, I know it sounds pretty lame. But hear this one out before passing judgement.

The Air Force policy at the time was that security police units could exercise the option of going from wear of the standard-issue security police beret (see previous picture of Andy Brown) or a locally-designed ball cap that would be worn only at the local installation and while wearing the battle dress uniform (Photo below).

The unofficial ball cap of the 92nd Security Police Squadron
around the 1994 era.

Once again, this may not sound like much, but this singular issue drove the entire squadron nuts for months. This single (rather trivial) matter completely consumed us. I formed a Process Action Team with representatives from the flights, both security and law enforcement, back-office troops, all ranks, and all levels of career field experience. They held meetings, debated the issue and conducted flight votes. Finally, after almost three months, they presented their results to me. I'll admit here that at every opportunity, Chief Joe Markin and I fanned the flames of dissention over this issue – just to keep the process moving along (but slowly). At the same time, we continued to move the squadron forward, reconstituting/re-emphasizing training and readiness while keeping the daily mission focused. In the end, we allowed the ball caps to be worn.[130] It wasn't to last long because the Air Force published a uniform change within a year or so mandating that all security forces members wear the beret with the new SF flash sewn on.

This is just one example; we employed numerous. Smoke and mirrors? Maybe, but it keeps them focused. In this particular circumstance, the unit had just experienced back-to-back tragedies, with a major crime incident and an aircraft accident (all in one week) that involved significant loss of life. We felt it was extremely important to keep them focused…on something, other than just pushing them back into the monotony of work. This is not to suggest you find trivial issues or "busy work" for them to focus on; although, as I've demonstrated that sometimes works as well. To the extent possible, find team-building issues. Perhaps they can find a charity to support (one directly related to the incident?). But you, as their leader, need to exercise that vision and innovation mentioned earlier.

## Defend Yourself

Unfortunately, that's the world we live in. It's okay to take the high road and not get mired in the nastiness that may be surrounding you… for a while. But at some point, you have to fight back. At some point, the "fight or flight" instinct needs to kick in. If your reputation, your good name, and your livelihood are in jeopardy, it's time to act in self-defense.

It happened to me! In a previous chapter I highlighted an event in my civilian career where someone (or some people) wrote anonymous letters to the FEMA Director accusing me of ridiculous, unsubstantiated things; none of them even remotely true. But it put me in a position of having to

---

130 Truth is, I was going to allow them to wear both. Baseball cap in the summer and beret all other seasons.

deny and defend. As told earlier, I did so vigorously. Regardless, I felt at the time that it had compromised my standing in the organization, and since I was unable to muster support from my leadership to refute the allegations (I wanted an investigation), I chose to leave. In hindsight, not what I'd recommend now. But I'd reached a point of exhaustion over the issue (from years of running the Region without adequate staff), and decided it was a good time to retire.[131]

Conversely, I'll share a story of a woman that I know who faced a similar circumstance. She had worked for me for a few years and I had great confidence and trust in her, and a belief that she would continue to rise in the organization (and at that point she had). But she called me one day seeking advice because her very existence within the organization was now in jeopardy. From her account, key subordinates were feeding senior leadership outrageous allegations about her specific leadership style, from her actions to her temperament. Moreover, her immediate supervisor had developed a chummy relationship with her subordinates, and she felt the entire gang was closing in on her; her boss had already stripped her of some supervisory responsibilities. As a note, I knew all parties involved and believed her account on its face.

As I'm hearing the details of her concerns and the circumstances surrounding the events, I began to realize a dynamic here that she wasn't articulating (a road she hadn't gone down yet in the conversation). I finally stopped her and reminded her that everyone involved in this situation were men in power positions. I asked her if, at any time, did she feel that the work environment had become hostile to her because of her gender. She said yes! Absolutely! And then she began to detail specifics.

We talked for a while longer. I gave her some advice on how to deal with each of the personalities involved, but I also told her she shouldn't follow my example (of just leaving) …she should consider going on the offensive! Perhaps the time for defense was over; maybe she'd reached a point where she needed to take the fight to them. I gave her some guidance on who to call for trusted legal and personnel advice, and then I (appropriately) backed away. I have strong feelings about meddling in the affairs of an organization to which I no longer belong.

---

131 I left for retirement in July of 2011. By October of 2012 I had returned to the Department of Homeland Security as Regional Director for the Office of Infrastructure Protection. During the interview, I was asked if there was anything I'd ever failed at. After thinking about that answer carefully for a moment, I said yes…retirement.

As in her case, sometimes (although rarely) you need to come out of your defensive crouch and go on the offensive. There might be a time when you need to stop being the nice guy and have to become as ruthless as they are. That's a sad commentary, I know. Nevertheless, it's the world we live in. Just please make sure it's because you're right, and that you're not just being vindictive. Hopefully, your morality (integrity, ethics, honesty) will guide you. Don't live the rest of your life in regret, but make sure you can still look yourself in the mirror every morning.

In all cases like these, again, just do the right thing.

# 7

# Professional Development

## *(It Doesn't Mean Just Yours)*

*"Before you are a leader, success is all about growing yourself. When you become a leader, success is all about growing others."*
—Jack Welch

I love people. I love troops. I love the opportunity to lead, mentor, and develop those subordinates I've been blessed to have under my charge. It's something I've realized profound personal reward in, and something I've also taken very seriously. In short, I'd say that mentoring young leaders has been the most rewarding aspect of my professional, and to some extent personal, life. In doing so, I've tried to concentrate on building character; learning from experience that many parents never instilled in some of my employees the concepts of duty, honor, loyalty, compassion, commitment (I've talked about that), or many of the other elements essential to good leadership. Believe me, over the years, I've had to supplement leadership mentoring with parental advice on more than one occasion. But I also believe it's equally important to one's development that they do as much as possible for themselves in terms of professional education. What schools, courses of study, certifications, or licenses have they pursued? What have they done for themselves to learn how to become an effective leader? Who have they chosen as their mentor[132], and how is that mentor really serving them?

A standard by which I've always led, one which I've always used in terms of developing and promoting future leaders, is to reward performance and to promote potential. Think about that one for a moment. When you're sitting on a hiring panel, and you have a superbly qualified individual in front of you, how do you judge that person? Based on what criteria do you say this is <u>the</u> guy or gal? If you do think about that for a moment, you'll realize that certainly every level of government (and most

---

132 Mentorship is a personal choice. Don't let yourself be assigned one. You should seek out someone that interests and inspires you; someone whose judgement you highly respect.

corporations) have personnel programs (incentives) to reward an employ-ee's performance; everything from reward-based suggestion programs to end-of-year performance bonuses. We have means by which we recognize employee achievements. Should one such award also be that we then pro-mote them because of their annual accomplishments? I don't think so.

Here's an example to illustrate: You're sitting on the hiring panel to promote or hire the next Branch Chief under you. In walks a guy who has been a great performer, is very loyal, has actively pursued an advanced college education, has attained professional certification in your particular field, and proceeds to wow you with a list of everything he's done this past year to meet his performance objectives. Then, next, another guy enters who has similar qualifications, but doesn't go too deep into the year's ac-complishments. Instead, he begins to describe where the branch has been, where it is today, and where he sees it 3-5 years from now; he begins to lay out a <u>vision</u> for where he'd like to take this particular unit in the coming years. Now, we can argue all day about whether or not you like this person's "vision." Regardless, which approach demonstrates potential to you? What type of person do you want to hire? The person who measures things, or the person who weighs the future and its direction? I'll take the latter al-most every time.

The bottom line here is that development of <u>potential</u> is what we, as senior leaders, should be striving for. All employees should be working on their own to ensure an acceptable standard of performance, or they prob-ably shouldn't be there; some might need help with that too. Nevertheless, leaders need to realize there's a difference between talent and potential, and they better start focusing on the right one of the two.

## *Your Development (or at least mine)*

I guess you might say my professional development began at the age of 20. At the time, I was working for my father-in-law in his lumber mill on Whidbey Island. My initial job with the company was to wash logs. As the logging truck would dump its load on to an inclined loading deck, my job was to wash the mud and gravel off each log and to keep them rolling down the deck toward the head saw. Monotonous work, but I soon graduated to the green chain; using a trim saw to cut the ends of dimensional lumber as it came off the head saw, and then stacking it in its appropriate pile.

That wasn't as monotonous, but it certainly was far more labor-intensive (wow…what a work-out every eight hours!). For a while, toward the end of my time there, I packed a chain saw in the woods while thinning trees (I never became competent enough to fall big trees), and I operated the logging truck and its loader, loading and hauling logs to the mill.

After working in the mill for about six months, and with my wife four months pregnant with our first child and no way to pay for the impending hospital bills, I walked into an Air Force recruiting office. I had checked out a couple of the other recruiters. The Army had a "high school to flight school" program that interested me. But the war in Viet Nam was still going on at the time and, to my regret now, I had friends that talked me out of doing that.[133] Nevertheless, I saw no long-term future as a mill worker (nor was it something I was interested in doing at the time), so I joined the Air Force as the best opportunity to educate and develop myself. I also saw it as the best way to provide for my young family; a path, perhaps, towards a stable future. If you notice, I didn't say anything about wanting to serve my country; that core value came later. But I was a 20-year-old at the time and only thought about money, food on the table, and a roof over our heads (already more than most 20-year-old kids concern themselves with).

I entered the Air Force in April of 1973 and shipped off immediately to basic training at Lackland Air Force Base in San Antonio, Texas. I'll never forget the day my fixation on education and development hit me like a lightning strike from the heavens. Simply put, after a long hard day of training, we basic trainees were <u>marching</u> in formation toward our evening meal at the dining hall. I glanced toward the parade grounds and saw a bunch of officer trainees <u>walking casually, laughing and joking</u>, toward the Officer Training School Club for a leisurely evening. I turned to a buddy who saw the same thing and said to him "I'm wanna be one of those guys!" Up to that moment, I'd always been, admittedly, a marginal student. I was a C student in high school; focused more on sports and just having fun.[134] When I got into college, I really didn't do much better; more interested in rowing crew at Western Washington University,

---

133   Sure, I've done well since. But my regret now is that I let others influence my life decision that way. I certainly would have been on a different path. But moreover, that I now see no honor in having ducked harm's way at the time.

134   Another aspect of my life's story; I came from a broken home. My parents were divorced when I was six. I changed schools every six months or so until my freshman year of high school. At that point, my high school years became the best years of my life.

for example, than attending classes. However, between junior college and my time at Western, I had amassed about two years worth of transferable credits. Now, I had a career goal…I'm going to OTS and live like one of those guys!

After basic training and technical training school, I showed up to my first assignment at March Air Force Base in Riverside, California. What I remember of that hot August day, so long ago, was this…I had driven on to base, my wife and three-month-old son with me, and proceeded directly to the barracks (nowadays it's called a dormitory; I guess that's much softer sounding for the snowflakes). The procedure in those days was to report to the Charge of Quarters (CQ), who was someone on duty to manage the barracks and be the official greeter of new arrivals to that squadron. I signed in officially, and then he directed me to the base hospital where I was to work, and to contact my supervisor.

MSgt Cariou was a fine NCO, as I learned throughout my assignment at March. But on that day, I made an almost fatal, dumb, green airman mistake. When he was done giving me an overview of the squadron, the hospital and what my duty assignment would be, I finished the conversation by asking him where the base education center was. He asked me why and, of course, I blurted out that I wanted to enroll in college immediately because my goal was to become an officer! Now, this is something a young, newly minted, United States Air Force airman, should <u>never</u> say to a crusty old NCO on the first day. At best you invite ridicule. At worst, you're seen instantly as not properly focused, not a team player…and not one of them.

Sgt Cariou sat me down and gave me a lecture on where my focus needed to be, and it wasn't with the base education center. He all but commanded me, then and there, to give up the notion of a commission, but instead, focus on my Career Development Course (CDCs) and my present career as an Air Force enlisted person.[135] Frankly, Sgt Cariou was right. That was my current job, that's what the Air Force was paying me to do, and that's where my focus should've been. Let's just say, my attitude was adjusted on-the-spot. I said "yes MSgt" and I jumped into my CDC studies within a couple of days (and breezed through them in no time).

135 Every new airman graduates from their respective tech training school with a 3-skill level (apprentice) rating. Once you get to your first duty station you are enrolled in your CDCs; an extension, self-study course that leads to your 5-skill level (journeyman rating). You need your 5-skill level before you can be promoted to Noncommissioned Officer (NCO).

Notwithstanding Sgt Cariou's direction, I still went down to the base education office and quietly enrolled in a night education program to finish my bachelor's degree. I didn't feel then, nor do I today, that I disobeyed any mandate from my boss. I did, in fact, put my CDCs first, as well as everything related to my job as an airman working for him. And I kept quiet about the rest. He was a great boss, and I think I served him well. But that first encounter with him, as well as his failure to realize how easily someone in his position can dash the hopes and dreams of a very junior subordinate, had the opposite effect; it just inspired me to push harder (I wanted to be an officer and there was no way the NCO mafia was going to derail that). It took me about a year and a half to quietly finish my education and build a reputation as an outstanding airman. Toward the end of my college program, and when I began to resurface the notion of a commission, I had all the support, from NCOs up through the command chain, that I needed.

In my case I had a career vision in mind. I was trying to develop my potential while also trying to show it. I saw a brighter future ahead of me and was determined to pursue that. It's amazing what a sudden family responsibility can do to your outlook on the world around you. You begin to look at concepts of accountability, duty, and obligation differently. You begin (at least in my case) to look at things with a slightly more conservative view; views toward money, safety, security, and values – both yours and what you're trying to instill in your child. When I was first married, my perspective on life hadn't really changed that much. Instead of living with my Mom, I was now living with my girlfriend. I was probably still as selfish as I ever was. I certainly didn't take college (or much else) very seriously. But things suddenly became different in my life. I had a <u>family</u>, and the awesome responsibilities that go along with that. It was time to make something of myself. [136]

## The guy that the guy depends on

One night, years ago, I was watching the TV show "West Wing." It was a big hit for a while (running from 1999-2006), and it was about the comings and goings of the White House (all the drama that apparently occurs). It was pure fiction, but it made a nice story, and Martin Sheen

---

[136] I've always said the day Don was born was the happiest day of my life. It was the day I became a father and we became a family. The saddest day of my life was, and will probably always be, the day we lost him 21 years later.

played the President. I didn't watch it regularly, but I caught this particular episode, and it was about Sam Seaborn (played by Rob Lowe), one of the President's top aides, wrestling with the decision about what he should do next in his professional life. The episode went on and on about everyone trying to guess what Sam's decision would be. The path facing him was to remain loyally by the President's side as a top (and very influential) aide, or go home to California and seek the open Congressional seat in his district. Toward the end of the episode, the President called Sam into his office and asked him if he'd decided yet. Sam was still pretty ambivalent. It was at this point the President told Sam that all his life he'd always wanted to be "the guy!" All of his career, leading up to the Presidency, in every position he had, he wanted to be the person in charge, not somebody's deputy or aide; he wanted to be "the guy!" Then he said, "Sam, all you've ever wanted to be is the guy the guy depends on. It's time for you to be <u>the guy</u>."

I was stunned. I sat there on the couch for a moment and then re-wound those last few minutes of the episode. I can't begin to tell you what a profound effect those words had on me then, and still today. All of the training, experience and education I've had over my life and career, and I get a monumental life lesson from a damn TV show! It was one of the greatest wake-up calls that anyone had ever handed me.

I began an immediate self-assessment. Sure, I'd been "the guy" a few times. In the military I'd been in command on four occasions (two Squadrons and two Groups), and my last job was to be the Director of Security Forces for a Major Air Command. But I'd never really been at the top of an organization. And at the time, I was somebody's deputy; watching younger, more politically connected people shoot past me on their way to bigger and better things[137]. I was the guy the guy depended on. By the time this happened I was well into my mid-50s; and, I was leading a personal life that didn't lend itself to relocation. I lived where I lived for a reason and wasn't going anywhere else. That, in itself, was a life (and career) choice. We all face them. Luckily for me, I had a senior leader leave their position early and I became the "acting" leader of the organization for almost two years before moving on. Not exactly how I would have wanted my professional life to end but, again, sometimes personal life <u>situations interv</u>ene.

---

137  To be fair, they were some pretty talented and amazing people (for the most part), and I can't discount the possibility that I had reached my peak; the Peter Principle if you will, where one gets promoted to one position above what they're really competent to perform.

I had a close family member, not long ago, tell me that his boss was starting to add more and more responsibility to his plate. On the one hand, he was excited that he was being seen as someone who could be trusted to handle the added workload, but on the other hand, it might mean less time available for the family. I told him that I couldn't really help him with that decision; everyone who faces this choice has to weigh the pros and cons (if not consequences). It's a personal choice. What I did offer was my own personal history. I told him that <u>not once</u> in my career, did I ever decline additional responsibility. I've always told my bosses "yes, give me whatever you're willing to give up."[138] If they've approached you, then that's certainly an indicator of their faith and trust in you. In this family member's case, I told him that if he did accept the additional responsibility, at some point his leadership would realize the only thing they hadn't given him is the title (promotion) that goes along with it. When I saw him a few days later, he told me that he'd accepted the challenge; he told his boss to give him whatever they were willing to give up. He'd taken the next move on the path toward being "the guy."

Again, everyone has to figure out what motivates them to get ahead; what drives you and what's important to you. The opportunities that are afforded you and your willingness to embrace them as they come will determine how far you go. But I guarantee you, as I sit and write this, chances are <u>you will go nowhere</u> if you squander your professional development obligations, as well as the opportunities that come your way.

The point to this story, and my personal experience, is that you should begin an early mapping of both your professional and personal goals. If you want to be a senior leader down the road, then you need to put yourself on a track that finds, and then takes, the right fork in the road when it is presented; both in opportunity and development. When it's there, take the fork that moves you from being the guy the guy depends on to "the guy."

*"The best way to predict your future is to create it."*
—Abraham Lincoln

---

138  Although there was that time I worked for two guys that I thought abused me. More in a later chapter.

# *Their Development*

*"When you were made a leader, you weren't given a crown, you were given the responsibility to bring out the best in others."*
—Jack Welch

Notwithstanding what I covered in the previous section, I've worked for too many leaders that are far too busy thinking about themselves (their next move, their next promotion, their next pay raise or bonus). I've seen leaders who will hang on to people for the sake of the organization (deny them an assignment essential to their growth, or even a promotion). The truth is, they won't let the person leave (or they certainly won't help them leave) because it might threaten their job security. It's pure selfishness on the leader's part, and I've seen it time and time again.

I was part of an organization not long ago that had elevated a relatively young man (about 40) into a leadership position. The history of that position had been one of instability; it was almost a revolving door. Partly, perhaps primarily, because it was a "burn out" job. It was one that required long days and the rigors of a very fast-paced, if not contentious, political climate. The person in that job was being asked to serve as director of all field operations, which meant also serving as the reporting official for ten regional directors. After a year in the job, this particular individual decided there was more to life than that type of work, in that type of pressure setting. Moreover, he had a very young family and needed to be more available to his kids than the job was allowing. He decided that he needed to get his family out of the Washington DC environment, so he began the process to compete for one of the field positions that was open.[139]

As this young leader applied for that open position, he was blocked at every turn. Senior leadership (and there were two or three above him that were complicit) refused to allow him to apply. When advised they couldn't legally block him from applying, they did refuse to give him an interview (legally their discretion). Why did they do this? They were selfish and irresponsible. They were bureaucrats (in the worst sense); only concerned about the mission, and didn't give a damn about this employee or his

---

139   He was willing to take a step down, literally, as the subordinate for one of the regional directors he was currently supervising. There was a position as the agency's representative in Maine that interested him, so, he applied.

needs, his personal development, or the morale of the larger organization.

What did he do? He quit! He moved his family to Idaho and took a job as a contractor. We, as an organization, lost one of the brightest minds and burgeoning leadership talents that I've ever seen in our business. This guy was the complete package. Had we paid attention to his personal goals we could've kept him within the organization. I was as sure then as I am now that, once his kids were of a certain age, we stood a decent chance of enticing him back into a leadership position somewhere in the organization. Perhaps not, but at least we wouldn't have lost a tremendous resource and talent. Besides, we would've been doing the right thing. Instead, we had leaders that took care of their interests, not those of their employees.

While some bosses will ride a good horse until it drops and then find another horse (like the situation above). I've also seen the opposite of this. My former boss, Colonel Sam Stocks would often say "I'll get rid of my best people first." He was all about developing people and moving them quickly on to bigger and greater things. He felt that if he sent a Stocks protégé out into the world, the return on investment would be exponential. He saw a larger, broader, visionary picture of what could be best for the organization; to have as many allies placed in key positions as possible. That's why, after only working on his staff for a year, he "kick me out" to a joint staff job at CINCPAC headquarters in Hawaii (and there were no complaints from me). Throughout my professional life I've tried to subscribe to the Sam Stocks philosophy of building allies by pushing my best and brightest out of the nest as early as possible.

Let me foot-stomp this point. It's your job as a supervisor, at any level, to make every effort possible to develop your employees. This is one of the key principles of the "sacred trust"; more on that soon. But as a teacher-leader, you should want diverse, talented people that want to be part of a team in search of a common goal; people that want to learn and grow along with you. And make no mistake, learning and growing should definitely include you. You should want people in your workforce that want to be there to work, yes, but to get an education as well; and that education comes in more ways than one.

*"Your reputation and success in life is more often based on choices not chance."*
—Joe Markin, Command Chief Master Sergeant,
United States Air Force (Retired)

## Too cool for school kids

One of my greatest challenges during my years in the FEMA region was in trying to break the culture of "hiring the next up." I'm sure you've heard of the concept, particularly as it relates to furloughs and lay-offs, that "last in, first fired" is how you reduce your workforce in most businesses or corporations. Unions don't like it, but they accept it as the most reasonable way to cull the workforce in hard times. I doubt you could really imagine how many people in FEMA believed that concept to be the unofficial, yet long-practiced, hiring policy for the Agency. Throughout my years, I faced countless challenges over that mindset. Yes, I took guff from rank and file employees that felt "it's my turn" to be hired into that recent opening. Afterall, "I've been here the longest and have put my time in." But often times the most crap I took was from their supervisor who didn't have the foresight to begin a development program for that employee early on, nor did they have the necessary fortitude to look that employee in the eye and explain why they were <u>not</u> the next up. That, my friends, is piss poor leadership at the intermediate level.

Hand-in-hand with that culture was one where many thought continuing education was either unnecessary for a successful career in FEMA, or was just uncool. There was a faction in the region that I dubbed the "too cool for school kids." Convincing them that education was a good thing was an almost impossible task.[140] Once again, it begins with their early development; what their parents taught them.[141] It's also the product of an institutional culture that had not only tolerated but reinforced the notion by years of hiring and promoting under-skilled, under-educated employees for the positions and grades they were holding (some in leadership positions!). I often felt that many of those who might be disgruntled and want to move on would never had been hired by any other agency. As a GS-12 through GS-15, they'd never meet the rigid experience, skill, and educational levels demanded elsewhere in government.

---

140 There was the occasion where they wanted to hire a young kid to be our GIS specialist. He had no formal education in that area, but they "liked him." On another occasion I had a GS-14 supervisor (actually two instances of this) who wanted to compete for a GS-15 position but didn't have any college education. I laid out a path to promotion that was completely unpopular. After I left, I learned that both employees were promoted to GS-15; one without any college education and the other with a degree from an on-line diploma mill. The culture continues.

141 To be clear, I understand the uneven availability of educational opportunity in our nation. It's inconsistent, socially, culturally, economically, and yes, racially. But what I'm referring to here, is a parent's need to instill the drive to dream and pursue.

You've already seen me say that your job as a supervisor is to develop your employees. You want to, you need to, do that for the health of your employees and for that of your organization. Without a diversity of skills, experiences, knowledge, and education, how can you possibly expect to refresh your business practices and to grow; how do you bring in new perspectives and ideas? How do you prepare your employees for the next opportunity in their careers? My biggest frustration was that all of this was disconnected. That last part (preparing employees) was made irrelevant by a culture that didn't push it, recognize it, or reward it; we just promoted people because of their time, not their potential! Even sadder was my realization that if we didn't develop our employees, then we'd probably <u>never</u> get to all those things necessary to move the organization forward. The lesson here? If you have people who fight you every step of the way on employee (moreover, their) development, particularly education and training, perhaps it <u>is</u> time to get rid of them! At least I tried.

## Helping the Marginal or Struggling Employee

My boss called me in one day and told me she had an intermediate supervisor who was struggling and needed direct supervision and guidance. She said that, in fact, what she wanted me to do was take this person under my control, document the incompetency of this supervisor, and develop a case so we could ultimately fire her. I nodded and left the boss's office with an understanding of what she wanted, but to be clear, approaching the issue with an end goal of termination was not how I do business. So, I decided to focus on the supervision and guidance part with a goal of seeing if I could develop and turn this supervisor in the right direction.

I'll cover metrics and performance measures in a later chapter. But if you want to know my views on the ultimate performance measure, it's this: <u>My measure of success is, and always has been, how well I "make" others around me succeed</u> (sometimes in spite of themselves); if they don't, I don't. I take it very personally when any part of the organization fails, or even one individual. I've never placed blame, or deflected my responsibility as a leader. If someone fails, then I failed to take some action that might have corrected that early. Some will say that I'm too hard on myself in this regard, and there are always cases of certain incorrigible individuals. I understand that, but I also believe that it's my job to make every effort before surrendering to defeat.

The long and short of this story is that I took this supervisor under control, developed and implemented a formal performance improvement plan (laying out goals, objectives and timelines for accomplishment). We met, at first, daily. Then later it was weekly. I gave her constant feedback while setting her on a course toward redemption. The result? She flourished under those conditions. Within a few months she was back in her old position and continued on with her career; we kept her.[142]

Don't be so quick to give up on people that are seemingly problems. That's nothing more than a cheap, coward's way out. You're being paid to be a supervisor and leader. Supervise and lead! Besides, when you dig deeply into some of these issues you might find there are other underlying causes than simple incompetence or even intransigence. There might be something else going on in the individual's life that's affecting their performance. Dig deeper.

**Other Things to Consider**

As you approach your style of leadership mentoring and development, consider some of these things:

Give them candid advice about everything. In my view, "too much" advice is never too much. Share your stories about even the most mundane of things if it leads to their better understanding of how things work and/or how they might be perceived (Um, like what I'm doing with this book?). I used to counsel young security forces officers on the importance of knee-high socks and V-neck tee shirts. You're probably saying what? Yes, socks and tee shirts. I was counselled by a General Officer one time that the unwritten rule of dress and appearance among Air Force officers was that senior leadership doesn't want to see skin when you sit and cross your legs, nor do they want to see a white tee shirt showing when you wear an open collar shirt. I said "yes sir", and filed that away as an important tip. My counsel to young officers was this; we already wear a funny looking beret (in the view of others), so we need to do whatever subtle things we can to blend in with the rest of the Air Force. Afterall, it's those guys that are going to determine how far up you move in your career. The more important point to this is, in most cases, people won't get tired of you talking to them; they'll enjoy the fact that you take the time to do so. Tell your little stories!

---

142 My boss wasn't very happy with me. All she ever saw was a problem she didn't want to deal with and she wanted me to make it go away. My boss retired shortly thereafter.

At least you'll entertain them, and you might even impart a few nuggets of wisdom in the process.

Give them duties that are commensurate with their grade and position, but duties that might teach them a positive lesson and will help them grow; sometimes duties that will test, stretch and challenge both their skills and temperament. I was a young second lieutenant, just signed into McChord Air Force Base in 1975, when my squadron told me to report to the Wing Protocol Office for an additional duty.[143] They also told me I'd needed to wear my dress blues. When I got there, I was told that I'd be accompanying the base honor guard that day for a graveside service at a local cemetery; I would be the officer in charge of the burial service. They handed me a 3x5 card with these words on it; "This flag is presented on behalf of a grateful nation, in honor of the faithful and dedicated service of your loved one." (I still have the card.) The protocol officer told me to memorize those words.

On the way over, the NCO in charge of the honor guard told me the sad story of a young active duty couple who were stationed in Germany. They were involved in a car wreck. She survived, but he didn't. When we got to the cemetery, the Chaplain met me and said that after the flag folding, I was to present the flag to the young lady, dressed in green at the end of the front row; she was the surviving spouse. As the ceremony started, I stood at attention at the head of the casket. Let me tell you now, this whole thing was a set-up from the start. Not that it was fake, because it certainly wasn't. It was very real and sad. But the honor guard knew what was in store for me and didn't say a word.

I stood at the head of the casket, at attention, when the first volley was fired. I think we all flinched, at least I did. More importantly, the crying (which had been muffled to that point) really started in earnest. Then the second volley, and a little more crying. Then the third volley, and even more crying. Then the bugler began to play taps. By this time, the family and friends were in a full-on wail, and were primed and ready for my follow-on act. Hell, I was almost crying at this point! The honor guard carefully folded the flag, passed it on down to the NCO in charge, who, with a smirk on his face, handed it to me. I did a right-face maneuver and

143 Every base has additional duties that need to be done, commensurate with rank. I was once tasked to be a team member for an independent audit of the Officers Club; we counted every knife and fork, every chair, and even the carpet and the parking lot (yes, even that had a stock number attached to it. I went outside and said "yup, still there, one each parking lot. Check!")

what did I see? A front row of grieving, crying family members…with a girl in a green dress…on each end! I did a quick "eany, meany, minnie, moe" in my head and went to the right end of the row, took a knee, and began…"This flag is presented on behalf of…" It was at this point the Chaplain, at the other end of the row, cleared his throat and said "Um, Lt…down here." It had suddenly gotten quiet. The crying had stopped. I looked up at the crowd and they were aghast! You should've seen the looks on their faces.

With a mortified look on her face, I snatched the flag out of the hands of the girl in the green dress and hustled on down to the other end of the row. I took a knee, recited the words, handed the flag over, and then headed straight for the bus (just about as fast as you just read it). By the time I got to the bus, most of the honor guard was rolling on the ground with hysterical laughter. I was pissed!

When we got back to base, I walked into the protocol office and told them, I quit![144] I said do with me what you will; file charges against me if you must, but I'm never doing that again. I told them that never mind how embarrassing it was to me, it ruined a ceremony that should have been somber, dignified, and respectful. We failed at that. I failed because I wasn't properly trained, or even briefed. My suggestion was to find a Lt on base that loves the drill and ceremonies type of work and make them the permanent officer in charge of the honor guard. Such a person would be able to train and practice with the team regularly. This is pretty much how the Air Force does it now, and I certainly don't take any credit for that. But this incident was, and still is, the most embarrassing moment of my entire professional career. Yet, sometimes it does take embarrassing moments for lessons to be etched deeply into your psyche.

Honestly, I laugh about it all these years later. But the point to this story was supposed to be about giving employees duties that will test, stretch, challenge, and help them grow. This certainly did for me. It stretched me in ways that I never thought possible, at least at that point in my young life. It also taught me about the things one should or should not include in the portfolio for training a young leader.

---

144   I was supposed to do that duty for another week.

# *Our Development*

I worked for an Air Force Colonel by the name of Loren Rodway. In my eyes, this man was, is, a prince among men. I owe an awful lot to Colonel Rodway; my assignment to the Pentagon, my early promotion to Lieutenant Colonel, my senior service school selection, the freedom he gave me in and out of the office to represent him and the organization with only the slightest (but when necessary) bit of guidance and direction, his mentorship (about so many things), and most of all his true friendship.

What Loren Rodway taught me was to <u>push</u>, not just help, the truly deserving people around you; to take exceptionally good care of all your subordinates. I worked for him for a couple of years in the Pentagon, when we were both assigned to the Office of the Assistant Secretary of Defense for Special Operations and Low Intensity Conflict (ASD-SOLIC). He ran the counterterrorism office for a while, and I served as one of his CT officers.[145] Of the many things I learned from him was the concept of servant leadership…at least how he practiced it. More than anyone I ever worked for, he taught me there is (or at least should be) more of a symbiotic relationship between leader and employees. You need each other. You, as the leader, have what they want and they have what you need as well; that we're all in this thing together. It's the <u>one big thing</u> I've been leading up to.

## The Sacred Trust of Leadership

Have you ever thought about what really motivates you to go to work every day? Perhaps even more important, why you work so hard to climb your respective ladder? Even more important than that, how did it all happen, and what is my responsibility regarding all this?

The fact is, people helped you along the way. Sometimes it was in small, subtle gestures. Other times it was a major boost. But to get where you're at right now, someone helped make that happen. Name me one person in this world that was truly a self-made man or woman. If you do, I guarantee you that if we pour over their life, we'll see several critical points where there was a hand extended somewhere along the way.

I remember when, while on the campaign trail in 2012, President

---

145 He was the third of my three bosses while there (Boink and Woolard), but he was assigned to the office for most of the time I was there.

Obama said "You didn't build that." He took a lot of heat for it, and in proper context, that quote related to rich people growing their businesses on their own. At the time, the President was trying to make his point that government also had a hand in helping the rich succeed. That statement resonated with me at the time, as it still does today. Many small business owners took great offense to his assertion that they weren't the ones that put all the hard work into building their businesses. But I look at it in a broader context of opportunity, not just how hard you worked to get it done. So, when you really think about it, somewhere along the line, someone gave you a hand-up. Big or small, somebody created an opportunity for you.

What is the sacred trust of leadership that I've been alluding to? If I needed to put it into one word, simply put, it would be <u>opportunity</u>; and, that you have a responsibility to provide the same opportunity to others that you had. More than just opportunity, or even professional development, it's a genuine sense of taking care of your troops. It's your opportunity now to build that trust they ultimately put into you, your mission, and your goals and objectives. It's where they learn to follow you because they know you have their interests at heart.

So why are we all in this game? We all want a better life for ourselves, and in many cases, for our families and loved ones. We're no different than the other guy or gal next to us, above us, or yes…especially below us. They all want the same things you want. <u>The people that work for you want what you have.</u> You, in turn, aspire to have your boss's job. The "sacred trust of leadership" is recognizing early, and embracing, the concept of developing your employees for that next step. Yes, your boss also hired you to get the mission accomplished. But the sacred trust is as equally important. That's your job too! You owe it to your workforce to provide them opportunities! What they do with those opportunities is completely up to them, but make sure the opportunities are there. I've held this belief close to my heart for decades. I learned it a long time ago, but it was reinforced by the way good bosses treated me and bad bosses didn't. Driven home by the way leaders like Colonel Rodway took care of me, I began to realize that in developing employees, you had to start inwardly with an understanding and acceptance that we're all in this for the same things. I want to move up, and the people working for me do too! I have an obligation to take care of that need (even before mine). Somewhere along the line, someone helped you. Now pay it forward!

There are definitely times when honoring the sacred trust means a sacrifice of your own. Several years ago, Harvard started a Senior Leadership Program in Homeland Security. Its inaugural class was held in the fall of 2004. I applied and was accepted, and then the hurricanes of 2004 hit Florida and the deep south and I found myself deployed. My participation was cancelled. I was told sometime later by a senior FEMA member that Harvard had called directly to the FEMA Director, Mike Brown, to plead on my behalf. They told him it was the inaugural course, they needed a FEMA representative, and with my experience and education, I was the guy they wanted. Mike Brown refused to yield; citing the on-going hurricane support.[146] I harbored no real ill feelings about that; although I'm convinced that if I'd been one of Mike's political appointees, the response back to Harvard would've been different. There were other opportunities over the subsequent years to go to Harvard, but I didn't pursue them. Instead, as class slots were given to the Region, I sent my subordinates. While a plum career credential, Harvard was needed more by my younger employees, at that point, than it was by me. Please don't take this as some kind of "woe is me" self-martyrdom. I did it because I thought it was right and I wanted to do it. I felt then, as I do now, that I was fulfilling the sacred trust, and I'd do it again and again.

To the extent that you are able to genuinely convey this heartfelt goal (promotions, awards, good assignments, better education, professional development), the more success as an organization you will realize. You'll also feel pretty damn good about yourself too.

Conversely, there are people who will just sap the life out of their employees. Years ago, I worked for a couple of Army Special Forces Lieutenant Colonels while working in the Special Operations Division at USCINCPAC in Hawaii. Now, I'd say, as an Air Force guy, that it's an Army thing. The truth is, I've worked for some pretty spectacular Army guys.[147] But these two guys were a different breed. Accomplished war heroes in their own right, they nevertheless were not polished in the intricacies of human resource management; they were not people people. On one occasion, during the party celebrating my promotion to Major, they left me in the office to run a last-minute package (getting all the necessary staff coordination, and then the four-star signature) while they went over to the club and drank all the liquor and ate all the food that I'd paid for in

---

146 Ironically, I had already been released from Florida and back to the Region as all this was going on.

147 LTC Joe Jakubowski was one. When I finally go him as my boss for my last year in Hawaii, we finally started having a blast.

advance. When I got there, everything and all the people were gone except these two guys. They had nothing to say except "sorry you missed it." On every occasion, their policy was that if you flew all night from the far east back to Hawaii and arrived early morning (which is the only way you can do that from most locations), you should come into the office and work all day; that's after having worked all day at the other end. These may seem like just minor nuisances, but they treated me like their personal servant. They did nothing for my personal or professional growth. While I've resented them for that, I thank them for the many things I learned from that experience that I never wanted to do as a leader.

Yes, a good leader will focus on the care and needs of his employees. It's as easy as that. Yet, as demonstrated above, it seems like it's one of the hardest qualities to find in leaders at every level. Even within the most senior positions of government or private business we find occasional leaders that are indifferent to their employees.

Again, we're all in it together. Everyone working for me, to include me, and those over me, all come to work every day for the same things. We all want to get ahead. We all want to provide for our families. We all want to be successful. We all want material things and non-material satisfaction in what we've accomplished. And we all want the same opportunities that our boss got to achieve all that. My job as a leader (my sacred trust to employees) is to provide them the same opportunities I got (that includes their personal and professional development). The same opportunities that Loren Rodway (and countless others in my career) ensured that I got. Employees are hoping I'll deliver, and I MUST do so. There's no reason for me not to; I need to do it only because it's the right thing to do! When I do deliver, I'm certain my employees will follow me anywhere.

To be clear here, I'm talking about providing opportunity, not what this nation seems to have devolved into; handouts and free stuff. And I'm not talking about just your favorite, most trusted troops. I'm talking about every cat that's working for you; across the board. If you fail in this endeavor you are a failed leader. Period. Nothing else in this book will help you. Give it up and go home! Put the tools in your employees' hands, give them guidance and direction, and allow them the space to grow. It boils down to this, the one question all subordinates ask: "You're going to take care of me, right boss?" Depending on how you answer that question, in words and deeds, will dictate your success. When it's no longer about you, but about everyone around you, then you've truly become a leader.

## Self-Promotion

I've never had the stomach for self-promotion. I don't particularly like seeing it in others, but more importantly, I try to completely avoid exercising it myself. To me, it's repugnant. It makes me more than uncomfortable. I've seen more than one leader tactically position himself in front of the boss just to be noticed. He wants to be seen as the guy with all the answers, and more often than not, to take all the credit. It's very unbecoming.

Me? I want to dish the credit out and, where possible, push the troops in front of the boss. Consequently, I never took much credit for <u>anything</u> and it was probably detrimental to my career. I don't want to sound overly magnanimous or heroic, but it's the truth. I don't necessarily recommend it in every case. You probably need to be a self-promoter (or at least visible) to some extent or they'll never know who you are. However, my philosophy was to spread the credit not only where credit was due but, to some extent, to who needed it the most.

I discussed in a previous chapter, the Nuclear Surety Inspection (NSI) we went through at Fairchild Air Force Base in 1995. It was a glorious performance in a critical inspection, at a critical time, by an entire 440-person unit. I doubt that, still today, any unit has ever achieved the same. We were rock stars on base, as well as throughout the entire major command. The higher headquarters inspection team chief designated each member of the squadron, Exceptional Performers! Usually this designation only goes to a handful of people. My wing commander held a very high opinion of me, and my just rewards were realized a few months later when I received his highest recommendation for my promotion to Colonel. But I took every opportunity I could to down-play my role in the outcome, and deferred that glory to others. Here's an example of that, and one of my greatest triumphs:

Benny Martin had been my Operations Officer for almost a year. Benny was a prior-enlisted Captain who had been passed over to Major for two cycles in a row. The Defense Officer Personnel Management Act (DOPMA) of 1980, the federal law standardizing military personnel actions, mandated that anyone being passed over twice would need to separate within a specified period of months. However, in Benny's case, he had 18 total years of service. In those cases, the individual is allowed to remain on active duty to complete a 20-year career. By all accounts, Benny's career was done. He would never get promoted, and would retire as a Captain. In fact, he had already begun job interviews.[148]

Benny walked into my office one day with a personnel notice that said he was being considered for promotion to Major on the upcoming board. He and I were confused by that, so I called the director of personnel on base. Benny and I were both shocked to learn there's a seldom used clause in the regulations that said if a person was still on active duty, their records would meet every promotion board until they were no longer on active duty, regardless of how many times they'd been passed over. Benny kind of shrugged it off, but I immediately went into high gear. We put together a promotion package for the Wing Commander with a recommendation that he push Benny this one time for promotion. It wasn't long before I got a call from the boss…"What the hell are you doing?"

My promotion announcement in 1996.

I went to the boss's office and only needed to make one short argument. "Boss, we gave you probably the greatest triumph in NSI history. You and this wing are the toast of the command right now. This is the guy that made it happen. He's a dynamic leader, and the troops followed him to victory. He gave his all for the wing, and it's time (and right) for you to give

148 Benny's failure to get promoted had nothing to do with his performance. It was the result of a board system that reviewed a person's educational experience (officers were expected to have a masters degree at the time). Benny had never completed a graduate degree. That system has since changed to mask any civilian education.

him your endorsement." The General thought about it for a moment, and then signed the promotion recommendation and handed it back to me. He said "you realize that without a masters degree he's likely to be non-selected again." I said "perhaps, but your recommendation carries a lot of weight, so we'll see." Three months later Benny was on the promotion list with a line number of 1 (meaning of the couple thousand Captains being promoted, he'd be first!). Benny Martin got the credit he deserved, and went on to retire as a Lieutenant Colonel.

A similar opportunity came very late in my career. In fact, it was my last assignment on active duty. I was the Director of Security Forces for a Major Command. As the senior security forces Director, and senior security advisor to the 4-star Commander, I led a staff of approximately thirty-five commissioned and non-commissioned officers. Our job was to provide support and guidance to twelve major installations in the US as well as thousands of deployed forces around the globe. Now, it's important to frame this story, by saying this up front; the men and women working at a Major Command are hand-picked by their Director with the goal of finding senior staff that are highly self-motivated, dedicated, and totally committed to the mission. Simply put, these are people the Air Force sees as possessing the <u>most potential</u> for success.

One of these professionals was a Lieutenant Colonel who was coming up for promotion to Colonel. This officer was the text book role-model; motivated, loyal, committed to his superiors and subordinates, and above all else possessed the highest integrity. The phrase "Right Stuff" was often used to describe him. In the Air Force that phrase is reserved for individuals possessing traits like those portrayed by such legends as Brigadier General Chuck Yeager, the first man to break the sound barrier. And while this guy didn't come from the hills and hollers of West Virginia like Yeager, he did grow up in deprived regions of the South. He knew disparity, but rather than let it drag him down, gained strength from its challenges. So when it came time for his records to go before the board for promotion, he was my first choice...a logical choice! However, there was only one snag, he was struggling with his required education (Air War College by seminar) and wasn't scheduled for final testing until after the cut-off for indorsement by a General Officer.

I worked for an archaic thinker (in my opinion); a 3-star General who was not sympathetic to the situation or this officer at all. So, going into the meeting I suspected I had a fight on my hands. To this day, I struggle as to why the General was reluctant to recommend this officer for promotion. I can only speculate that it was because of preference or bias towards non-flyers, lack of first-hand knowledge regarding the individual's career accomplishments, or he failed to see the individual's full potential. If you lead people long enough, you're going to encounter these sorts of professional challenges. And if you cave to the pressure early in your debate, you've simply given validation to your boss that you weren't totally committed to your position. I watched several young officers fall into this trap on occasion. And before they knew it, they carried the reputation within the organization as…weak on leadership, weak on confidence, weak on commitment and weak on loyalty.

I went to see the 3-star and as I entered his office, I was greeted with almost outright hostility…so my instincts were right. He was hell-bent on resisting my efforts to push this officer. It was probably the tensest meeting I've ever had with a General Officer. The words we exchanged, about whether or not my guy was worthy, aren't nearly as important as the tenor and tone of the meeting. At a point in the argument, the General grew tired of my persistence and, despite his own objections, grabbed his pen, signed the promotion recommendation and threw it at me…"Get out of my office." My mission was a success, but the stakes were high. If my guy failed the final exam, and failed to get promoted, then both of our careers would be over.

And now, as Paul Harvey would say is, "the rest of the story."[149] The Lieutenant Colonel went on to make Colonel that promotion cycle; and, to validate my instincts and recognition of the highest <u>potential</u>, he went on to even bigger and better things. The most valuable lesson I took from this experience was this: When a subordinate is as committed to you as you are to him or her, don't let anything stand in your way when it comes to mutual respect. Fight the fight, winner take all! Why, because eventually you'll have to look at yourself in the mirror and ask the question, would he have done the same for me? Yes, he would have. Good Day!

I've already said it, my style was to use our accomplishments to promote others, not myself. I did that on active duty and again in my civilian federal job. I don't know if I was naïve through all those years, but I seemed

---

149 Paul Harvey was an American radio broadcaster who was famous for his *"The Rest of the Story"* broadcasts. You millennials probably need to go ask your parents about this one. He'd always end his program with a resounding "Good Day!"

to come out of it ok. I certainly miscalculated when I thought the system would take care of me. As for you, just understand as a leader at any level, it's a world of self-promotion. All you have to do is look around you. I don't discourage you from self-promoting. Some of it is necessary. Again, your bosses need to know who you are and what you've been doing. Just don't become obsessed with it at the expense of your troops. At some point, you have to look in the mirror and ask yourself how much of that (self-promotion) is really in your character as well. It wasn't in mine. I don't want to make myself out as some kind of hero, because I'm not. Maybe just dumb. It just wasn't, isn't, in my DNA. It's not who I am. For that reason, I'm probably lucky to have gotten as far as I did.

*"The day the soldiers stop bringing you their problems is the day you stopped leading them. They have either lost confidence that you can help them or concluded that you do not care. Either case is a failure of leadership."*
—Colin Powell

# 8

# Leadership Cop-Outs

## (TQM, MBO, meta-leadership, telecommuting and other administrative nonsense)

*"Management is doing things right; leadership is doing the right things."*
—Peter F. Drucker

First off, the title of this chapter was just to get your attention. I'm really not that opposed to some of tools of the trade that have surfaced over the past few decades. Things like Total Quality Management (a focus on customers, suppliers, and continuous improvement), or Management by Objectives have been wonderful tools to help leaders apply form and function to their organization. That said, I've seen senior leaders go all in on some of these, to the point of relinquishing their own artful style of leadership in favor of the more precise methods of one of these "crutches." In my view, these are just support mechanisms to help you determine the health of your organization, or aids to help you measure your progress; all valuable if applied responsibly. Nevertheless, <u>a leader still has to lead</u>. Sorry, millennials, no there hasn't been an App developed yet to help you with this.

Dallas Willard talks about how Christians should not be counted, but weighed. In an article in *"Leadership* Journal", Dr. Willard said "Many churches are measuring the wrong things. We measure things like attendance and giving, but we should be looking at more fundamental things like anger, contempt, honesty, and the degree to which people are under the thumb of their lusts. Those things can be counted, but not as easily as offerings."[150] This is a concept that I've long agreed with. Christians shouldn't be measured by how many times they've been seen at church or by what they put in the collection plate. If that were the case, then it's no wonder why so many people think I'm such a heathen. In fact, they shouldn't be measured by man at all. Instead, whatever judgement is passed

---

150 "How Do We Assess Spiritual Growth?: An interview in *Leadership* Journal", May 2010, Dallas Willard, http://www.dwillard.org/articles/individual/how-do-we-assess-spiritual-growth

shouldn't be in terms of quantity, but in quality; what's in their heart. Only God knows that.

The same could be said, perhaps should be said, for leaders as well... their leadership prowess should be weighed, not measured. For far too long senior leadership at every level and throughout every sector (from academia to business to government) has placed an extraordinary level of emphasis on <u>counting</u> our performance. Goals, objectives, performance measures, and metrics by which to measure have, over decades, become the standard. Somehow, we've lost focus on what truly counts…how well does a man or woman lead? And how do you truly measure that? I think it's measured in the <u>quality</u> of a leader's performance. Is he or she a calming influence over the temperament of the organization? Does the organization reflect the personality of the leader, and just what does that personality look like? Is the leader caring, compassionate, decisive, fair and consistent? Are they a "team" under this leader? How well does this leader develop his or her employees? It's this last question that tells me the most about an organization and its leadership. As mentioned previously, are they more focused on their careers or those of their employees? Just look around to see who's getting all the good school slots.

Don't get me wrong, at least part of my focus has always been on the extrinsic, objective performance measurements handed down by my senior leadership; it's been mandated, forced on me, so I've obediently complied throughout the years. But I've also tried to equally divide my attention toward building and mentoring good leaders through some of the artful tools I've discussed in previous chapters.

## *Technology*

Without question, advances in technology have made the modern leader's job a whole lot easier. It's also made life for workers easier and more comfortable and, consequently, has aided in mitigating long-standing morale issues.

As a young airman, I was never more excited than the day the Air Force took away my old Royal manual typewriter (yes, we had those when I first came in) for a new IBM Selectric (yes, those have been long gone for some time now too). I remember my first computer, and so many other tools that made my job easier.

I'm standing in front of a static display Turkish F-86 at Erhac AB in 1979. Sometime after this photo was taken, we had a young troop get drunk, climb into the airplane, close the canopy, and then couldn't get out. In his panic he began to pull every lever he could find. None of us were aware (including the Turkish officials) that the airplane still had an active ejection seat. The Airman ejected himself through the canopy and was killed instantly. It was tragic for all of us, and was the only instance in my 42-year career that I ever lost someone.

In 1979, as a young officer, I spent a year in northeastern Turkey at a very remote site at Erhac Air Base; a Turkish base with a small American detachment. In those days, to call home, you were patched through our operations center, to the international operator in Ankara, to the nearest Air Force base in the states, who would dial your home phone number for you. We were given 5 minutes a month! Five minutes to say hi to your wife and each of the kids and then goodbye to your wife; with all those connections, on what was effectively a party line.[151] Then fast-forward to 1996, when I spent a year on the Arabian Peninsula and had both internet and email. Life was much better for the deployed troop then, when you could communicate daily with family and friends. Today, troops (as I

151 We would send our "Airman of the Month" to another remote site in eastern Turkey (Diyarbakir) because they had a direct satellite link into Cheyenne Mountain, and their troops could talk as often and for as long as they wanted.

understand) are able to call home via cell phone as often as they need; not to mention video chats.

So, things have gotten better over the years through technology, and leaders today need to be thankful for relief of some of the challenges their predecessors faced. However, if you're an Air Force senior commander today, and you've never seen troops "hump" a post in the weapons storage area for an eight-hour shift, day after day, often in a driving rain storm (or worse yet, a blizzard) because sensors didn't exist yet, you have no real idea what morale issues are. For that matter, if you haven't taken the time to see what today's security forces member goes through on post, in most deployed areas around the world, you probably have no real appreciation for what a true leadership challenge is.[152]

Air Force security troop on the hump at Dover AFB in the late 1970s. Also, the same type of post where I found a troop kicking a pebble along the miniature golf course he'd built. (Official U.S. Air Force photo)

Don't get me wrong on this issue either. I'm extremely happy our career field, our Air Force, has developed to the point it has. We have sensors, cameras and other technology that makes life on post so much better for our troops. In the late 1990's, I was pushing for better weapons (we fielded the M-4 rifle by the time I left), and better gates (I pushed for heated

152 Admittedly, I'm biased. I like to think I came from the meanest, toughest career field the Air Force ever had to offer. But there are, certainly, others in and out of the military that face their own unique challenges.

sidewalks for gate guards to stand on) among many other things. My argument in the security business has always been: We, as humans, are horrible detectors, but we're great responders. Let, technology do the hard, tedious stuff (with fences, walls, gates, locks, alarms, sensors, cameras), and let the troops focus on the things we do well (human reaction, discrimination, and then response).

All of this said about technology, don't allow it to somehow lull you into a false sense of responsibility when it comes to making the hard decisions involving people. With all the toys in the world, it's still Airman Snuffy that's playing with them! He needs, deserves, and will respect your attention.

## *Metrics*

Metrics are a way of life in the Air Force (the military in general), most government, and probably most businesses as well. They are, in fact, a valuable tool for showing comparative trends (from month to month or year to year) on all aspects of an operation. In the Air Force, they're used to track flying hours, fuel consumption, accident rates, budget expenditures, and so on. As I said, they're a valuable tool, but not a replacement for good old-fashioned leadership. I've seen senior leaders get so wrapped-up in managing their organization with metrics they've forgotten how to get down into the trenches and communicate with their employees on real and personal issues. Or, perhaps like water always looking for the path of least resistance, they've found it much easier and far less stressful to just focus on a bunch of charts as their measure for success. If you recall, my measure of success is how well I've made/helped others succeed; not in just the things measured by metrics, but in their personal and professional development as well. You can't do that by sitting in your office and flipping slides!

Next, is a short story (my favorite) about my long-standing regard for the over-importance that management by metrics carries. Read on for another example of "it's a wonder he got as far as he did."

In 1984, as a young Captain and commander of the Security Police Squadron at Peterson AFB, I was not a huge fan of metrics. We (the Wing staff) presented a metrics presentation to the Wing Commander twice a month (half of the Wing's metrics at one meeting and then the other half two weeks later; every month). It was monotonous and tedious. Moreover, I thought at the time that it was a level of micromanagement that was unnecessary. To top all that off, it exposed me to public criticism twice a month for sometimes things I couldn't control (Why did Airman Smith from the maintenance squadron get busted for a DUI? "Umm…his commander is sitting in the room. Maybe we should ask him?"). Anyway, now you know how I felt about metrics at the time.

Brigadier General Ralph Spraker was a crusty old guy with a serious personality and demeanor, but he did (luckily for me) have a sense of humor. As I sat in a staff meeting one morning where countless slide after slide kept coming up on various measures of performance throughout the Wing, they finally got to the Transportation Squadron's slides reflecting vehicle abuse rates for the previous month. So you know, vehicle abuse was a big deal in the Air Force at the time, and I assume it still is. The combination of accident damage, poor or inappropriate maintenance, and outright malicious destruction can cost tax payers millions, and often that comes directly out of the Wing's budget. Every month when these slides were presented, Gen Spraker would become furious; sometimes at the circumstances of the incident and sometimes at the action (or lack of) that a particular commander would take to correct it. Well, this month I had a vehicle that was about to be briefed, and I had personally seen to this particular slide.

As soon as the slide appeared there was a muffled laugh across the room. The format for the slide reflected several columns; date, location, vehicle type and registration number, damage, and corrective action. My slide reflected all the appropriate information, but for vehicle type it listed pickup, for damage it listed "padded dash destroyed beyond repair", and for corrective action it said "offender has been castrated."

Now, Gen Spraker always sat at the head of the table, but my seat in the conference room was always directly behind him. He studied that slide for a moment and then spun his chair around and looked at me. Then he looked at the slide again, and then back to me. With a slight grin he said "you wanna explain that Captain?"

As straight-faced as I could be, I said "Sir, this was a K-9 patrolman and his dog. The Handler had gotten out of his truck to write a traffic ticket and left his dog in the front seat of the truck.

My Wing Commander at Peterson in 1983,
Brigadier General Ralph Spraker.

The dog became agitated and destroyed the entire dash before the patrolman could get back to the truck in time. We've fixed the problem...the Vet castrated the dog and we shouldn't have any further issues."[153]

By this time, General Spraker could hardly constrain himself. He spun back around in his chair and looked out over all the other squadron commanders and said "Jesus! The next time one of you sons of bitches has a vehicle abuse I'm sending you to Hunsinger!" It was hilarious. I was a sudden metrics hero. For years, as I saw former Peterson colleagues around the Air Force, they'd bring up that staff meeting. I just thought it was the most appropriate use of metrics at the time.

---

153 Anyone that knows dogs will understand what neutering of an adult male dog will do to his disposition.

## *Telecommuting*

Okay, call me a dinosaur. I don't really like telecommuting either. Sure, it's a wonderful tool to allow employees the comforts of home, from time to time. Notice I said "allow" and "time to time." The problem with telecommuting, as we get deeper into the 21st century, is that it's almost become an employee right, and it's more and more all the time. Worse yet, it's been abused incessantly. In my last job, the agency was trying to save money. In order to curb administrative and real property expenses, they allowed many of us to work out of our homes. I dedicated a spare bedroom as my office and did that for three years. Since I was three hours behind Washington DC, I can't remember how many times I crawled out of bed at 6 AM to be on a conference call in my pajamas.[154] Sounds great, right? Well it was! But throughout the day, nobody knew where I was or what I was doing. I could've been out walking my dog, running errands at the store, or working a part-time job from that little bedroom office. I wasn't! I was one of the diligent ones that accounted honestly for every hour. I sat at my computer addressing the mountain of paperwork sent to me by headquarters, as well as conversing with my field employees, sometimes hourly. But there's no proof of that. You'll just have to take my word for it, as headquarters did at the time.[155]

Others were not so honest and, occasionally, we'd catch them goofing off and then lying about it. I had one employee report that his government vehicle had been broken into. His credentials, computer, cell phone, and other items were all stolen. As it turns out, he was in a part of town that was never addressed on his calendar (he had no appointments there for that day). There were other irregularities about his story (like, why was he anywhere without his credentials and cell phone?). In the end, our investigation found that he had a gym membership across the street from where his car was parked. On government time, he was going to the gym everyday for a couple of hours.

As you can see, from just my experience, how easy it is to abuse the concept. During my final years at FEMA we were beginning to allow employees to telecommute more and more. It was a program that headquarters

154 I feel no guilt about that since my official duty hours were 7:30 to 4. Nevertheless, I use it to make a point about both the flexibility and potential
155 I have admitted the biggest danger to telecommuting as being the proximity of the refrigerator. It was far too easy to get hungry and go grab a snack.

was beginning to embrace as a morale booster and, from their perspective, something that would be extremely efficient as the agency was beginning to issue government cell phones to every employee. I think we were also trying to recruit and retain more millennials at that point and studies, as well as social media evidence, suggested that more quality time at home was more attractive to prospective employees than more pay. So, we jumped on the telecommute bandwagon.

As a leader, at any level of an organization, have you ever had a situation come up where you needed to respond to a customer <u>right now</u>? You walk (sometimes run) down the hall to find "the guy that knows everything" about this issue, only to find that he's telecommuting today. I can't begin to tell you how many times that has happened to me. My primary argument against telecommuting has always been one of quality (and timely) customer support. How can you run a customer service agency when your primary customer (ours was any one of the four states or the 273 federally recognized tribes in Region 10) calls to find their designated liaison, and he's out for the day telecommuting? In many cases, even if they contacted him at home, there wasn't much he could do for them if the issue required documents or maps back at the office. That said, I'm sure as time moves on, technology advancements will probably resolve many of my concerns.

I do, however, agree that telecommuting does have its place. There are industries where telecommuting is highly efficient; those where everything is done in isolation, either by phone or computer (telemarketing calls, for instance). I knew a person whose job was to take court audio transcripts and transcribe them into written documents. She did this at home on her computer. In her case, telecommuting made sense. There are certainly other cases where working from home makes sense, occasionally, within government. But I urge leaders to allow its use judiciously.

## *Cell Phones, email, and Social Media*

Don't let your employees communicate with you exclusively by texting. None of us like bad news to begin with. If I'm getting bad news (or giving it), there are often more questions that come up than you can effectively deal with through a text message. Texting, as well as email, are best used in those situations as a vehicle for setting up a follow-on call or meeting.

But when it's important stuff, call me! Better yet, come and see me. I have a friend who runs a small business that said he's told his employees "I don't want you texting me to tell me you're home sick for the day. I want to hear it directly from you."

Email and, especially, Twitter (if not more dangerous) are as ineffective as texting. So much is lost in an email exchange; context and tone being the two biggest. You wouldn't believe how many times I've had to read an email (over and over) in an attempt to decipher its meaning. Similarly, I've had employees come into my office (some after agonizing over it for days) sheepishly thinking I was upset with them over an issue. "No, don't ever read into one of my emails for some hidden message. If I'm dissatisfied, you'll hear about it in person." In the case of Twitter…it lends itself to even more misinterpretation when you're limited to only 140 characters. Use these platforms sparingly, and with absolute discretion, at all times, but particularly when trying to convey messages to your employees.

## *Other Unnecessary Distractions*

Asbestos, perfume, dogs, dust…yes, these are just some of the many seemingly minor irritants that can blow up and ruin your day if you're not paying attention. There are countless others, and it's a failure of leadership (at every level) to not address these issues before they get to the hysterical stage.

We had a contractor come in to re-design our restroom facility in the basement floor of our building. It was a 1950s vintage underground bunker. As the contractor got into the demolition phase, he found asbestos in several locations. At the very moment that he posted a sign "Do not enter—Asbestos abatement in progress" panic began to spread throughout the building. Now, I've been in a number of locations where asbestos had been found and measures taken to correct the problem (you should spend some time in the Pentagon). I know it's a serious, but totally treatable situation. In fact, my own home in Virginia was built in the early 70s with air conditioning duct work that was asbestos-based. I was advised to just leave it alone and make no attempt to disturb it. Similarly, when I was a kid, my grandmother had a stove with a sheet of asbestos abutting one wall next to it. It is, and has been, around for a long time. Today, when found, we contract (very expensively) to have it removed.

As the asbestos situation in our building began to unfold (as the hysteria began to escalate), I brought the contractor, select members of the staff, and a representative from the Occupational Safety and Health Administration (OSHA), into my office for a thorough briefing on the issue, and our course of action. The contractor said he had complied with all of the industry-mandated safety measures (screening, taping, controlled entry to the affected part of the building, air filtration for workers, etc.). The OSHA rep told me that she'd done extensive air quality testing and determined the environment to be safe for workers outside the confined space of the construction area. In other words, office workers on the bottom floor were completely safe so long as they stayed out of the construction zone. I left the meeting feeling I'd done all that was prudent and necessary to ensure everyone's health and safety. I later held a short briefing with the entire staff, and made all of the relevant reports available to them.

Despite all my efforts to do the right thing (keep the employees apprised and, moreover, keep them safe), it wasn't long before someone contacted the DHS Inspector General with a complaint… "We've been exposed to toxic carcinogens, and Hunsinger doesn't care!"

We (I) eventually worked through this issue. In the end, everything came out just fine. The contractor finished his work (we ended up with a beautiful, functioning, restroom), the OHSA rep monitored throughout the construction phase, and (years later now) there hasn't been a single health-related issue; at least that I'm aware of.

I guess the moral to this story is the old adage that "no good deed goes unpunished." No matter how hard you try to bring change or improve their work conditions, some employees will find something to complain about. In fact, there are some instances where trying to improve a work condition without consultation with the union will result in a grievance (I'm not making this up!).

Nevertheless, this was another classic case for the need to think three steps ahead and two layers deep on every issue. Try to anticipate, ask yourself, with every move you make, "what could possibly go wrong here?" I guarantee you, with every move you make, there is a fork in the road of that decision process. If you take the wrong fork, it's likely to hurt.

# *Final Thoughts*

Whether TQM, metrics, or other aids you use to help you in your leadership endeavors, just don't lean too hard on them. There's no substitute for an old-fashioned conversation with your employees. Sure, you can use Survey Monkey (or whatever the platform of the day is), but there's nothing like sitting down with them and talking about the issues that are really bugging them. Try it. You might be surprised at what you get.

Nor do you need some self-assessment tool; one that gives you a cute little window with panes for each concept, or a hierarchical "ladder", or even a pyramid of success. Yes, it's fun to do those sometimes, but you don't need these clever little marketing toys the academia world (with no leadership experience, by the way) is using to sell their book on a newly discovered leadership concept.

I'll just give it plain and simple. Don't overly rely on a bunch of ridiculous management "crutches" to relieve you of the vulnerabilities inherent in relying on just your leadership skills. Instead, trust your instincts a little more..."Use the force, Luke!"

# 9

# If You Aren't Having Fun, Neither Are Your Employees

*"The Constitution only gives people the right to pursue happiness. You have to catch it yourself."*
—Benjamin Franklin

Not too long ago, I was reading the story about Van France, founder of Disney University, who said "a maxim of the movie industry is that it takes a happy crew to produce a happy show."[156] This has long been proven true within the customer service aspect of any organization. However, Disney U approaches the issue from a slightly different angle; teaching employees that their primary job (from janitor to performer) is to put on the best show possible for their guests, and that every employee is part of the show.[157] Part of the Disney U mandate is that employee training and education must be engaging, memorable, and fun. Walt believed "laughter was no enemy to learning."[158]

People at the Disney corporation are genuinely happy to be there. But it's Disneyland! It's supposed to be the happiest place on earth. Who wouldn't be happy to go to work every day at Disneyland (or in my son-in-law's case, a major league ballpark)? Regardless of where you're working, there's no reason why you can't have fun in any organization or any job if only the right circumstances are presented...if leadership places an emphasis on that type of culture.

I mentioned in a previous chapter the two Special Forces guys I worked for in my first couple of years in Hawaii. Not to re-visit that issue, but an important point about their leadership negligence included the hours they kept; whether implicit or explicit, the message a leader conveys to his troops is that "you need to keep pace." In my case, I was in freakin Hawaii! I couldn't help that they weren't happy going home at night. But I was.

---

156 *Disney U: How the Disney University Develops the World's Most Engaged, Loyal, and Customer-Centric Employees* by Doug Lipp, McGraw Hill, New York, 2013, p. 29.
157 Recall, in a previous chapter, what I said about an organization having to define who they are, and how the Marines and FEMA had done that.
158 Ibid, P. 26

Besides, I had a 12-year-old son at home that was waiting for me to hit fly balls and grounders every night. I did keep up their pace for a year or so, and then I rebelled. I just gradually started scaling back my hours to accommodate my family. Yet, there were times I just got up at 5 pm and said "sorry sir, I have to go." It was another pivotal moment in my leadership development. Years later, in more senior positions, I adopted a personal policy of last in and first out.

Hawaii, 1988, getting ready for an equipment jump. On jump status, we had to jump at least quarterly. It wasn't until LTC Joe Jakubowski got there that we actually started having fun doing these "office jumps."

Hawaii, 1988, on my way for an equipment jump.

To be clear, in my later leadership roles I certainly put in my 8-hour day, and often times more. But if official hours were 7:30 am to 4 pm, I didn't come in at 7 or stay until 5 or 6 on a routine basis. There were times when that needed to be done; and, in the disaster response business, I expected people to stay as long as we had to at times. But overall, I expected people to go home at the end of the duty day and spend time doing other things. I came to realize that if I didn't make that effort, some people would grow up like my two Special Forces bosses. I didn't want anyone developing those types of habits.

My advice to all leaders is to get past the career issues and all of the intimidation that goes along with that, and just do (again) what's right and good…and have fun! None of us are perfect. We're all fallible. We'll all make mistakes. As long as your heart is pure…and you want to do good, always…you can look yourself in the mirror every day and be proud. As for the rest? Just have fun doing it!

## *"How Can We Piss-Off the Joint Staff Today?"*

One of my favorite bosses was a Navy (SEAL) Captain by the name of Lou Boink. Captain Boink was one of the legends of the SEAL community, and it was truly an honor to work for him.[159] For years I'd tell people that going to work for him every day was like being on an episode of Letterman. I thought he even resembled David Letterman in looks and mannerisms a bit.

Captain Boink made going to work fun. You never knew what was going to happen from day to day; what flippant saying might come out of him or what crazy action we'd suddenly be involved in. We worked in the Office of the Secretary of Defense, and there was always a fierce (but unneeded) rivalry between our office and the Joint Staff's Special Operations Division. Whenever I had an issue to work or a package to run with them, Boink would ask "Well, Dennis, what's the piss-off factor on this issue? How pissed off will the Joint Staff boys be with us? Can we work it up to maybe a 9 or so?" It was all in good humor (at least on our side), but it also made it fun. What Captain Boink taught me was to work hard, have fun doing it, and don't take yourself too seriously.

## *Targets are up!"*

When Lou Boink left the Pentagon for another assignment, I went to work

---

159  I also worked for Captain Rick Woolard, Rear Admiral George Worthington, and Rear Admiral Cathal (Irish) Flynn. All great men, and SEAL legends.

for Captain Rick Woolard, another SEAL, and former commander of SEAL Team 6. We got a call one day from the DOD liaison to Hollywood. Yes, there is one of those. I can't remember his official duty title, but that was about it. He worked for the Assistant Secretary of Defense for Public Affairs, but is office location was in Hollywood, California.

DOD has a program where they offer assistance to movie production companies. The company reimburses DOD for the costs, but DOD reserves some rights (although often negotiated) to review and insist on edits to scripts if the movie presents a negative image of the military. If parties can't come to an agreement, DOD will walk away.[160] This call was a request for our Assistant Secretary's office (more specifically, the counterterrorism guys) to review a script for a movie to be titled "Toy Soldiers." The movie was a story about a boys school in southern Virginia, filled with kids from affluent families. In the scenario, there'd been a Noriega-style snatch of a drug cartel leader by US forces in South America, and now his son was attempting to seize the school, hold the kids hostage, and gain the release of his father. Lou Gossett Jr played the school's headmaster, Sean Astin was the lead student, Andrew Divoff was the terrorist, and R. Lee Ermey was the response force commanding general.

In all his infinite wisdom, Captain Woolard handed the script to my office mate, Lieutenant Colonel Moe Elmore, and me. He told us, essentially, that we had it; follow it through to its conclusion.

Mo and I read the script, made a few small edits, and then at a follow-on meeting told the director and producers it was good to go…our job was done. It was at that point, the director (Daniel Petrie, Jr) asked the liaison officer if Mo and I could go to Charlottesville with them to serve as DOD liaisons for the shoot. The liaison looked at us, we looked at each other (some words to the effect "Well, the boss told us to follow it to its conclusion"). Sure, we can go!

Mo and I ventured on down to Charlottesville, checked into a hotel, and made our way to the film location the next morning. I have to tell you two things, right off, that struck me most about that experience. First, what a production! A lot of people (caterers, construction workers, wardrobe, drivers, hair and makeup, camera/production people, extras, administrative people, and the list goes on). It was a busy place with a lot of activity,

---

160 Members of our office had read the script for "Navy SEALS", starring Charlie Sheen, but walked away. It was too over the top. Before I left the Pentagon, we had read the script for "Clear and Present Danger", starring Harrison Ford, and agreed to assist.

yet, surprisingly organized. I was also surprised at how gracious people were to Mo and I; they treated us with great respect. Second, (and rightly or wrongly) my perception was, in spite of their courtesy to Mo and I, these people thought they were doing a great service to society and the country; they were doing God's work here. I, on the other hand, felt like I was on a six-week boondoggle (and I was), not accomplishing anything worthwhile or meaningful to the world (I wasn't). I walked away from the experience thinking…here's an industry that offers no real value added. Notwithstanding, Mo and I had a blast.

Throughout filming, we offered a few suggestions from time to time on things we thought would be a little more realistic. Most of time we just watched and stayed out of the way. Both Mo and I recognized that not all movies are factually correct; there's always some artistic license involved by the Director.

Somewhere into week three, there was a scene where the actual assault by US troops to re-take the school was about to be filmed. Out walked two actors, dressed in camouflage paint and ghillie suits, ready to film their roles as snipers. Their role in the movie was to begin the assault by taking two terrorist lookouts off the building's roof. As they got into position and began reciting their lines, Mo stepped up to the 1st Assistant Director and whispered to him that the sniper commands were all wrong. So that you understand, Mo was a special forces officer and a former Delta operator.[161] The 1st AD went running up to the Director and told him what Mo had said. The Director stopped filming and walked over to Mo and I and asked Mo "Well, what are the right commands?" At that point, Mo gave him the most eloquent, yet succinct, tutorial I'd ever heard on the art of sniper operations. The Director said "Ok, we'll re-write and do just that."

Mo and I started to walk off, when the Director asked "Wait, why don't you guys just do it? I don't need these actors. I've got the real deal right here." We looked at each other, almost dumb-struck by it, and agreed we'd do it. Mo wrote the command lines for them, and then coached them a little on the sequence. While the cast and crew took a short lunch break, we ran down to the wardrobe and make-up area and got into costume. When lunch was over, Mo and I got into position, each one of us behind

---

161  So that you also know, Mo and I realized early on that our names would appear on the credits as technical advisors. So, we were a little concerned about our professional integrity, within our own communities, if we were to allow too much "hokey" stuff.

a 50 caliber Barrett sniper rifle, and shot the scene over a matter of about 30 minutes (several takes from several different angles). My three words of fame were "targets are up!"

Mo and I started to walk off again, when the Producer said "Oh no, not so fast. You guys need to come with me." I learned two very important lessons about the movie industry that day. First, if you utter a single word on screen, the production company has an obligation to immediately enroll you in the union. He ushered Mo and I down to their administrative offices and had us fill out all the paperwork to become immediate members of the Screen Actors Guild[162]. They were also obligated to pay us the daily union minimum for an actor (I think it was $450 in those days). The movie industry is a classic catch 22; you can't get a part unless you have a SAG card, and you can't get a SAG card unless you have a part. Mo and I just fell into it…unintentionally for sure.

The second thing I learned about the movie industry that day was a hard lesson about their culture. Remember the gracious and respectful environment toward Mo and I, described earlier? That suddenly changed. Not only did we rather unceremoniously displace two other union actors, we stepped in front of more than a hundred people who felt they were ahead of us. Has it ever occurred, have you ever wondered, what attracts so many crew members to live the nomadic life of a movie production company? It's because almost all of them are aspiring actors; taking menial jobs with the crew, hoping the Director will turn to them one day and say "get in there." Again, Mo and I just fell into it, and never intended to usurp someone else's opportunity (or life dream). There were some upset people that gave us the cold shoulder for the rest of the production.

Toward the end of filming came the final US counterterrorism assault on the school. The extras we used for the assault were an Army Special Forces reserve unit out of West Virginia. As we stepped up to do that filming, the Director stepped out to give them a pep talk, and then launched into specific moves he wanted them to do. As he's describing things, several of the soldiers started looking at Mo and me, as if to say "Help! This is not going to look right." Mo just nodded at them and let the Director finish his talk. When he was done, and walked off, Mo gathered the troops around and said "Ok, forget everything you just heard. This is how we're gonna do it."

---

162  I still hold a union card today.

Me, Lou Gossett Jr, and LTC Moe Elmore on location for the filming of
*Toy Soldiers* in 1991.

As you watch the movie and get to the scene where the troops deploy
from their helicopters…from that point forward is everything that Mo and
I (mostly Mo) scripted for them to do. We did the shot in one take and,
at the end, the Director came running out yelling "Perfect, perfect!" Our
work was <u>finally</u> done!

I thank our boss, Rick Woolard, for recognizing what a treat this was
for a couple of his troops. He could have easily said no, we're a small office
with a heavy workload. But, instead, he sucked it up back home, and let us
go out and have some fun. It's bosses like that who realize too much work
and not enough fun can burn out your workforce in short order.[163]

---

163 We were sitting in the ops center one night during Desert Storm. I had a headache, so Woolard reached into his bag and pulled out a bottle of Excedrin. I took two
and then he said "You know where I got these?" I said, "um, no???" He said "When we
were doing the assault of Noriega's house during the Panama operation, I had a split-
ting headache. I went into his bathroom and took those out of his medicine cabinet." I
said "With all due respect, Captain, you're giving me drugs from the house of one of the
most notorious drug bosses in all of South America!!?" I thought he was joking. He was
dead serious.

## *Some Final Thoughts*

As you reach a certain age, guys start calling you to reminisce about the old times. No one really remembers the bad times, unless it's to remember the good times that got you out of the bad times. They all remember the brotherhood; the times that they felt most like a team or even an extended family. In creating that type of culture, I'll go back to what I said in a previous chapter about focusing your employee's efforts on things you want them focused on. Whether it's subtle, innocuous conference room banter or more deliberate attempts at "fun stuff", keep it as light as you professionally can. Let your employees be themselves. There's plenty of time for the serious stuff.

*At the end of your life, you will never regret not having passed one more test, not winning one more verdict or not closing one more deal. You will regret time not spent with a husband, a friend, a child, or a parent.*
—Barbara Bush

# 10

# Final, Final Thoughts

*"Every man's work...is a portrait of himself."*[164]
—Samuel Butler (Novelist)

Have you ever seen the movie "Mr. Holland's Opus?" If you have, you know it's about a high school music teacher who kept wanting to move on to do other, bigger, things in his life. He took the teaching gig as a temporary step in his career ladder. His goal was to compose beautiful music, an opus; perhaps making the big time on Broadway. He never did. Decades later, he found himself retiring from that high school job, yet, in the end, realizing the tremendous effect he had on the lives of others. Metaphorically, <u>that</u> was the opus he had created.

Now, many years later, I'm just one small piece of an elaborate mosaic that many of my mentors have crafted for themselves; their opus, if you will. From my high school football coach[165] to the great mentors and leaders of my career, in every tiny portion of each masterpiece, you'll see the picture of countless faces throughout their communities and beyond whose lives were richly affected; collectively, having made a tremendous impact on the lives of others. I can only dream that someone will have seen that in me as the balance of my life is weighed and measured.

Like Mr. Holland, I never got rich or famous. I never completely fulfilled my dreams and aspirations (I'm not sure any of us really ever do). But I believe I've helped a few people reach some of theirs along the way; and for that reason alone, I have no regrets in what I have or haven't done personally.

---

164 This quote was used at the eulogy for Col Fred Walker. We served together 85-88 in the Special Operations Division at USCINCPAC. He died in 1990 of cancer. One of my great heroes. If ever a man's work were a self-portrait it would be Fred and his many accomplishments. A phenomenal patriot, warrior, and scholar. As the senior AF guy in our office I spent many hours being mentored by him.

165 Since I focused predominantly on my professional career, I didn't discuss Coach Jim Leierer in this book, or the tremendous impact he had on my early development. It was beyond measure. He was probably the greatest man I've ever known in my life.

## *Follow Your Own Personal Code (not someone else's)*

Throughout this book, I've stressed doing good and right things; and it comes down to this: Don't let your life be driven by draconian dogma, or any deep-seated belief for that matter. Political, religious, ethnic, cultural, and many other tribalisms can be destructive. If you're a conservative, that's okay; if you're liberal, then that's okay too. But <u>let your life be driven by your heart, and your heart driven by what is good and right always</u>; not by something someone tells you is the party line. Read! Keep yourself informed on both sides of every issue, then make your own decision. Do things for your troops, do things for your country, do things because they are right and honorable. But don't do things out of some misguided loyalty to Party or platform.

Doing good and right things doesn't mean having to come in and "make your mark." Too many leaders are driven to establish or leave their legacy. To many of them, "change" is the measure of how you make an impact. In fact, change for the sake of change is both disruptive and destructive, and nothing more than a self-aggrandizing effort. If that's what's important to you, or what you're focused on, then you'll fail as a leader on Day 1.

Doing good and right things is an act of nobility. If you look up nobility in Webster's it gives you two definitions. One definition describes elements of character; integrity, virtue, class, dignity and so on; to be noble or to do noble things. The inference being...to do right and good things. The other definition relates to one's position; a class distinction, suggesting a birthright to one's position in society. The inference being a titled and/or privileged person. So, the question is, which of the two definitions do you want your legacy to be associated with? Or perhaps a better question is, if a survey were conducted of your employees, which of these two definitions would they associate your leadership style with?

## *A Few Basic Principles by Which to Live*

**Civility always**: Public displays of anger are <u>never</u> appropriate. Expressions of disappointment are always more effective than insults.

**Dignity in all things**: You can't enjoy dignity in your life until you've extended it to others.

**Grace**: How you carry yourself says far more than what you say.

**Virtue**: Serve a cause greater than yourself; and that cause doesn't involve money, fame, or power for yourself. There is no greater, more noble, aspiration than to serve.

**Ego**: Set it aside. Be willing to accept, even embrace the thought (as hard as that may seem), that you may never be recognized for anything you've done or accomplished.

**Conviction**: Unwavering in what is right.

**Self-pity**: There's no room for it in leadership

Take time to talk to your employees! I never once turned someone away that wanted to talk. Even if I was embroiled in some issue, I'd always put my pen down, or push away from the computer screen, and give them my undivided attention. I've often found this to be the most difficult, but probably one of the most important, things a leader should discipline themselves to do. The virtues of grace, dignity, civility, and others, should never be seen as signs of weakness. Practicing the golden rule <u>never</u> makes you a weak leader.

## *When it's Over, Say Goodbye*

I think it's necessary to provide you a note of caution when moving on from the old job. There will always be loyalists who'll still want to reach out to you, to continue to engage you. Most of this is usually to seek advice. Some of that is either personal career advice, or perhaps a "what would you do in this situation" type of advice related to the old office. I urge you to be careful. Some of it, perhaps most of it, is okay...as long as you're mindful of the potential minefield you're traversing. However, don't engage in commiseration. It's bad form, if not unfair, to do so when usually the facts are that you're not aware of all sides of the issue. Moreover, you're gone now. Resist the temptation. It's not fair to current leadership (no matter how good or bad you think they might be), and it diminishes your stature. I've been successful at holding the line here. But there have also been times over the years where I've had to catch and remind myself to not get caught up in these conversations. It's an easy trap to fall into, so don't be "that guy."

## *Conclusion*

I've laid the foundation for you throughout the previous pages on trust, loyalty, integrity, ethics, responsibility, accountability, sound decision-making…on leadership. Now, it's up to you on how much of what I've had to say makes any sense; if any of it is applicable to your leadership style or the daily issues you face.

What's the bottom line to this whole story? Yes, leadership comes down to getting the job (the mission) done, while successfully motivating your employees to do so. However, it's more than that too. It's about how you go about motivating your employees. It's about demonstrating to them that you truly care about their welfare. It's not about organizing ice cream socials; nor is it about having everyone's birthday on your calendar so you can give them all the same canned greeting throughout the year. It's not about having free food for lunch or quiet rooms to meditate (some corporations actually do this). It's about developing, grooming, and nurturing your employees to seek and achieve their potential; and then providing them opportunities to do just that. It's the sacred trust of leadership…to help them along the path to achieve what you've already gotten. It's all of these things wrapped up in a leader that is honest, forthright, trustworthy, and fair. If you can accomplish all of that, you may never become rich or famous. You may not even achieve your personal dreams. But you'll feel so much better about yourself and the world you've left behind.

In the end, I miss the camaraderie of it all. I miss my band of brothers. I miss being in charge of a mission greater than myself, as well as the people. I miss having a well-defined mission, the resources and the freedom to get it done. I miss the intensity and the stress of it all; the responsibility and accountability. I miss the action, and I miss that "whiff of grapeshot."[166]

I used to have a screen saver on my computer that said simply "What have you done for your troops today?" I miss them most of all.

*"Nothing in life is more liberating than to fight for a cause larger than yourself, something that encompasses you but is not defined by your existence alone."*
—John McCain

---

166 A term attributed to Napoleon to invoke the essence of battle.

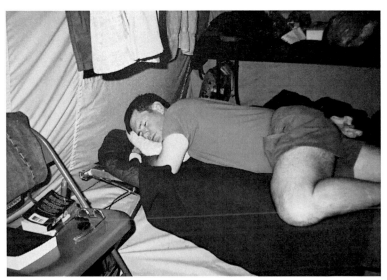

Tent city, Thumrait, Oman, 1998. Demonstrating a little leadership.

# Bibliography

Anonymous, retrieved 7 September 2018, *"What I learned from Pete Rose"*, http://www.wowzone.com/peterose.htm

Batura, Paul J., *"Remembering the space shuttle Challenger: a bold prayer in a public school that brought comfort amidst the grief"*, Retrieved 27 January 2019, Fox News, https://www.foxnews.com/opinion/remembering-the-space-shuttle-challenger-a-bold-prayer-in-a-public-school-that-brought-comfort-amidst-the-grief

Brown, Andy, *"Warnings Unheeded: Twin Tragedies at Fairchild Air Force Base"*, 2016, WU Press, Spokane

Department of Defense Pamphlet GEN-1A, *"Duty, Honor, Country Address at West Point"* by General Douglas MacArthur (1962), US Government Printing Office, 1964.

Fielkow, Brian, retrieved 23 July 2018, *"The 20/60/20 Rule: How to Handle Misaligned Employees"*,

https://www.entrepreneur.com/article/316461

Ferebee, Andrew, 10 June 2018, *"Here are the 7 rules of success"*,

https://www.theladders.com/career-advice/here-are-the-7-rules-of-success

Lipp, Doug, *"Disney U: How the Disney University Develops the World's Most Engaged, Loyal, and Customer-Centric Employees"*, McGraw Hill, New York, 2013

MassCommons, retrieved 15 August 2018, *"Fear & Loathing On The Campaign Trail: Make Them Deny It"*, https://masscommons.wordpress.com/2012/03/15/fear-loathing-on-the-campaign-trail-make-them-deny-it/amp/

McGregor, Douglas, *The Human Side of Enterprise*, 1960, McGraw-Hill, New York

Newman, Romy, retrieved 18 July 2018, *"Successful bosses run their most effective meetings exactly like this"*, https://www.theladders.com/career-advice/successful-bosses-run-their-most-effective-meetings-exactly-like-this

"Owen Honors", retrieved 10 April 2018, https://en.wikipedia.org/wiki/Owen_Honors

Powell, General Colin L., *"18 Lessons of Leadership"*, April 2011, Air University, http://www.airpower.au.af.mil/apjinternational/apj-s/2011/2011-4/2011_4_02_powell_s_eng.pdf

Rowe, Mike, retrieved 30 March 2019, "Mike Rowe on why you shouldn't follow your passion" https://www.wimp.com/mike-rowe-on-why-you-shouldnt-follow-your-passion

Robinson, Melia, 11 January 2017, *"Tim Ferriss: 'You are the average of the five people you most associate with"*, https://amp.businessinsider.com/tim-ferriss-average-of-five-people-2017-1

Rumsfeld, Donald, retrieved 7 July 2018, *"There Are Known Knowns"*, https://en.m.wikipedia.org/wiki/There_are_known_knowns

The Hatch Act of 1993, titled "An Act to Prevent Pernicious Political Activities" (Pub. L. 76-252)

The University of Virginia, retrieved 8 November 2018, *"The Papers of George Washington, Farewell Address – Transcription"* http://gwpapers.virginia.edu/documents_gw/farewell/transcript.html

Trengriffin, *"A Dozen Things I've Learned from Charlie Munger about Inversion (including the Importance of being Consistently Not Stupid)"*, retrieved 21 October 2018, https://25iq.com/2015/09/12/a-dozen-things-ive-learned-from-charlie-munger-about-inversion-including-the-importance-of-being-consistently-not-stupid-2/amp/

U.S. Army War College, retrieved 21 September 2018, *From the Archives: Battling the Bureaucracy* https://ssi.armywarcollege.edu/pubs/parameters/articles/04spring/archives.pdf

*"Who Are The Ten FEMA Kings?"* 17 April 2010, https://forum.prisonplanet.com/index.php?topic=167164.0

Willard, Dallas, An interview in *Leadership* Journal, May 2010, http://www.dwillard.org/articles/individual/how-do-we-assess-spiritual-growth

# Index

# About the Author

Dennis Hunsinger is a Northwest guy. Born in Southern California, Dennis but spent his teen and young adult years on Whidbey Island (just north of Seattle). While Whidbey has been his primary residence throughout most of his life, and still is, he says "there was that time I enlisted in the United States Air Force and didn't come out again until 29 years later." A retired Air Force Colonel, with another 13 years in federal government as a civilian employee, Dennis served this great nation for 42 years in a variety of senior leadership positions.

An experienced and proven leader, his distinguished Air Force career included four assignments as a commander (two Group and two Squadron commands), as well as several Air Force and joint staff positions. His final Air Force position was as Director of Security Forces for the Air Mobility Command. Serving for two years as Acting Regional Administrator (and five years as Deputy) of the Federal Emergency Management Agency (FEMA) in Region 10, he was responsible for all FEMA activities in Alaska, Idaho, Oregon and Washington. Dennis finished his federal civil service career as

Regional Director for the Department of Homeland Security's Office of Infrastructure Protection.

Dennis holds bachelor's and master's degrees in criminal justice from Chapman University, and a doctorate in Sociology from The American University. He is a graduate of the FBI National Academy, the Department of Homeland Security Executive Leadership Program, and the Industrial College of the Armed Forces.